The Web Publisher's Illustrated Quick Reference

Springer

New York
Berlin
Heidelberg
Barcelona
Budapest
Hong Kong
London
Milan
Paris
Santa Clara
Singapore
Tokyo

Ralph Grabowski

The Web Publisher's Illustrated Quick Reference

Covers HTML 3.2 and VRML 2.0

Springer

Ralph Grabowski
XYZ Publishing, Ltd.
34486 Donlyn Avenue
Abbotsford, British Columbia V2S 4W7
Canada

On the cover: VRML logo placed in the public domain by Kevin Hughes <kevinh@eit.com>.

Library of Congress Cataloging-in-Publication Data
Grabowski, Ralph.
    The Web publisher's illustrated quick reference: covers HTML 3.2 and VRML 2.0/Ralph Grabowski.
      p.   cm.
    ISBN 0-387-94831-7 (pbk.)
     1. HTML (Document markup language) 2. World Wide Web (Information
retrieval system) 3. Electronic publishing. I. Title.
QA76.76.H94G72 1996
005.7'2–dc20   96-25481

Printed on acid-free paper.

Production managed by Francine McNeill; manufacturing supervised by Jacqui Ashri.
Camera-ready copy supplied by the author using PageMaker.
Printed and bound by R.R. Donnelley and Sons, Harrisonburg, VA.
Printed in the United States of America.

9 8 7 6 5 4 3 2 1

ISBN 0-387-94831-7 Springer-Verlag New York Berlin Heidelberg SPIN 10542973

Table of Contents

How to Use This Book

The *Web Publisher's Illustrated Quick Reference* is an alphabetical summary of two important elements in creating a Web site on the Internet: HTML v3.2 (Hyper Text Markup Language) and VRML v2.0 (Virtual Reality Modeling Language). The format of this quick reference book is especially clear because each HTML tag and VRML node starts on its own page.

The Internet is characterized by constant change; the HTML and VRML specifications are no different. HTML v2.0 and VRML v1.0 are stable specifications. The next stages for both, HTML v3.2 and VRML v2.0, were being developed while this book was being written. In addition, vendors have created proprietary extensions, most notably Netscape and Microsoft. This book included the most recent draft for each specification, HTML v3.2 preliminary and VRML v2.0 Draft #3, as well as the HTML extensions created by Netscape and Microsoft.

Each page of the HTML reference section includes:

DESCRIPTION

This concise description tells you the purpose of the HTML tag, whether it is obsolete (not found in HTML v3.2) and the meaning of its abbreviation. Tags are identified if they are unique to HTML v3.2, Netscape Navigator v1.1 or v2.0, and Microsoft Explorer.

REQUIRED ATTRIBUTES

This section tells you when the HTML tag requires one or more attributes.

EXAMPLE MARKUPS

Example markups are actual HTML code that shows you how the tag is used. The tag is printed **boldface** to help you find the tag more quickly.

SCREEN GRAB

Almost every HTML tag includes one or more screen grabs to help you instantly see the effect of the tag on the document.

OPTIONAL ATTRIBUTES

This section lists the optional attributes that can be used with the HTML tag. Many attributes include an example of its usage, a table of attribute values and their meaning, and whether the attribute is specific to HTML v3.2, Netscape Navigator v1.1 or v2.0, or Microsoft Explorer.

TIPS

Every HTML tag includes one or more tips on using the tag. Heeding these tips and warnings will save you valuable time in developing your Web site.

RELATED HTML TAGS

Related HTML tags are provided for easy cross-reference.

Each page of the VRML reference section includes:

DESCRIPTION

This concise description tells you the purpose of the VRML v2.0 node, the meaning of its abbreviation, and the node type. The node's name under VRML v1.0 is noted here.

SCREEN GRAB

Many VRML nodes include a screen grab to help you instantly see the effect of the node on the scene.

VRML 2 SYNTAX

This section tells you the node syntax and default field values, as specified by VRML v2. 0 Draft #3. Included is a table listing the type, name, default value, and meaning of every field.

VRML 1 SYNTAX

This section briefly describes the node syntax as specified by VRML v1.0c.

NODE GEOMETRY

This section supplies detailed information about every field found in the VRML node.

RELATED EQUATIONS

The geometry-related VRML nodes include geometric equations, such as surface area and volume.

TEXTURE MAPPING

Similarly, the geometry-related VRML nodes describe how texture maps are applied to the node.

TIPS

Every VRML node includes one or more tips on using the node. Heeding these tips and warnings will save you valuable time in developing your Web site.

RELATED NODES

Related VRML nodes are provided for easy cross-reference.

Ralph Grabowski
Abbotsford, British Columbia, Canada
Email: ralphg@xyzpress.com

HTML

HTML is the basis of everything on the World Wide Web (*short for hyper text markup language*).

SAMPLE MARKUP

■ All HTML documents have two parts, the Head and the Body:

```
<HTML>
  <HEAD>
    <TITLE>This Title Appears on the Browser's Title Bar.</TITLE>
  </HEAD>
  <BODY>
    <P>This is paragraph of text is displayed by the HTML browser.
    It can contain text, images, and hyperlinks.</P>
  </BODY>
</HTML>
```

TIPS

■ HTML is based on SGML, short for structured generalized markup language, which was created in 1988.

■ HTML was invented by Tim Berners-Lee in 1989.

■ The HTML v1.0 specification was finalized in March, 1993.

■ HTML+ was an advanced specification proposed in 1993 but was never implemented. Nevertheless, it is useful to read the spec to see the future direction of HTML.

■ HTML v2.0 was the first commonly-accepted specification; the specification was finalized in November, 1995.

■ HTML v3.0 was proposed in early 1995 but expired on September 28, 1995, because it contained — like HTML+ — too many new tags for browser programmers to assimilate.

■ HTML v3.2 was accepted in May, 1996, and is the current specification that this book is based on.

■ Both Netscape and Microsoft added extensions to the HTML spec that only their browsers understand; many of the Netscape extensions were adopted in HTML v3.2.

■ This book includes the Netscape extensions found in Navigator v1.1 and v2.0, as well as most Microsoft extensions found in Explorer v2.0.

■ While the HTML specification tends to add new tags and attributes, some are removed. The following tags were removed from HTML v3.2:

Tag	Meaning
<DIR>	Directory-style list; use <OL> instead.
<FIG>	Figure; replaced by the <IMG> tag.
<LISTING>	Display text with line breaks; use <PRE> instead.
<PLAINTEXT>	Display text with line breaks and ignore all HTML tags; use <PRE> instead.
<XMP>	Display text with line breaks; use <PRE> instead.

■ The following tags have been proposed in expired HTML proposals; they may appear in a future HTML specification:

Tag	Meaning
<ABBREV>	Definition of an abbreviation.
<ACRONYM>	Meaning of an acronym.
<AU>	Name of the document's author.
<BANNER>	A portion of the document that does not scroll.
<COL>	Definition of a table column.
<COLGROUP>	A group of table columns.
<CREDIT>	Credit of the document's creation.
<DEL>	Deleted text.
<FN>	Footnote.
<INS>	Inserted text.
<LANG>	Language specification.
<LH>	List heading.
<MATH>	Mathematical symbols.
<NOTE>	A note in the document.
<OVERLAY>	Overlay one item over another item.
<PERSON>	Name of a person.
<Q>	A quotation.
<RANGE>	Indicates a range within the document.
<TAB>	Specifies tab spacing.

■ To read the latest status of HTML, check the **http://www.w3.org** Web site.

<!DOCTYPE ... >

Declares the document to be an HTML document (*short for DOCument TYPE*).

EXAMPLE MARKUPS

- To declare the document as an HTML document:

  `<!DOCTYPE HTML PUBLIC>`

- To declare the document as compatible with HTML v2.0:

  `<!DOCTYPE HTML PUBLIC "-//IETF//DTD HTML 2.0//EN">`

- To declare the document as compatible with HTML v3.2:

  `<!DOCTYPE HTML PUBLIC "-//W3C//DTD HTML 3.2//EN">`

TIPS

- The **<!DOCTYPE>** element is optional but is helpful in reporting the document type to applications.

- If you use this tag, it must the very first tag in the HTML file and located before the initial **<HTML>** tag.

- DTD is short for "document type definition."

- W3C is short for "World Wide Web Consortium."

- HTML is short for "hyper text markup language."

- IETF is short for "Internet Engineering Task Force."

RELATED HTML TAGS

`<!- ->`	Comments in the HTML document.
`<HTML>`	Encloses all of the HTML code.
`<TITLE>`	Document title.

<! - - *str* - - >

Marks the string *str* as a comment, not to be displayed by the HTML browser.

SAMPLE MARKUP

- To indicate a comment:

```
<!-- This document is missing a reference. -->
```

OPTIONAL ATTRIBUTES

none

TIPS

- The comment tag should cause the browser to ignore everything within the starting and ending - - (double dash) marks; however, some browsers incorrectly consider the closing > (right angle bracket) as the end of the comment.

- Use this tag to temporarily disable HTML code.

- A comment can span more than one line:

```
<!-- Author:       Ralph Grabowski
     Date created: 15 April, 1996
     Last update:  24 June, 1996 -->
```

RELATED HTML TAGS

<!DOCTYPE>   Indicates an HTML document.

<CITATION>   Indicates a citation.

<A ... > ... </A>

Indicates a hyperlink to a URL (uniform resource locator) via text or an image (*short for Anchor*).

REQUIRED ATTRIBUTES

You must use either HREF or NAME – but not both – within the <A> tag:

HREF   Identifies the destination URL (*short for Hyperlink REFerence*).

NAME   Identifies a destination tag within the current document.

EXAMPLE MARKUPS

■ To jump to a document using an *absolute* URL named "http://www.strokeofcolor.com/garage.html":

```
Read  <A HREF="http://www.strokeofcolor.com/garage.html">  The
Garage Entrepreneur </A> (TM) by Jake Richter.
```

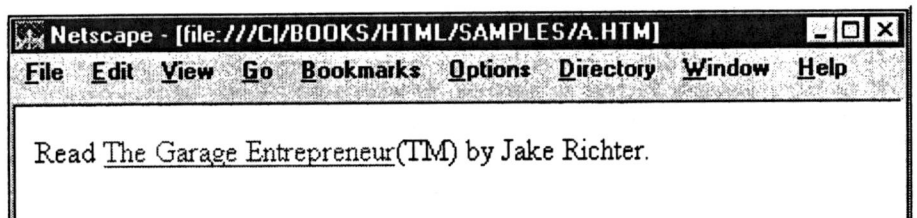

■ To jump to a document using a *relative* URL named "upf-001.htm":

```
The Upfront eZine dated <A HREF="upf-001.htm">1 May, 1995</A>.
```

■ To jump to another location named "ue" *within* the document:

```
Got to the <a href="#ue">Upfront eZine</a>.
   . . .
<a name="ue">
```

■ To send the viewer back to the top of the document:

```
<a name="welcome">
   . . .
Back to the <a href="#welcome"> top</a>.
```

■ To send email by clicking on text, prefix the email address with the **mailto:** resource:

```
Comments? Email me at  <A HREF="mailto:ralphg@xyzpress.com">
ralphg@xyzpress.com</A>
```

■ To indicate a hyperlink by displaying a thumbnail image named "th.gif" (instead of text), which then jumps to an image named "fig.gif":

```
Click this image <A HREF="fig.gif"> <IMG SRC="th.gif"> </A> to
view the figure in full size.
```

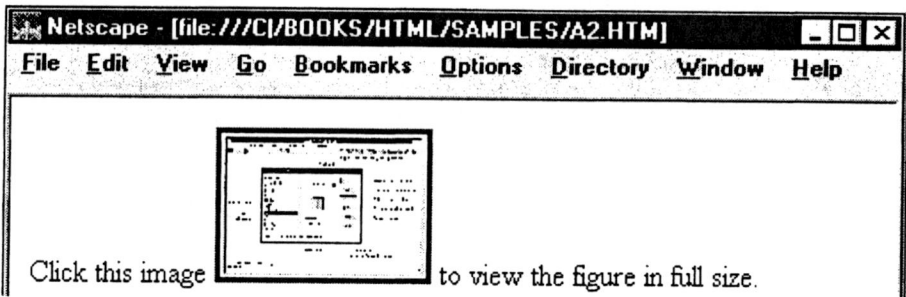

OPTIONAL ATTRIBUTES

BASE TARGET (*Netscape v2.0*) Defines the default window that displays links.

Example: **BASE TARGET="windowname"**

METHODS (*Removed from HTML v3.2*) Specifies the HTTP communications method for requesting (or sending) data from (or to) the server.

REL Describes the relationship of the destination document to the current document (*short for RELation*).

Example: **REL="next"**

REV Describes the relationship of the current document to the destination document (*short for REVerse relation*).

Example: **REV="previous"**

Rel and Rev	Meaning
"next"	The next document of the series.
"previous"	The previous document of the series.
"parent"	The parent to the subdocument.
"made"	Alternate to the author, "made by".

TARGET (*Netscape v2.0*) Display the document in the window described by **TARGET**, such as a named **<FRAME>** element or another instance of Navigator.

Example: **TARGET="frame2"**

Four target names have special meaning:

Target	Meaning
"_blank"	Display document in a new, unnamed windows.
"_parent"	Display document in parent of the current document; if parent not available, defaults to "_self".
"_self"	Display document in current window.
"_top"	Display document in the top document; if top not available, defaults to "_self".

TITLE	Gives a title to a document that otherwise can't have a title, such as an FTP site or an image. *Example*: **TITLE="Figure 1.2"** displays Figure 1.2 on the title bar.
URN	(*Removed from HTML v3.2*) A server-independent reference to documents; an alternative to URLs (*short for Universal Resource Name*).

TIPS

- The **<A>** element must have either the **HREF** attribute or the **NAME** attribute.

- When the URL is suffixed with #*name*, the document is loaded and positioned to display starting at the *name* tag rather than at the top of the document.

- Within a document, the **<A>** element with an **HREF** attribute jumps directly to the destination tag when the URL is #*name* ; the jump can be further down or higher up in the document.

- The destination tag is constructed as **<A NAME="*name*">**

- The resources allowed in the URL:

URL	Meaning
file:	Host-specific file.
ftp:	File Transfer Protocol.
gopher:	Gopher and Gopher+ protocol.
http:	HyperText Transfer Protocol.
mailto:	Electronic mail.
news:	USENET news.
nntp:	USENET news using NNTP access.
prospero:	Prospero directory service.
telnet:	Telnet protocol for interactive sessions.
wais:	Wide Area Information Servers protocol.

- You can use the **<FORM>** and **<INPUT>** tags to create a hyperlink button:

```
<FORM Action="http://www.url.com/">
  Click here to jump to
  <INPUT Type="submit" Value="your URL destination.">
</FORM>
```

RELATED HTML TAGS

<BASE>	Base URL of the document.
<LINK>	Relationship to other documents.
<TITLE>	Document title.

\<ADDRESS\> *str* \</ADDRESS\>

Marks the string *str* as an address and displays it in italics (*level 0*).

SAMPLE MARKUP

- To indicate an address:

```
<ADDRESS>XYZ Publishing, Ltd.<BR> PO Box 3053<BR>
Sumas WA 98295-3053</ADDRESS>
```

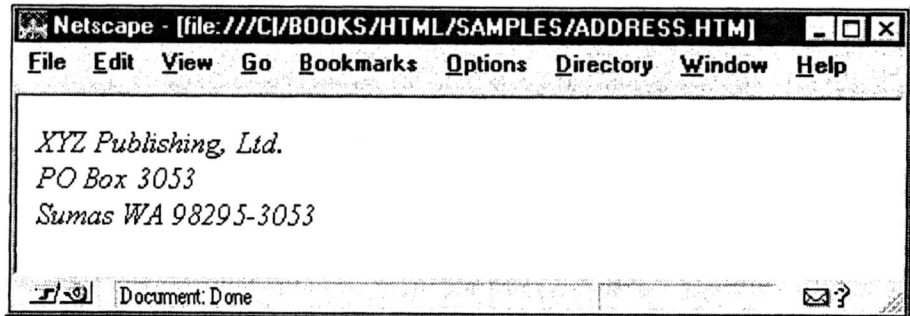

OPTIONAL ATTRIBUTES

none

TIPS

- This tag causes the browser to render the text appropriate for an address.
- Navigator v2 renders the text as left-justified, italic text.

RELATED HTML TAGS

\<AU\>	Indicates an author.
\<CITATION\>	Indicates a citation.

<APPLET CODE HEIGHT WIDTH ... >
... </APPLET>

Identifies and invokes a Java application.

REQUIRED ATTRIBUTES

CODE — Name of the Java code to execute, often an URL; equivalent to using **CODEBASE** and **NAME**.

HEIGHT — Height of screen required by application, in pixels.

WIDTH — Width of screen required by application, in pixels.

SAMPLE MARKUP

- To run applet AudioDat.Class in a 250- by 400-pixel window:

```
<APPLET CLASS="audiodat.class" WIDTH="250" HEIGHT="400"></APPLET>
```

OPTIONAL ATTRIBUTES

ALIGN — Alignment of the display. *Example*: `ALIGN="left"`

Align	Meaning
left	Left justified.
right	Right justified.
top	Top justified.
texttop	Top of adjacent text.
middle	Middle justified.
absmiddle	Middle of document window.
baseline	Baseline of adjacent text.
bottom	Bottom justified.
absbottom	Bottom of document window.

ALT — A string that describes the application displayed by browsers that cannot execute the applet; substitutes for invoking the application.

Example: `ALT="The AudioDat applet"`

CODEBASE — Specifies the base URL of the application.

HSPACE — Reserve blank space (a margin) around the application, in pixels.

NAME — Application name; allows reference to other apps in the same document.

VSPACE — Reserve blank space (a margin) around the application, in pixels.

TIP

- Other programming languages, in addition to Java, may be supported in the future.

RELATED HTML TAG

PARAM — Defines a parameter for an applet.

HTML A

<AREA COORDS ... >

Specifies an area within a mapped image; optionally executes a hyperlink to URL when user selects area.

REQUIRED ATTRIBUTE

COORDS   The x,y-coordinates of the area:

Coords	Rectangle	Circle	Polygon
"x1,y1"	Upper-left corner.	Center.	First vertex.
"x2,y2"	Lower-right corner.	Radius.	Next vertex.
"x3,y3"			Next vertex.
"x4,y4"			Next vertex, etc.

SAMPLE MARKUP

■ To link a rectangular area with corner coordinates (10,20) and (100,150) to http://haven.uniserve.com/~ralphg/:

```
<AREA COORDS="10,20,100,150" HREF="haven.uniserve.com/~ralphg">
```

OPTIONAL ATTRIBUTES

ALT   Alternate character data that describes the area displayed by a browser in text-only mode; substitutes for displaying the image.

Example: ALT=" [Click here to jump.]"

HREF   Name of the URL; see Appendix A.

NOHREF   Specifies that this area should not generate a link.

SHAPE   Type of shape of the area.

Example: SHAPE="rect" for a rectangular area.

Shape	Meaning
"rect"	Rectangular or square shape (default).
"circle"	Circular shape.
"polygon"	Multi-sided shape.

TIPS

■ This tag is usually used with the <MAP> tag.

■ A partial URL in <AREA> is relative to the URL specified by <MAP>.

RELATED HTML TAG

<MAP>   A client image map.

`<B>` *str* `</B>`

Displays the enclosed text with a boldface font (*short for Bold*).

SAMPLE MARKUPS
- To boldface a portion of text:

```
The <B>HTML-Java-VRML</B> Quick Reference.
```

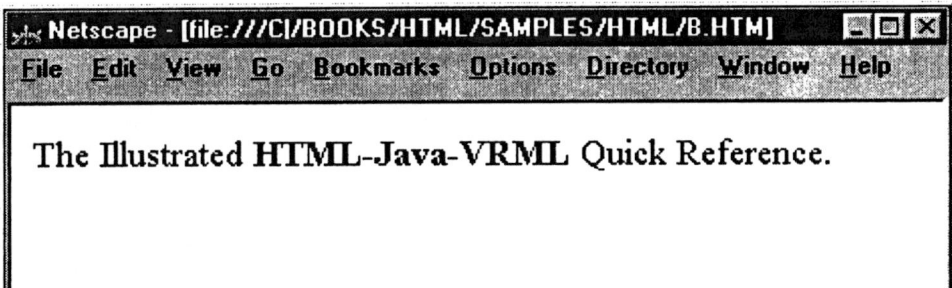

- To boldface an anchor:

```
<a href="#ue"><B>Upfront eZine</B></a>
```

OPTIONAL ATTRIBUTES
none

TIP
- Most browsers display text within this tag in boldface; some browsers might not be able to — in that case, the browser must render the text differently from italicized text.

RELATED HTML TAGS
`<I>`	Display enclosed text in italics.
`<STRONG>`	Display text in a strong font.

<BASE HREF ... >

Specifies the absolute URL for relative URL links in the document.

REQUIRED ATTRIBUTE

HREF   Identifies the destination Uniform Resource Locator (*short for Hyperlink REFerence*); see Appendix A.

SAMPLE MARKUP

■ To indicate a base URL (*http://haven.uniserve.com*), then specify a relative URL (*upf-001.htm*):

```
<BASE HREF="http://haven.uniserve.com">
...
<A HREF="upf-001.htm">Next document</A>
```

OPTIONAL ATTRIBUTE

TARGET   (*Netscape v2.0*) Display the document in the window described by **TARGET**, such as a named **FRAME** or another instance of Navigator. Four target names have special meaning:

Target	Meaning
"_blank"	Display document in a new, unnamed windows.
"_parent"	Display document in the parent of the current document; if parent not available, defaults to "_self".
"_self"	Display document in current window.
"_top"	Display document in the top document; if top not available, defaults to "_self".

TIPS

■ This tag is useful when documents might be moved to a different location, such as another subdirectory, hard drive, or computer; you need only change the one URL within this **<BASE>** tag, rather than search and change every URL throughout the document.

■ When this tag is missing and there are relative URLs in the document, then the browser assumes the URL first used to access the document.

RELATED HTML TAGS

<A>   Indicates a hyperlink.

<LINK>   Indicates the relationship between documents.

<BASEFONT SIZE>

Specifies the size of normal text.

REQUIRED ATTRIBUTE

SIZE   Size of the font ranges in seven relative sizes from 1 through 7:

Size	Meaning
1	Minimum size.
3	Default size.
7	Maximum size.

SAMPLE MARKUP

■ To make text larger for the visually impaired:

```
<BASEFONT SIZE=7>
```

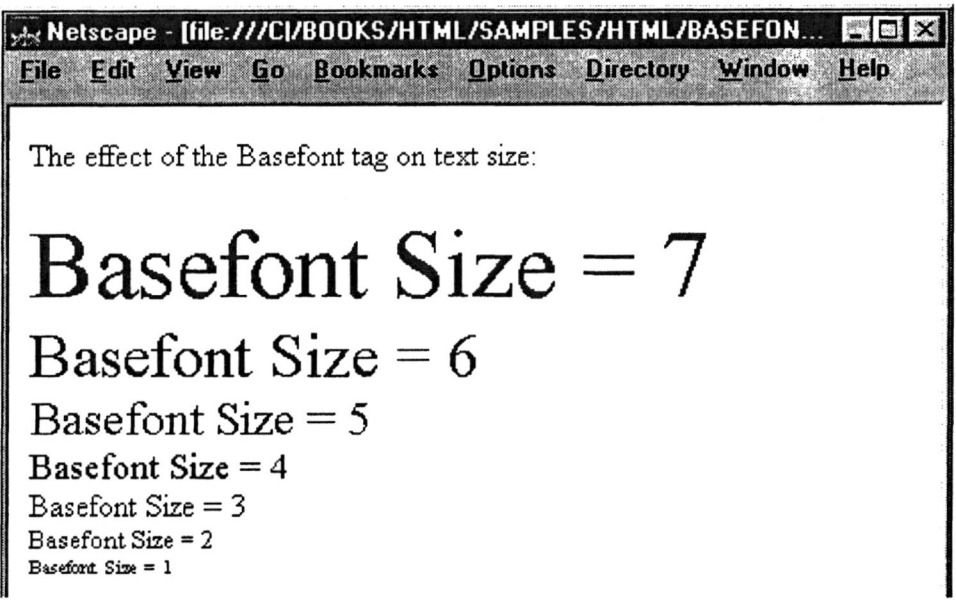

OPTIONAL ATTRIBUTES

None.

TIP

■ This tag affects the size of all text displayed by the browser.

■ Use the <FONT> tag instead of this tag.

RELATED HTML TAGS

<FONT>   Sets the default font size and color for the entire document.

<H*n*>   Displays text in a variety of six headline sizes, from small to large.

<BIG> *str* </BIG>

Displays text with a larger font.

SAMPLE MARKUP

■ To display the first letter of each word larger:

```
Welcome to <BIG> T</BIG>he <BIG> B</BIG>ig <BIG> W</BIG>eb <BIG>
P</BIG>age.
```

OPTIONAL ATTRIBUTES

none

TIPS

■ Navigator v2.0 displays this tag in boldface.

■ This tag overcomes the problem of not being able to display larger text with the <H*n*>
tags.

RELATED HTML TAGS

<FONT> Specifiies a default size for the font.

<H*n*> The headline tags.

<BLINK> *str* </BLINK>

Causes text within the tags to blink, flash on and off.

SAMPLE MARKUP

- To make the name blink on the screen:

    `<BLINK>Ralph Grabowski</BLINK> wrote this document.`

OPTIONAL ATTRIBUTES

none

TIPS

- Don't use this tag since it irritates the viewer.

- This tag only affects text and not other objects inside the tag, such as images.

RELATED HTML TAGS

<B>	Make text boldface.
<H*n*>	Make text larger and boldface.
<I>	Make text italic.

HTML B

<BLOCKQUOTE> *str* </BLOCKQUOTE>

Displays a block of text as a quotation.

SAMPLE MARKUP

■ To quote a block of text:

```
Quote of the Month:
<BLOCKQUOTE>Never underestimate the bandwidth of a speeding truck
full of DAT taps.</BLOCKQUOTE>
-- Zap Anderson
```

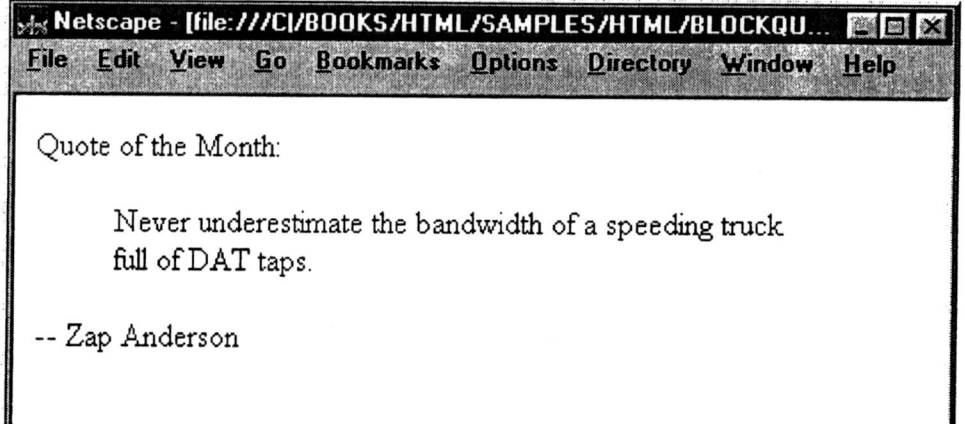

OPTIONAL ATTRIBUTES

none

TIPS

■ This tag may perhaps be replaced by the **<BQ>** tag in a future version of HTML.

■ Single-font browsers prefix each line of the blockquote with the **>** character.

RELATED HTML TAGS

<I>	Make text italic.
<LI>	Indent text.

<BODY ... > ... </BODY>

Contains all the content of the HTML document.

EXAMPLE MARKUPS

■ Every HTML document must surround its content with the <BODY> tags:

```
<BODY>
    . . .
</BODY>
```

■ To display the background color in white:

```
<BODY BGCOLOR="#ffffff">
```

■ To display a repeating "wallpaper" pattern of image file "bg.gif" in the background:

```
<BODY BACKGROUND="bg.gif">
```

OPTIONAL ATTRIBUTES

ALINK (*Netscape v1.1; HTML v3.2*) Changes the color of text that indicates an active link in a document; default color is red (short for Active LINK).

Example: **ALINK="#000000"** creates black text.

BACKGROUND (*Netscape v1.1; HTML v3.2*) URL of the image used as wallpaper, a repeating pattern displayed in the background of the document; usually a GIF or JPEG file.

Example: **BACKGROUND="image.jpg"**

BGCOLOR	Color code for the background color using the a color name or code number.

(HTML v3.2) The valid color names are based on the 16 VGA colors: aqua, black, blue, fuchsia, gray, green, lime, maroon, navy, olive, purple, red, silver, real, white, and yellow.

Example: BGCOLOR="white"

(Netscape v1.1; HTML v3.2) The color code "#rrggbb" in the hexadecimal range from 00 to ff (0 to 255 in decimal). This format allows for 16.7 million different colors:

Format Code	Meaning
#	Hexadecimal numbers follow.
rr	Range of red.
gg	Range of green.
bb	Range of blue.

Example: BGCOLOR="#ffffff" produces a page with a background color of white. Here are the hexadecimal codes for 12 common colors:

Color Code	Meaning
"#000000"	Black.
"#909090"	Dark grey.
"#bfbfbf"	Grey (default).
"#dfdfdf"	Dark grey.
"#ffffff"	White.
"#ff0000"	Red.
"#ff00ff"	Magenta (pink).
"#00ff00"	Green.
"#ffff00"	Yellow.
"#00ffff"	Cyan (light blue).
"#0000ff"	Blue.
"#bf00ff"	Purple.

BGPROPERTIES	*(Explorer)* Toggles whether the background image scrolls with the text to create a watermark effect; currently takes a single value:

BgProperties	Meaning
...	Background scrolls with text (default).
"fixed"	Background does not scroll with text.

LINK	*(Netscape v1.1; HTML v3.2)* Color of text for unvisited links, using the "#rrggbb" format.

Example: LINK="#0000ff" is blue, the default color.

TEXT　　　　　(*Netscape v1.1; HTML v3.2*)　Color of text for normal text, using the "#rrggbb" format.

Example: **LINK="#000000"** is black, the default color.

VLINK　　　　(*Netscape v1.1; HTML v3.2*)　Color of text for visited links, using the "#rrggbb" format.

Example: **LINK="#00ff00"** is green, the default color.

TIPS

■ This tag surrounds everything displayed by the browser.

■ Make sure you don't end up with low-contrast text, such as yellow text on a white background, or blue text on a purple background. Some high contrast combinations can be hard to read, such as boldface yellow text on a black background.

■ See Appendix D for a listing of 500 named colors that correspond to #rrggbb hex codes.

RELATED HTML TAG

\<HEAD\>　　　　Defines the type of document.

HTML B

str <BR ... > *str*

Forces a break in the text (*short for BReak*).

SAMPLE MARKUP

- *The text* `The HTML-Java-VRML <BR> Quick Reference` *is displayed as:*

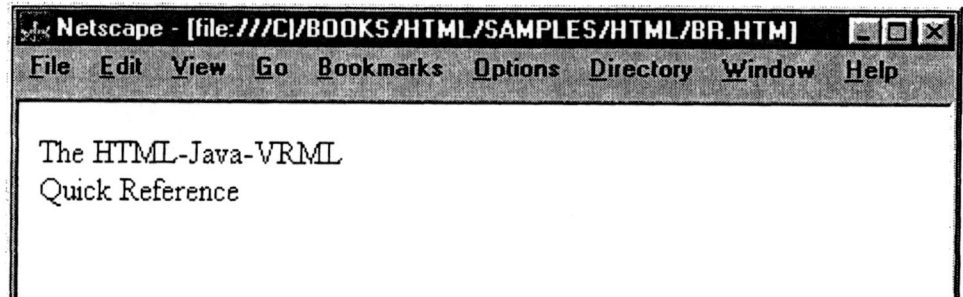

OPTIONAL ATTRIBUTE

CLEAR   (*Netscape v1.1; HTML v3.2*) Force line break to clear floating graphics

Clear	Meaning
all	Move text down until flush with both margins.
left	Move text down until flush with left margin.
right	Move text down until flush with left margin.

TIP

- Normally the HTML browser automatically formats text to fit the window; this tag lets you force the end of a line. For example, use the <BR> tag to separate lines in a poem, while the <P> tag separate the poem's verses.

RELATED HTML TAG

<P>   Signal end of paragraph: breaks line and inserts a blank line.

<CAPTION ... > ... </CAPTION>

Caption for a figure or table.

EXAMPLE MARKUPS

■ To add a caption to a figure:

```
<FIG SRC=bg.gif> <BR>
<CAPTION> This is a caption to the figure </CAPTION> <FIG>
```

OPTIONAL ATTRIBUTES

ALIGN   Alignment of the display.

Example: **ALIGN="right"** right justifies the element.

Align	Meaning
center	Centered
left	Left justified (default).
justify	Justified full column width.
right	Right justified.

TIPS

■ This tag is placed inside the **<FIG>** and **<TABLE>** tags; the best location is at the beginning or end.

■ Although **<CAPTION>** is an HTML v3.2 element, it works in Netscape v2.0 and up.

RELATED HTML TAGS

<FIG>   Places a "formal" figure.

<TABLE>   Creates a table, for which the <CAPTION> tag can be used with.

<TITLE>   Creates a "caption" for the HTML document on the browser's title bar.

HTML C

<CENTER> ... </CENTER>

Centers the text, image, or table between the left and right document edges.

EXAMPLE MARKUP

■ To center some text:

```
This is normal text, <CENTER> followed by centered text
</CENTER> and back to normal again.
```

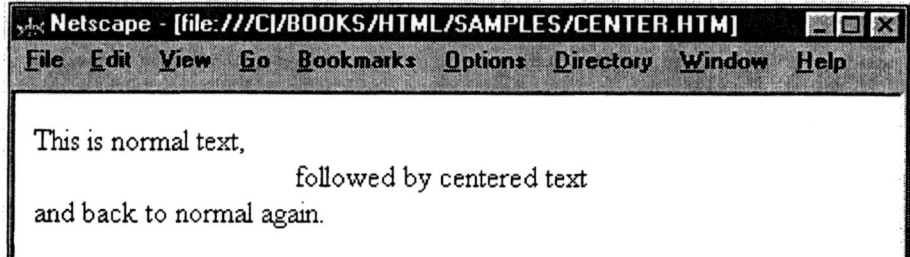

OPTIONAL ATTRIBUTES

none

TIPS

■ This tag does not override the **ALIGN** attribute, if found in another tag.

■ The **<CENTER>** and **</CENTER>** tags cause lines breaks in the flow of text.

■ Use this tag to center a table in the document.

■ The **<CENTER>** tag might be discarded in favor of the **ALIGN="center"** attribute.

RELATED HTML TAGS

none

\<CITE\> *str* \</CITE\>

Marks the string *str* as a citation, typically in italics (*short for CITation*).

SAMPLE MARKUP

■ To indicate a citation:

`This is normal text, <CITE>followed by cited text</CITE>.`

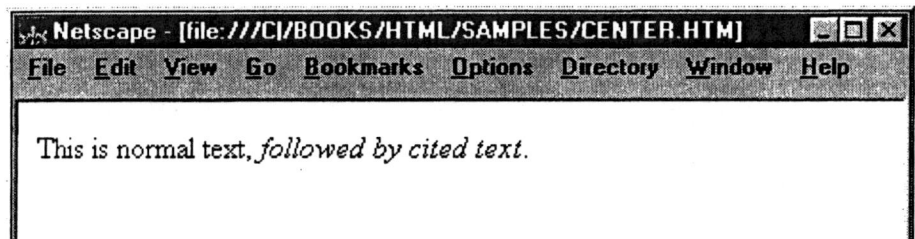

OPTIONAL ATTRIBUTES

none

TIPS

■ This tag causes the browser to render the text appropriate for a citation, typically in italics.

■ The \<CITATION\> tag is typically used within a line of text.

RELATED HTML TAGS

\<ABBREV\>	Indicates an abbreviation.
\<DFN\>	Indicates the definition of a term.
\<Q\>	Brief line of quotation.
\<SAMP\>	Sample of text.

HTML C

\<CODE\> *str* \</CODE\>

Marks the string *str* as programming code and displays it in a fixed font.

SAMPLE MARKUP

- To indicate a fragment of code in the body of text:

```
A fragment of code <CODE>(defun c:id (x y / x1 y1) (command
"ID")) </CODE> that shows a simple AutoLISP function.
```

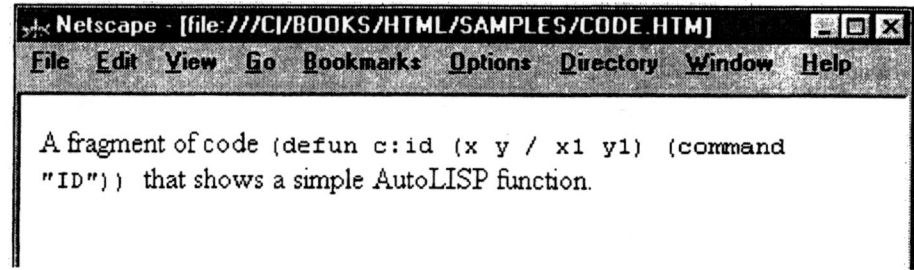

OPTIONAL ATTRIBUTES

code

TIPS

- This tag causes the browser to render the text appropriate for programming code, typically in a fixed font, such as Courier.

- This tag is intended for a single line of code; use the **\<PRE\>** and **\</PRE\>** tags for more than one line of code.

RELATED HTML TAGS

\<PRE\>	Indicates more than one line of code.
\<VAR\>	Indicates a variable.

<DD> ...

Definition of a term; must be used within the **<DL>** tag and preceded by the **<DT>** tag (*short for Definition Definition*).

EXAMPLE MARKUPS

- To create a definition list:

```
A definition list:
<DL>
  <DT> The DL tag:
  <DD> Defines a definition list; or
  <DD> A glossary list.
</DL>
```

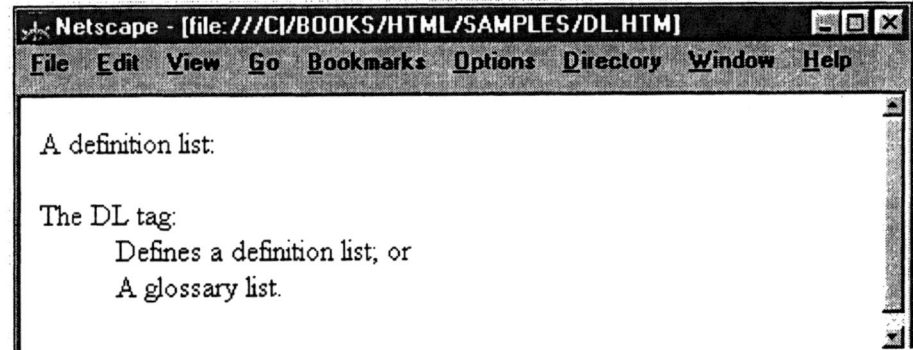

OPTIONAL ATTRIBUTES

none

TIPS

- Use this tag to create a list without bullets or numbers.

- This tag is placed inside the **<DL>** tag; this tag should be preceded by the **<DT>** tag.

- This **</DD>** closing tag is optional.

- Browsers render definition text in different ways.

RELATED HTML TAGS

<DL>	Definition or glossary list.
<DT>	Definition term.

<DFN> *str* </DFN>

Marks enclosed text as a definition (*short for DeFiNed text*).

SAMPLE MARKUP

■ To indicate an definition:

```
Normal text <DFN> followed by definition text. </DFN>
```

OPTIONAL ATTRIBUTES

none

TIPS

■ This tag causes the browser to render the text appropriate for a definition, typically in bold or bold-italics.

■ Browsers that don't understand this tag, such as Navigator v2, render the text as normal.

RELATED HTML TAGS

<DL>   Definition list.

<SAMP>   Sample of text.

<DIR ... > ... </DIR>

(Obsolete) Defines a short, unordered list of items (20 characters or less) that are to be displayed in columns across the page (*short for DIRectory*).

SAMPLE MARKUP

- To create a directory list:

```
A directory list:
<DIR>
  <LI> Upfront #1: 1 May, 1995
  <LI> Upfront #2: 15 May, 1995
</DIR>
```

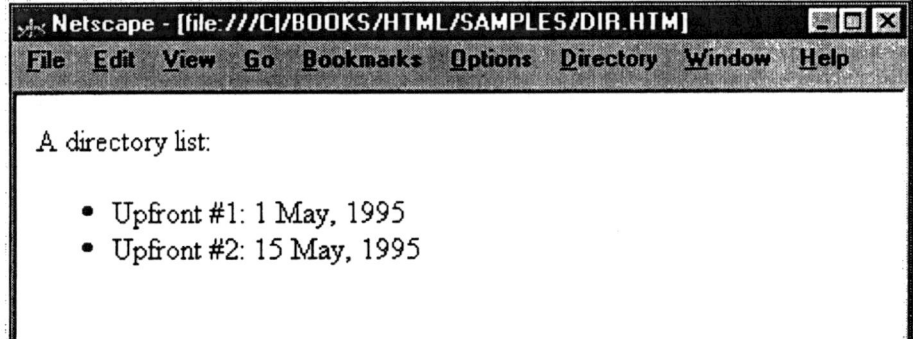

OPTIONAL ATTRIBUTE

COMPACT   Display list in a compact form; not understood by most browsers.

               Example: **<DIR COMPACT> ... </DIR>**

TIPS

- This tag is supposed to display short lists in columns across the document but this does not occur in Navigator v2.0.

- Use the **<LI>** tag to indicate individual list items inside the **<DIR>** and **</DIR>** pair.

- This tag is usually treated exactly like the **<UL>** tag.

- The **<DIR>** tag has been removed from the HTML v3.2 specification.

RELATED HTML TAGS

<LI>   Indicates a list item.

<OL>   Ordered list.

<UL>   Unordered list.

<MENU>   Menu list.

\<DIV ... \> ... \</DIV\>

Marks a block of the document as a logical group (*short for DIVision*).

SAMPLE MARKUP

■ To create an index and a chapter division:

```
<DIV CLASS="index">
  ...
</DIV>
<DIV CLASS="chapter_1">
  ...
</DIV>
```

OPTIONAL ATTRIBUTES

ALIGN   Alignment of the display.

Example: `ALIGN="right"` right justifies the element.

Align	Meaning
center	Centered
left	Left justified (default).
justify	Justified full column width.
right	Right justified.

TIPS

■ This tag allows you to divide the document into logical sections, such as table of contents, introduction, forward, chapters, appendices, and index.

■ The \</DIV\> ending tag is optional since the start of the next \<DIV\> tag implies the end of a paragraph.

RELATED HTML TAG

\<CENTER\>   Centers a block of text.

\<P\>   Breaks up a block of text into paragraphs.

<DL ... > ... </DL>

Defines a list with no bullets or numbering (*short for Definition List*).

EXAMPLE MARKUPS
- To create a definition list:

```
A definition list:
<DL>
  <DT> The DL tag:
  <DD> Defines a definition list; or
  <DD> A glossary list.
</DL>
```

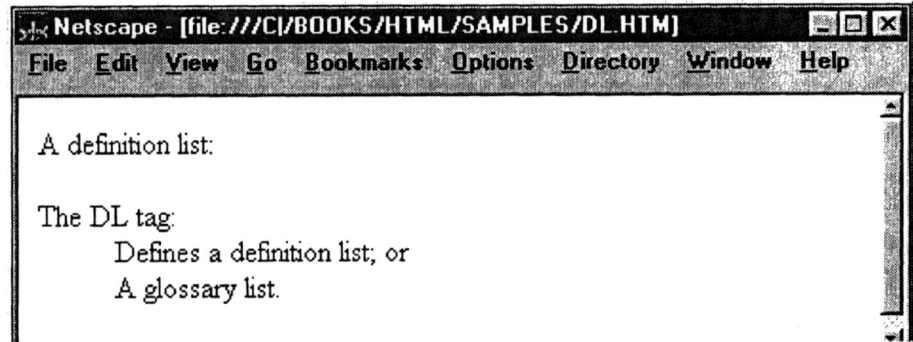

OPTIONAL ATTRIBUTE
COMPACT   (*Obsolete*) Display the text in a compact manner; ignored by most browsers.

TIPS
- This tag encloses the **<DT>** tag to indicate the term being defined, followed by the **<DD>** tag to define the term.

- You may use the **<LH>** tag to create a list heading within the **<DL>**.

RELATED HTML TAGS
<DD>	Definition of the term.
<DT>	Term being defined.
<LH>	List heading.
<OL>	Creates a numbered list.
<UL>	Creates a bulleted list.

\<DT\> *str*

Creates a title for the definition list (*short for Definition Title*).

EXAMPLE MARKUPS

■ To create a definition list:

```
A definition list:
<DL>
  <DT> The DL tag:
  <DD> Defines a definition list; or
  <DD> A glossary list.
</DL>
```

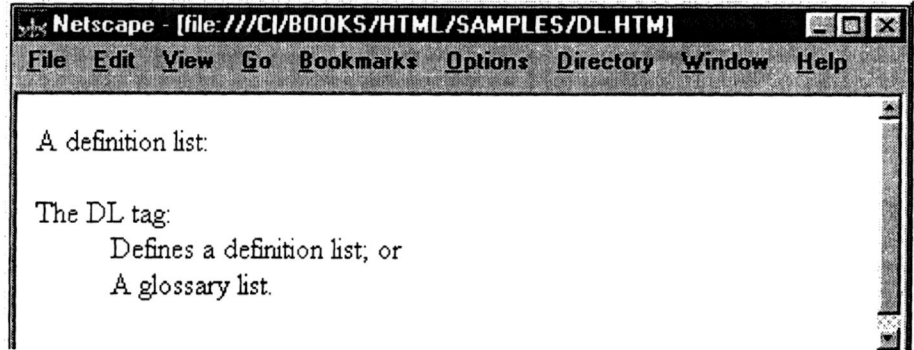

OPTIONAL ATTRIBUTES

none

TIPS

■ This tag is placed inside the \<DL\> tag; this tag should be followed by the \<DI\> tag.

■ The \</DT\> ending tag is optional since the \<DD\> tag is always next.

■ Browsers render definition text in different ways.

RELATED HTML TAGS

\<DL\>   Definition or glossary list.

\<DI\>   Term being defined.

<EM> *str* </EM>

Displays enclosed text as emphasized (*short for EMphasis*).

EXAMPLE MARKUPS
■ To emphasize text:

    This text is <EM> emphasized! </EM>

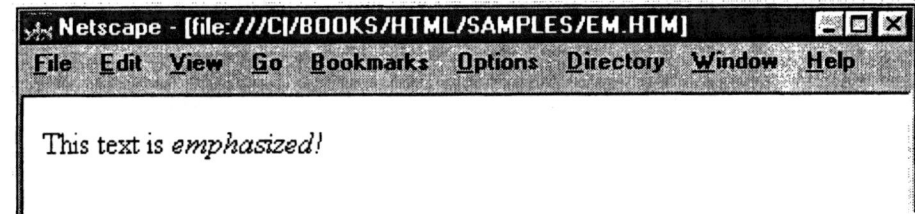

OPTIONAL ATTRIBUTES
none

TIPS
■ This tag typically displays text in italics.

■ Browsers are supposed to render <EM> text different from <STRONG> text.

RELATED HTML TAGS
<B>	Display text in bold face.
<BIG>	Display text in a larger size.
<STRONG>	Display text in a strong format.

\<EMBED SRC ... > ... \</EMBED>   Netscape v2.0

Displays an object — usually by means of a plug-in — that the browser normally cannot display.

REQUIRED ATTRIBUTE

SRC The source filename of the emdedded object in URL format.

Example: `<embed src="http://www.url.com/image.svf">`

EXAMPLE MARKUP

■ To embed an AutoCAD drawing in the HTML document:

```
An AutoCAD drawing embedded into the document:<BR>
<embed src="drawing.dwg" width=200 height=200>
```

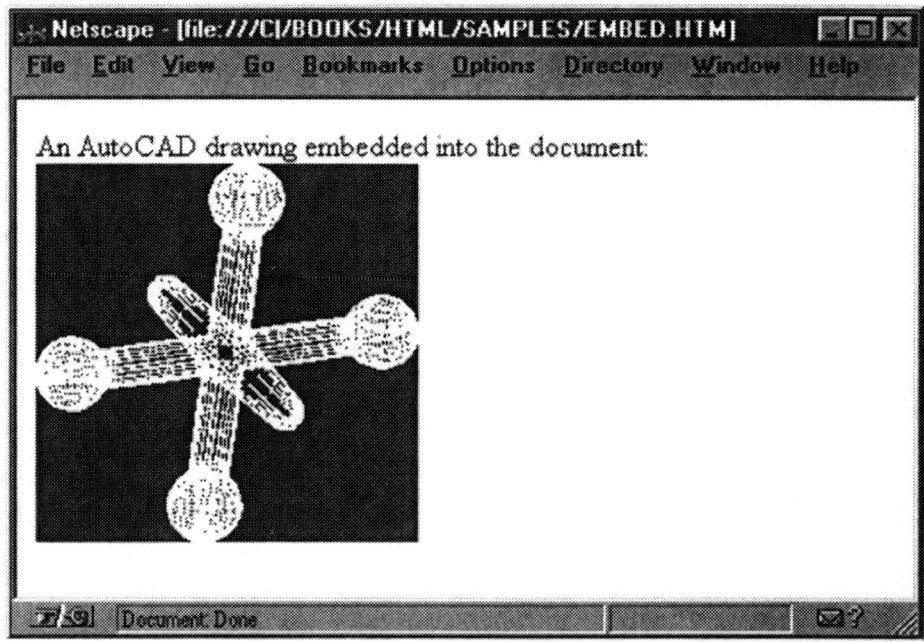

OPTIONAL ATTRIBUTES

HEIGHT Height, measured in pixels or in percent of screen height.

WIDTH Width, measured in pixels or in percent of screen width.

Example: `<embed src="drawing.dwg" width=30% height=40%>` scales the embedded objects to 30% of the width and 40% of the height of the page.

attribute Additional attributes required by the plug-in.

Example: `<embed src="file.dxf" layeron=a,b layeroff=c,d>` turns on layers a and b but turns off layers c and d.

TIPS

■ This tag only works when the MIME (short for Multipupose Internet Mail Extensions) type has been registered with the browser.

■ Through MIME, the browser knows how do deal with a file when the browser does not recognize the filename extension.

■ In Netscape, select **Options | Helpers** to match the filename extension with the plug-in or other action. This is similar to associating a file extension with an application under Windows:

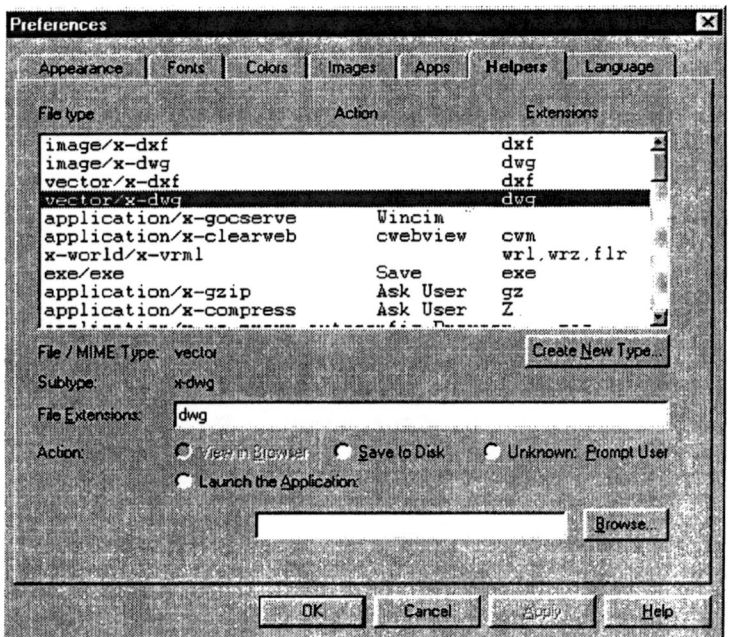

■ For example, Netscape Navigator loads the SoftSource DWG/DXF plug-in when it encounters DWG (AutoCAD drawing files) and DXF files, when these MIME types are associated:

Extension	MIME Type	Meaning
.DWG *or* .dwg	vector/x-dwg	AutoCAD drawing file.
.DXF *or* .dxf	vector/x-dxf	Drawing interchange format.
.SVF *or* .svf	vector/x-svf	Simple vector format.

■ Activate the embedded object by double-clicking.

■ Netscape plans that Navigator v4.0 will automatically load plug-ins, as required.

■ Many plug-ins are available from the Netscape Web site, including:

Plug-in	Meaning
Live3D	VRML (virtual reality modeling language).
Acrobat	PDF (portable document format).
SoftSource	DWG and DXF (AutoCAD drawing files).
QuickTime	Apple QuickTime for multimedia movies.

RELATED HTML TAGS

\<APPLET\>   Executes an application.

\<IMG\>   Imbeds an image in the document.

<FIG SRC ... > ... </FIG>

(*Obsolete*) Inserts a "formal" figure (*short for FIGure*).

REQUIRED ATTRIBUTE

SRC   The source filename of the figure in URL format; see Appendix A.

EXAMPLE MARKUPS

■ To display a figure and include a caption:

```
<FIG SRC="bg.gif">
<CAPTION> A figure with caption. </CAPTION> </FIG>
```

OPTIONAL ATTRIBUTES

CLEAR   (*Netscape v1.1*) Force line break to clear floating graphics

Clear	Meaning
all	Move text down until flush with both margins.
left	Move text down until flush with left margin.
right	Move text down until flush with left margin.

ALIGN   Alignment of the display.

Example: **ALIGN="right"**   right justifies the element.

Align	Meaning
center	Centered
left	Left justified (default).
justify	Justified full column width.
right	Right justified.

HEIGHT   Height, measured in pixels or in percent of screen height.

WIDTH   Width, measured in pixels or in percent of screen width.

Example: `<embed src="drawing.dwg" width=30% height=40%>` scales the embedded objects to 30% of the width and 40% of the height of the page. ^p UNITS="..."

IMAGEMAP   Indicates this is an active image; specifies the URL that the click coordinates should be sent to.

Example: `IMAGEMAP="http://xyz.com/cgi-bin/imagemap"`

TIPS

- This tag was removed from the HTML v3.2 specification.

- It is intended that this tag be used for "formal" figures while **<IMG>** be used for decorative images.

- To display text that identifies the figure (on text-only browsers), simply include text within the **<FIG>** tags, such as `<FIG SRC="image.fig"` **Figure displayed here** `</FIG>`

- This tag performs the same purpose as the **ISMAP** attribute of the **<IMG>** element without the need for a cgi-bin program.

- This tag can contain *all* HTML markup elements, including **<H*n*>**, **<HR>**, **<P>**, and **<OL>**.

- The **<FIG>** tag does not work with Navigator v2 (the figure, above, was faked).

RELATED HTML TAGS

<CAPTION>   Displays a caption to the figure.

<EMBED>   Embed a graphic not supported by the browser.

<IMG>   Display an image.

<FONT SIZE ... >

Displays text in a larger or smaller size.

REQUIRED ATTRIBUTE

SIZE   (*Netscape v1.1; HTML v3.2*) Size of the font.

Example: <FONT **SIZE=+4**> displays the font four times larger than specified by the **<BASEFONT>** tag.

Size	Meaning
+	(Optional) Larger size relative to <BASEFONT>
-	(Optional) Smaller size relative to <BASEFONT>
1	Absolute smallest size.
3	Default size.
7	Absolute largest size.

SAMPLE MARKUP

■ To size and color text:

```
A variety of font sizes:<BR>
<HR>
<FONT SIZE=1 COLOR=#0000ff>
Font size 1 ( the smallest and colored blue). <BR>
<FONT SIZE=3 COLOR=#000000>
Font size 3 (the default size and color, black). <BR>
<FONT SIZE=5 COLOR=#ff0000>
Font size 5 (larger and red). <BR>
<FONT SIZE=7 COLOR=#00ff00>
Font size 7 (the biggest and green).
```

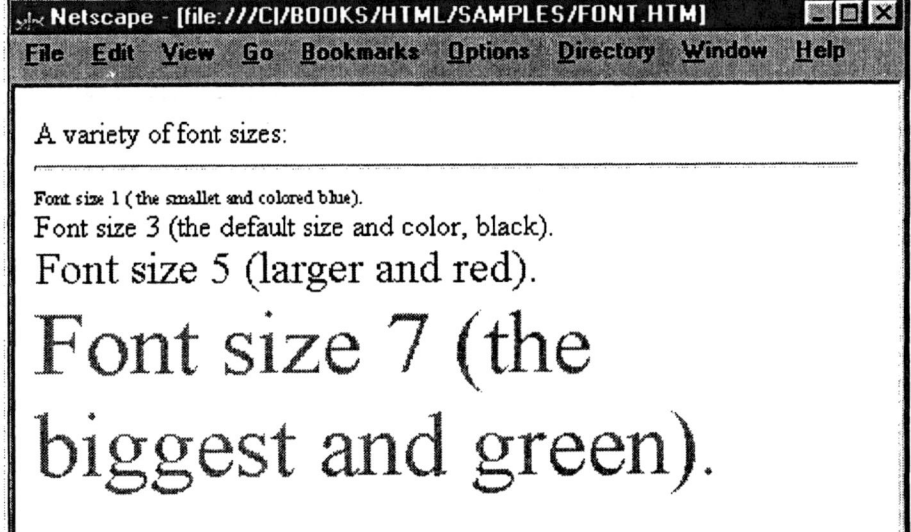

HTML F

OPTIONAL ATTRIBUTES

COLOR   (*Netscape v2.0; HTML v3.2*) Color name or code for the text.

(*HTML v3.2*) The color name uses one of the 16 VGA colors: aqua, black, blue, fuchsia, gray, green, lime, maroon, navy, olive, purple, red, silver, teal, white, and yellow.

(*Netscape v2.0*) The color code uses the format "#rrggbb" in the hexadecimal range from 00 to ff (0 to 255 in decimal). This format allows for 16.7 million different colors:

Format Code	Meaning
#	Hexadecimal numbers follow.
rr	Range of red.
gg	Range of green.
bb	Range of blue.

Example: BGCOLOR="#ffffff" produces a page with a background color of white. Here are the hexadecimal codes for 12 common colors:

Color Code	Meaning
"#000000"	Black.
"#909090"	Dark grey.
"#bfbfbf"	Grey (default).
"#dfdfdf"	Dark grey.
"#ffffff"	White.
"#ff0000"	Red.
"#ff00ff"	Magenta (pink).
"#00ff00"	Green.
"#ffff00"	Yellow.
"#00ffff"	Cyan (light blue).
"#0000ff"	Blue.
"#bf00ff"	Purple.

See Appendix D for the names of 500 colors in hex format.

FACE   (*Explorer*) Name of the type face in Microsoft Windows format.

Example: <FONT SIZE=1 FACE="Arial"> displays the Arial font at a small size.

TIP

■ Don't use difficult to read colors, such as yellow text on a white background.

RELATED HTML TAGS

<BASEFONT>   The font name and size to use as normal text.

<BIG>   Display larger text.

<H*n*>   Display headline text in seven sizes.

<SMALL>   Display smaller text.

<FORM ... > ... </FORM>

Creates a form for users to fill in and sends the data to a cgi-bin server.

SAMPLE MARKUPS
See <INPUT> and <SELECT> for many examples of using the <FORM> tag.

OPTIONAL ATTRIBUTES

ACTION   The URL to which the form data is sent.

METHOD   Determines how form data is sent:

Method	Meaning
GET	Data is sent as part of the URL (default).
POST	Data is sent in the message body.

ENCTYPE   Type of transaction:

EncType	Meaning
application/x -www-form -urlencoded	Single form (default).
multipart/form-data	Form consists of one or more files.

TARGET   (*Netscape v2.0*) Display form in the target frame.

TIPS

■ This tag is used to create forms, such as a subscription application form.

■ Forms cannot work on their own; they must be linked back to a cgi-bin program.

■ While **METHOD=GET** is the default attribute, **METHOD=POST** is preferred.

■ Form data is sent in the format of *name=value* pairs. Each pair separated by the & (ampersand) character. Each is URL-encoded so that spaces are converted to the + (plus) character; some characters are encoded in hexadecimal notation.

■ The **<FORM>** tag expects at least one of the following: **<INPUT>**, **<SELECT>**, or **<TEXTAREA>**.

■ You can use the **<FORM>** and **<INPUT>** tags to create a hyperlink button:

```
<FORM Action="http://www.url.com/">
  Click here to jump to
  <INPUT Type="submit" Value="your URL destination.">
</FORM>
```

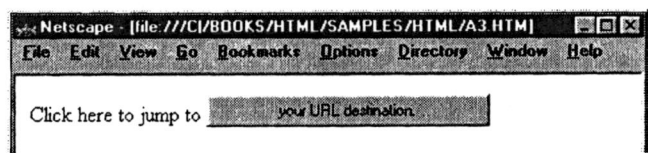

RELATED HTML TAGS

\<INPUT>	Specifies edit fields in the form.
\<OPTION>	List of options for the \<SELECT> tag.
\<SELECT>	Select one option from several options.
\<TEXTAREA>	Paragraph text entry field.

RELATED ENVIRONMENT VARIABLES

QUERY_STRING

Stores the value of the input information appended to the **ACTION=URL** attribute when **METHOD=GET** (the default).

CONTENT_LENGTH

The length of data stored in a data body when **METHOD=POST**.

<FRAME ... >

Defines a frame in **<FRAMESET>**.

SAMPLE MARKUP

■ To create three horizontal frames in one frameset:

```
<FRAMESET ROWS="30%, 40%, 30%">
  <FRAME SCROLLING="no" SRC="font.htm">
  <FRAME SCROLLING="yes" SRC="bg.gif">
  <FRAME SRC="th.gif">
</FRAMESET>
```

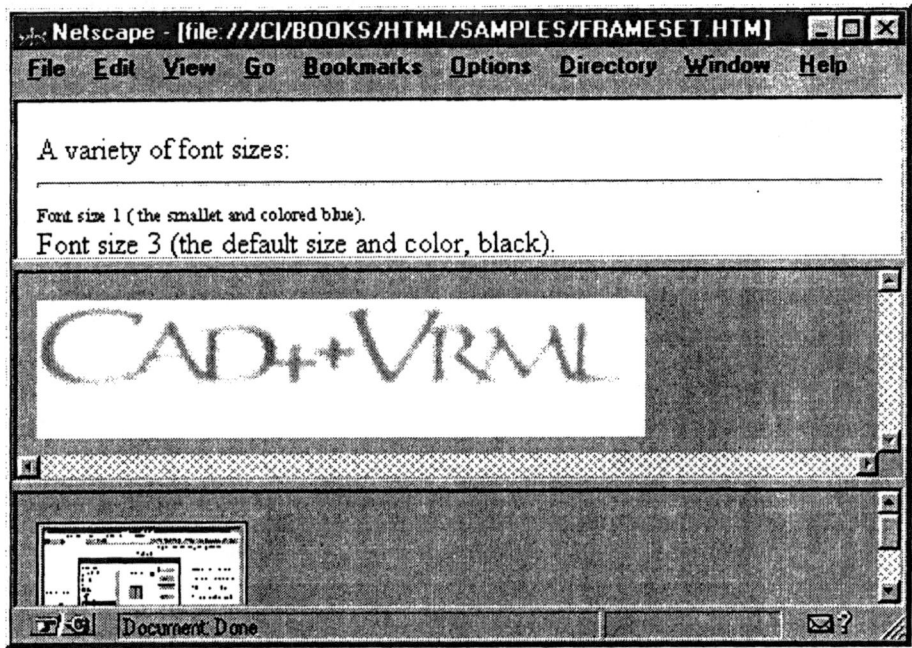

OPTIONAL ATTRIBUTES

SRC   URL of the document to be displayed in the frame.

NAME   Name that can be the target of a frame:

Example: **NAME="frame2"**

Four names have special meaning:

Target	Meaning
"_blank"	Display document in a new unnamed windows.
"_parent"	Display document in parent of the current document; if parent not available; defaults to **"_self"**.
"_self"	Display document in current window.
"_top"	Display document in the top document; if top not available; defaults to **"_self"**.

MARGINWIDTH
> Width of the horizontal margin between the element and the frame, in pixels.

MARGINHEIGHT
> Height of the vertical margin between the element and the frame, in pixels.

SCROLLING　Determines if the frame has scrollbars.

> *Example*: `<FRAME SCROLLING="yes">`

Scrolling	Meaning
yes	Always display scrollbars.
no	Never display scrollbars.
auto	Display scrollbar when necessary (default).

NORESIZE　Prevents the user from resizing the frame.

> *Example*: `<FRAME NORESIZE>`

TIPS

■ A **<FRAME>** with no **SCR** attribute is displayed blank.

■ The **<FRAMESET>** tag *replaces* the **<BODY>** tag; Navigator displays a blank document when both the **<FRAMESET>** and the **<BODY>** tags are present in the HTML file.

■ When a frame does not set **NORESIZE**, the user can resize them to suit; for example, if the frame displays an advertisement, the user can resize the frame to nothing to suppress the ad.

■ When **MARGINWIDTH** and **MARGINHEIGHT** are missing, the browser uses the value of 1 pixel for the margin.

■ The number of **<FRAMES>** must match the number defined by **<FRAMESET>**.

RELATED HTML TAGS

<A>　　　　　Hyperlink.

<BODY>　　　Defines a non-frame document.

<FRAMESET>　Defines a set of frames.

<FRAMESET ... > ... </FRAMESET>

Defines a set of frames.

SAMPLE MARKUP
- To create three horizontal frames in one frameset:

```
<FRAMESET ROWS="30%, 40%, 30%">
  <FRAME SCROLLING="yes" SRC="font.htm"b
  <FRAME SCROLLING="no" SRC="bg.gif">
  <FRAME SRC="th.gif">
</FRAMESET>
```

OPTIONAL ATTRIBUTES

ROWS   Describes the rows of frames in comma-delimited format.

Example: **<FRAMESET ROWS="100","100">** defines two frames, each 100 pixels high.

COLS   Describes the columns of frames in comma-delimited format.

Example: **<FRAMESET COLS="50%","50%">** defines two frames, each taking 50% of the available width.

Rows *or* Cols	Meaning
n	Size of frame in pixels.
n%	Size relative to available space in percent.
1*	Use remaining space equally among frames.
*n**	Use remaining space factored among frames.

TIPS
- The **<FRAME>** element defines the individual frames within a frameset.

- The **<FRAMESET>** tag *replaces* the **<BODY>** tag; Navigator displays a blank document when both the **<FRAMESET>** and the **<BODY>** tags are present in the HTML file.

- Additional **<FRAMESET>** tags subdivide frames into subframes.

- When **MARGINWIDTH** and **MARGINHEIGHT** are missing, the browser uses the value of one pixel for the margin.

- The number of **<FRAMES>** must match the number defined by **<FRAMESET>**.

RELATED HTML TAGS

<FRAME>   Defines a frame.

<NOFRAMES> Display content for browsers that cannot display frames.

<TABLE>   Create a table.

HTML F

<Hn ... > str </Hn>

Displays text in a prominent manner, in a range of six sizes, like a headline (*short for Headline*).

EXAMPLE MARKUPS

- To display headline text in all six sizes:

```
All of the headline sizes:
<H1><HR> Headline size 1 (the largest). </H1>
<H2> Headline size 2. </H2>
<H3> Headline size 3. </H3>
<H4> Headline size 4. </H4>
<H5> Headline size 5. </H5>
<H6> Headline size 6 (the smallest). </H6>
```

OPTIONAL ATTRIBUTE

ALIGN   (*HTML v3.2*) Alignment of the display.

Example: ALIGN="right"   right justifies the element.

Align	Meaning
center	Centered
left	Left justified (default).
justify	Justified full column width.
right	Right justified.

TIPS

■ The HTML standard calls for documents to use the H*n* tags in decreasing order: the first text uses **<H1>**, the next text uses **<H2>**, etc. However logical that may be, typographical considerations call for using whatever size of **<H*n*>** you think looks good in your document.

■ The **<H1>** tag is used for primary headlines; the correct display is supposed to be bold, a very large font, centered, and causes a page break when printed.

■ The display of the **<H2>** element by the browser is supposed to be bold, large font, and flush left.

■ The display of the **<H3>** element by the browser is supposed to be italic, large font, and slightly indented.

■ The display of the **<H4>** element by the browser is supposed to be bold, normal font, and indented more than **<H3>**.

■ The display of the **<H5>** element by the browser is supposed to be italic, normal font, and indented as **<H4>**.

■ The display of the **<H6>** element by the browser is supposed to be bold, normal font, and not indented.

■ Note that Navigator v2 uses a font size for **<H5>** and **<H6>** smaller than normal text; the font size for all headers is at least as large as regular text for most other browsers.

RELATED HTML TAGS

<B>	Displays text boldface.
<BIG>	Displays text big.
<STRONG>	Displays text strongly.
<EM>	Emphasizes the text.
<FONT>	Specifies a font size and color.
<I>	Displays the text in italics.

<HEAD> ... </HEAD>

Describes the contents of the HTML document.

EXAMPLE MARKUP

■ Even though this tag is optional, it makes good programming sense to include it as a form of identification. The most basic HTML file uses the following tags:

```
<html>
  <head>
    <title> The Short HTML File </title>
  </head>
  <body>
    <H1> The First Headline </H1>
    Text and other material making up this document. <P>
  </body>
</html>
```

OPTIONAL ATTRIBUTES
none

TIP

■ This tag surrounds information about the document; the **<BODY>** tag surrounds the content of the document.

■ The **<HEAD>**, **<HTML>**, and **<BODY>** elements are optional.

■ The tags permitted within the **<HEAD>** ... **</HEAD>** elements are listed below.

RELATED HTML TAGS

<BASE>	The absolute URL used with any relative URLs within the document.
<ISINDEX>	Indicates the document is keyword-searchable.
<LINK>	Specifies the relationship between this and other documents.
<META>	Non-HTML information.
<NEXTID>	The next identifier; for use by automatic HTML editors.
<STYLE>	Specify default formatting for the document.
<TITLE>	Document title displayed by browser.

<HR ... >

Draws a horizontal line (*short for Horizontal Rule*).

SAMPLE MARKUP

■ To size and color a horizontal rule:

```
A variety of horizontal rules... <BR>
First, the standard, default rule:
<HR>
Now, a rule with NOSHADE:
<HR NOSHADE>
A short rule, 50% of the width of the page:
<HR NOSHADE WIDTH="50%">
Another short rule, this one 50 pixels wide:
<HR NOSHADE WIDTH="50">
A 10-pixel-thick rule:
<HR NOSHADE SIZE="10">
Here is the ALIGN="left" attribute at work:
<HR NOSHADE WIDTH="50" ALIGN="left">
```

Netscape - [file:///C|/BOOKS/HTML/SAMPLES/HR.HTM]

File   Edit   View   Go   Bookmarks   Options   Directory   Window   Help

A variety of horizontal rules...
First, the standard, default rule:

Now, a rule with NOSHADE:

A short rule, 50% of the width of the page:

Another short rule, this one 50 pixels wide:

A 10-pixel-thick rule:

Here is the ALIGN="left" attribute at work:

HTML H

OPTIONAL ATTRIBUTES

ALIGN (*Netscape v1.1*) Alignment of the display.

Example: ALIGN="right" right justifies the element.

Align	Meaning
center	Centered
left	Left justified (default).
justify	Justified full column width.
right	Right justified.

NOSHADE (*Netscape v1.1*) Display rule in solid 50% grey; default is three shades of gray.

SIZE (*Netscape v1.1*) The thickness (vertical direction) of the rule, in pixels.

WIDTH (*Netscape v1.1*) The width (horizontal direction) of the rule across the page; default = full width.

Example: <HR WIDTH="50%">

Width	Meaning
n	Absolute width: in pixels.
n%	Relative width: percentage of the document's width.

TIPS

■ Use this tag to visually separate blocks of text.

■ The default rule is three pixels wide, consisting of (from top to bottom) a dark gray, medium gray, and light gray line, each one pixel high.

RELATED HTML TAG

<IMG> A long, thin image can be used to replace the horizontal rule.

<HTML ... > ... </HTML>

Contains the entire HTML file; the grandaddy of all tags (*short for Hyper Text Markup Language*).

SAMPLE MARKUP

■ Even though this tag is optional, it makes good programming sense to include it as a form of identification. The most basic HTML file uses the following tags:

```
<html>
  <head>
    <title> The Short HTML File </title>
  </head>
  <body>
    <H1> The First Headline </H1>
    Text and other material making up this document. <P>
  </body>
</html>
```

OPTIONAL ATTRIBUTE

VERSION   Declares the version of HTML being used.

Example: <HTML VERSION=""-//W30//DTD W3 HTML 3.0// EN"">

TIPS

■ All other tags are placed within this pair of tags.

■ The <HEAD>, <HTML>, and <BODY> elements are optional.

RELATED HTML TAGS

all

HTML H

<I> str </I>

Displays the enclosed text in an italic font (*short for Italic*).

EXAMPLE MARKUP

■ To display italic text:

```
Normal text, <I> followed by italic text. </I>
```

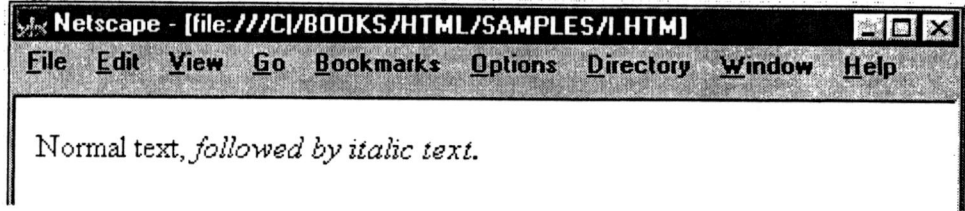

OPTIONAL ATTRIBUTES

none

TIPS

■ The HTML standard calls for browsers to display <B> text different from <I>.

■ While the <I> tag is supposed to display text in italics, some browsers may not be able to and will display text differently.

RELATED HTML TAGS

<B>   Displays text boldface.

<EM>   Emphasizes the text.

<FONT>   Specifies a font size and color.

<IMG SRC ... >

Displays an image in the document (*short for IMaGe*).

REQUIRED ATTRIBUTE

SRC   The source filename for the image file in URL format; see Appendix A (*short for SouRCe*).

EXAMPLE MARKUPS

- To display an image in the document:

  ```
  The simplest application of the IMG tag:
  <IMG SRC=th.gif>
  ```

- To display a text description of the image:

  ```
  The effect of the ALT attribute:
  <IMG SRC=bg.gif ALT="[Thumbnail Image]">
  ```

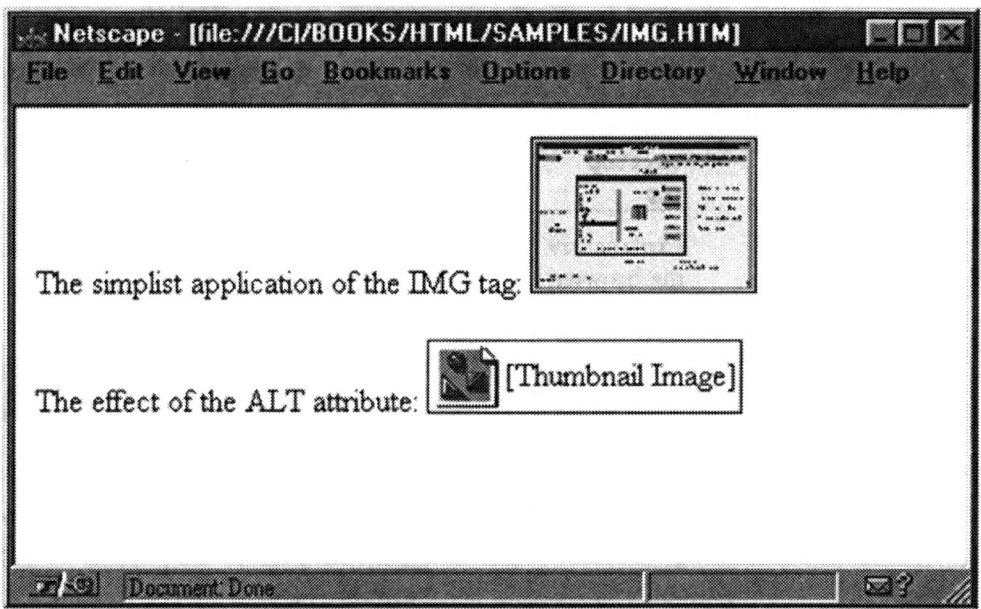

OPTIONAL ATTRIBUTES

ALIGN   Alignment of image with adjacent text. Your browser might interpret the alignment in different manners.

Align (HTML v2.0)	Meaning
bottom	Align with bottom of text.
middle	Align with middle of text.
top	Align with top of text.

(*Netscape v1.1*) Netscape refined the meaning of the **ALIGN** attribute's options to lessen confusion:

Align	Meaning
absbottom	Align image bottom with lowest text in the line.
absmiddle	Align image middle with the middle of text line.
baseline	Align the bottom of the image with text baseline.
bottom	Align bottom of image with text baseline.
left	Align image with left margin; wrap text to the right of the image.
middle	Align middle of image with text baseline.
right	Align image with right margin; wrap text to the left of the image.
texttop	Align image top with the tallest text in the line.
top	Align top of image with text baseline.

ALT   Explanatory text displayed if the image is not or cannot be displayed by the browser.

ISMAP   Turns the **<IMG>** element into an image map.

HEIGHT   (*Netscape v1.1; HTML v3.2*) The height (vertical direction) of the image.

WIDTH   (*Netscape v1.1; HTML v3.2*) The width (horizontal direction) of the image across the page; default = full width.

Example: **<IMG WIDTH="50%">**

Width *or* Height	Meaning
n	Absolute width: in pixels.
n%	Relative width: percentage of the document's width.

BORDER   (*Netscape v1.1; HTML v3.2*) The width, in pixels, of the border around the image used as a hypertext anchor.

Example: **<IMG SRC="img.gif" BORDER="2">** draws a two-pixel-wide border around the image.

Border	Meaning
n	Width, in pixels.
1	One pixel wide border; default.
0	No border.

HSPACE	(*Netscape v1.1; HTML v3.2*) Reserve blank space (a margin) around the application, in pixels.
VSPACE	(*Netscape v1.1; HTML v3.2*) Reserve blank space (a margin) around the application, in pixels.
USEMAP	(*Netscape v2.0; HTML v3.2*) Specifies a URL with a #*name* suffix to identify a file and map name, and is used with the **<MAP>** element.
DYNSRC	(*Explorer*) Specifies the URL of a video clip or VRML scene.
START	(*Explorer*) Determines when the video clip or VRML scene begins:

Start	Meaning
fileopen	Start when file opens.
mouseover	Start when mouse moves over image.

CONTROLS	(*Explorer*) Displays a set of controls appropriate for the image.
LOOP	(*Explorer*) Specifies the number of times the video clip repeats:

Loop	Meaning
n	Rerun the video clip *n* times.
INFINITE	Rerun the video clip an infinite number of times.
-1	Rerun the video clip an infinite number of times.

LOOPDELAY	(*Explorer*) The delay before the video clip repeats; in milliseconds.

Dir	Meaning
"ltr"	Left to right (default).
"rtl"	Right to left.

TIPS

■ The functions of the **<FIG>** element are replaced by the **<IMG>** element in the HTML v3.2 specification.

■ Specifying the **BORDER, HEIGHT,** and **WIDTH** attributes improves the download performance on some browsers.

■ If the **<IMG>** tag is used with the **ISMAP** attribute, then the x,y-coordinates of the upper-left corner of the image are (0,0).

■ The **ISMAP** attribute is only meaningful if the **<IMG>** element is within the contents of an **<A> element** is connected to a cgi-bin program at the URL identified by the **HREF** attribute of the **<A>** element.

■ To display the meaning of an image when the image is not displayed, the **ALT** text is commonly surrounded by square brackets, such as:

```
<IMG SRC=fig.gif ALT="[Explanation of Figure]">
```

RELATED HTML TAGS

<EMBED>	Displays images via browser plug-ins.
<FIG>	Displays a figure.

<INPUT TYPE ... >

Creates a user input area in a form, including radio buttons, check boxes, and text entry areas.

REQUIRED ATTRIBUTE

TYPE   Specifies the type of input form to display. The **\<INPUT\>** tag requires the **TYPE** attribute and one of these options:

Type	Meaning
text	Display a text entry box (default).
password	Display a password input box.
checkbox	Display a check box.
radio	Display a radio button.
submit	Displays the Submit button.
reset	Displays the Reset button.
hidden	A hidden element.
image	A clickable inline image.

SAMPLE MARKUPS

■ To create check boxes (allows one or more selections):

```
<FORM>
  Pick one or more: <BR>
  <INPUT TYPE="checkbox" VALUE="AutoCAD"> AutoCAD<BR>
  <INPUT TYPE="checkbox" VALUE="MicroStation" CHECKED>
    MicroStation<BR>
  <INPUT TYPE="checkbox" VALUE="Virtual Drafter">Virtual
    Drafter<BR>
</FORM>
```

- To create radio buttons (only one slection may be made):

```
<FORM>
  Chose one from the following:<BR>
  <INPUT TYPE="radio" VALUE="AutoCAD"> AutoCAD<BR>
  <INPUT TYPE="radio" VALUE="MicroStation"
    CHECKED>MicroStation<BR>
  <INPUT TYPE="radio" VALUE="Virtual Drafter"> Virtual Drafter<BR>
</FORM>
```

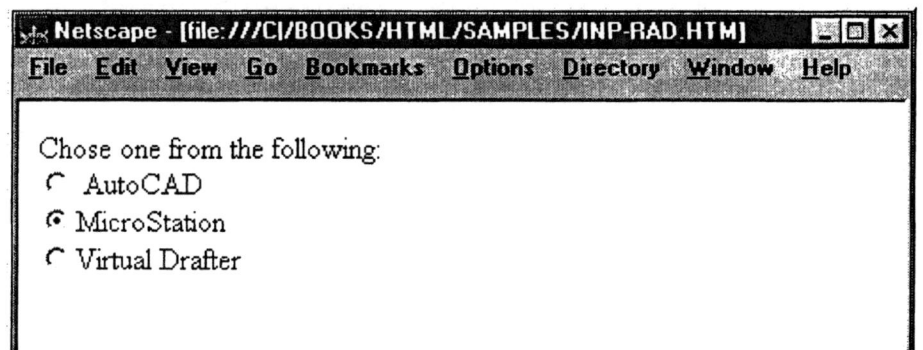

- To prompt for a password (text input is hidden by asterisks):

```
<FORM>
  Enter your password:
  <INPUT TYPE="password" VALUE="system" SIZE=8>
</FORM>
```

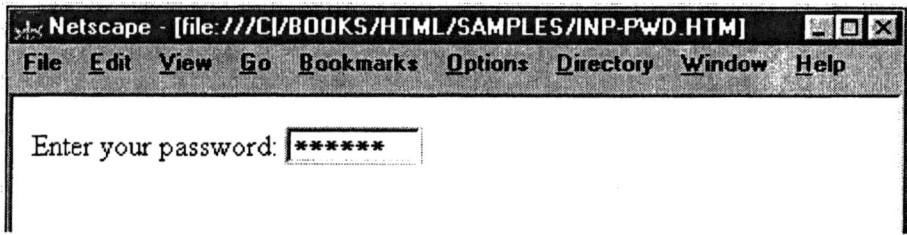

- To prompt for a text entry (a single line of text):

```
<FORM>
  Enter your userid:
  <INPUT TYPE="text" NAME="userid" VALUE="guest" SIZE=8>
</FORM>
```

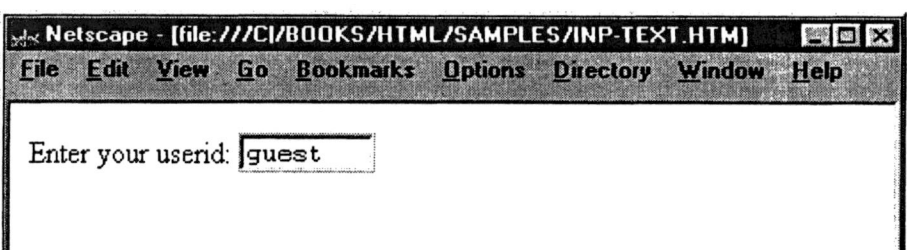

■ To display the **Submit Query** and **Reset** buttons:

```
<FORM>
  Click <B> Submit Query </B> to send data, otherwise click <B>
Reset       </B> to exit: <P>
  <INPUT  TYPE="submit">
  <INPUT  TYPE="reset">
</FORM>
```

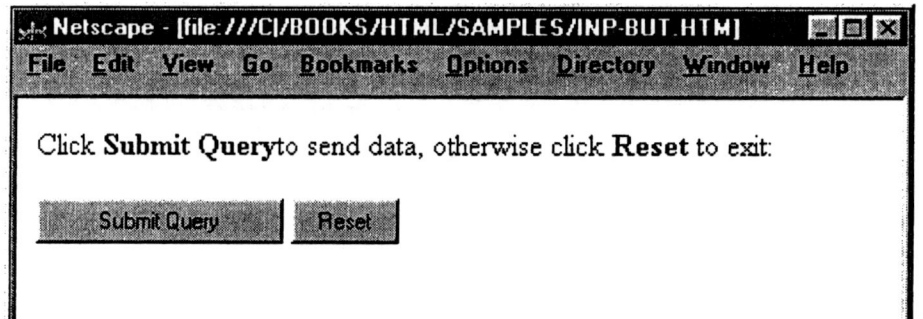

OPTIONAL ATTRIBUTES

ACCEPT   A comma-delimited list of acceptable MIME formats for the file **TYPE**.

DISABLED   Input item is displayed as disabled, usually grayed out.

ERROR   Displays an error message when input is incorrect.

■ *The TYPE=TEXT attribute takes these optional attributes:*

NAME   Assigns a variable name to the value entered into the input element.

MAXLENGTH   Maximum text buffer for text and password **TYPE**s.

SIZE   Size of displayed field; width of text and password **TYPE**s in characters.

VALUE   The initial value of an input element.

■ *The TYPE=CHECKBOX attribute takes these optional attributes:*

CHECKED   Indicates that the radio and checkbox **TYPE** is turned on.

NAME   Assigns a variable name to the value entered into the input element.

VALUE   The initial value of an input element.

■ *The TYPE=RADIO attribute takes these optional attributes:*

CHECKED   Indicates that the radio and checkbox **TYPE** is turned on.

■ *The TYPE=HIDDEN attribute takes these optional attributes:*

NAME   Assigns a variable name to the value entered into the input element.

VALUE   The initial value of an input element.

- *The TYPE=IMAGE attribute takes these optional attributes:*

ALIGN　　　　　Alignment of the display.

　　　　　　　　Example: ALIGN="right"　right justifies the element.

Align	Meaning
center	Centered
left	Left justified (default).
justify	Justified full column width.
right	Right justified.

NAME　　　　　Assigns a variable name to the value entered into the input element.

SRC　　　　　　Specifies the URL for an image that replaces the rule.

- *The TYPE=SUBMIT attribute takes these optional attributes:*

NAME　　　　　Assigns a variable name to the value entered into the input element.

VALUE　　　　　The initial value of an input element.

- *The TYPE=RESET attribute takes these optional attributes:*

VALUE　　　　　The initial value of an input element.

TIPS

- Use this tag to create a data entry input form.

- The longest text entry is 1,024 characters.

- This tag can only be used with a cgi-bin program to process the data generated by the user.

RELATED HTML TAGS

\<FORM\>　　　　Defines the form.

\<OPTION\>　　　Range of possible values.

\<SELECT\>　　　Select from a range of values.

\<ISINDEX ... >

An early version of the **\<FORM>** tag.

SAMPLE MARKUP

■ The \<ISINDEX> tag is simply included in the **\<HEAD>** section of an HTML file:

```
<HEAD>
  <ISINDEX>
  <TITLE> A File with IsIndex. </TITLE>
</HEAD>
```

OPTIONAL ATTRIBUTES

ACTION   The URL to which the data is sent.

PROMPT   (*Netscape v1.1*) Character string used by the browser as the query prompt.

TIPS

■ This tag has been replaced in practice by the **\<FORM>** tag.

■ This tag can be placed in the **\<HEAD>** or **\<BODY>** section of an HTML document.

■ When placed in the **\<HEAD>** section, this tag informs the browser this document can be examined using a keyword search.

■ When placed in the **\<BODY>** section, this tag requires that the **ACTION** attribute points to a cgi-bin program that handles the query.

■ In the **\<BODY>** section, this tag prompts the user: "This is a searchable index. Enter search keywords:"

RELATED HTML TAG

\<FORM>   Creates a form.

<KBD> *str* </KBD>

Displays enclosed text in a "keyboard" font (*short for KeyBoarD*).

EXAMPLE MARKUP

■ To display keyboard text in size six:

```
<FONT SIZE=6>
This is normal text, <KBD> followed by keyboard text. </KBD>
```

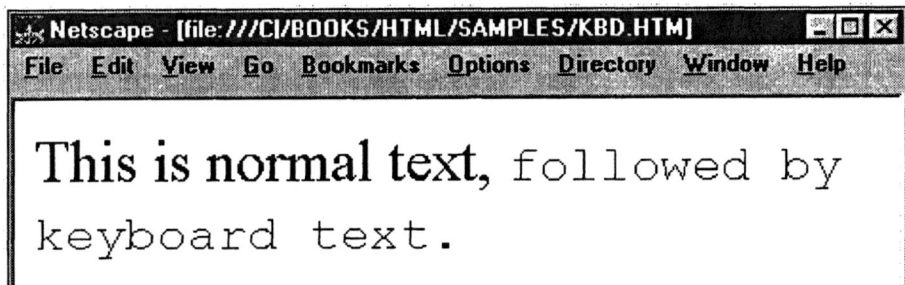

OPTIONAL ATTRIBUTES

none

TIPS

■ The HTML standard calls for browsers to display **<KBD>** text different from **<CODE>** but most browsers display the two the same.

■ You may want to use the **<B>** tag to help differentiate keyboard input from computer prompts, such as:

```
<KBD> Enter value: <B> 32.6540 </B></KBD>
```

■ This tag is intended to present text as entered by a user at the keyboard.

RELATED HTML TAGS

<CODE>   Displays text as a line of programming code.

<FONT>   Specifies a font size and color.

<PRE>   Displays text as several lines of programming code.

<LI ... > str

Defines an item in a list (*short for List Item*).

SAMPLE MARKUP

- To change the type of bullet in an unordered list:

```
The following unordered list:
<UL>
  <LH> This is the heading.
  <LI> The first item.
  <LI TYPE="circle"> The second item.
  <LI TYPE="square"> The third item.
</UL>
```

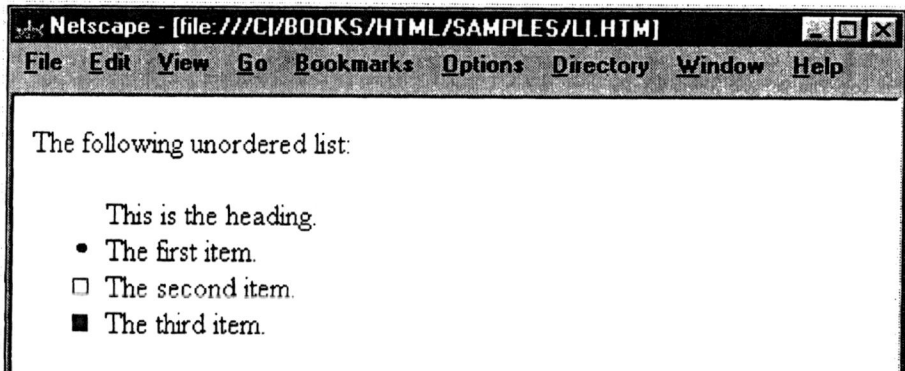

- To change the type of numbering in an ordered list:

```
Plus, the numbered list:
<OL>
  <LH> This is the heading.
  <LI> The first item.
  <LI TYPE="A"> The second item.
  <LI TYPE="i"> The third item.
</OL>
```

Plus, the numbered list:

    This is the heading.
1. The first item.
B. The second item.
iii. The third item.

OPTIONAL ATTRIBUTES

TYPE   (*Netscape v1.1; HTML v3.2*) Specifies the type of list marking within an
                <UL> unordered list.

                Example: **<LI TYPE="square">**

Type	Meaning
disk	Solid circle bullet; default.
circle	Open circle bullet.
square	Solid square bullet.

TYPE   (*Netscape v1.1; HTML v3.2*) Specifies the type of list marking within an
                <OL> ordered list.

                Example: **<LI TYPE="a">**

Type	Meaning
A	Uppercase alphabetical list (A, B, C, etc).
a	Lowercase alphabetical list (a, b, c, etc).
I	Uppercase Roman numeral list (I, II, III, etc).
i	Lowercase Roman numeral list (i, ii, iii, etc).
1	Numbered list (1, 2, 3, etc); default.

VALUE   (*Netscape v1.1; HTML v3.2*) Sets the value of the numeric counter for an
                <OL> ordered list.

                Example: **<LI TYPE="1" VALUE="4">** changes counter value to 4.

TIPS

■ The closing </LI> is optional.

■ The **START** attribute of the <OL> tag initializes the sequence number; use the **VALUE**
attribute of the <LI> tag to change the sequence.

RELATED HTML TAGS

<DL>   Directory list (no bullets or numbers).

<OL>   Ordered list (numbers).

<UL>   Unordered list (bullets).

<LINK HREF ... >

Describes the relationship of this document with other documents.

REQUIRED ATTRIBUTE

HREF   The filename of the linked document in URL format; see Appendix A.

SAMPLE MARKUP

■ To identify the next document:

```
<LINK REL="next" TITLE="Name of Document #3" HREF="http://
xyzpress.com/url-s3.html">
```

OPTIONAL ATTRIBUTES

REL   Describes the relationship of the destination document to the current
                    document (*short for RELation*).

                    Example: REL="index"

REV   Describes the relationship of the current document to the destination
                    document (*short for REVerse relation*).

                    Example: REV="begin"

Rel and Rev	Meaning
"meta"	Meta information.
"navigate"	Navigational aid, map, or index.
"begin"	The first document of a series.
"end"	The last document of the series.
"next"	The next document of the series.
"previous"	The previous document of the series.
"child"	A subdocument.
"parent"	The parent to the subdocument.
"sibling"	Subdocument with a parent in common.
"top"	The logical top document.
"contents"	Table of contents.
"index"	Index.
"biblioentry"	An entry in a bibliography or citation.
"citation"	A citation.
"definition"	A definition.
"bibliography"	The bibliography.
"glossary"	A glossary.
"author"	The author(s) of the document.
"made"	Alternate to the author, "made by".
"editor"	The editor(s) of the document.
"publisher"	The publisher of the document.
"copyright"	The document's copyright information.
"trademark"	Trademark information.
"disclaimer"	The legal disclaimer text.

URN	Universal Resource Name, the intended replacement for URLs.
TITLE	Displays a title, usually on the browser's title bar.
METHODS	Specifies the HTTP communications method for requesting (or sending) data from (or to) the server.

TIPS

■ One document may have links to many other documents.

■ To specify a sequence between documents, include two **<LINK>** elements identifying the next and previous documents with:

```
<LINK REL="next" TITLE="Name of Document #3" HREF="http://
xyzpress.com/url-s3.html">
```

```
<LINK REL="prev" TITLE="Name of Document #1" HREF="http://
xyzpress.com/url-s1.html">
```

■ Since it is more efficient to break up a large document into smaller HTML documents, use the **<LINK>** element to identify the relationship between the parent and subdocuments. For example, the parent document identifies subdocuments with the **REL** attribute:

```
<LINK REL="subdocument" TITLE="Name of Subdocument #1"
HREF="http://xyzpress.com/url-s1.html">
```

And the subdocument identifies the parent document with the **REV** attribute:

```
<LINK REV="subdocument" TITLE="Name of Parent Document"
HREF="http://xyzpress.com/url-p.html">
```

■ A typical use for the **<LINK>** element is to identify the owner of the document:

```
<LINK REV="owns" TITLE="WorldCAD Access" HREF="mailto:
ralphg@ xyzpress.com">
```

■ If you use the **REV="made"** attribute in **<LINK>**, some browsers expect the URL "mailto:name@e-mail_address" (which allows sending a comment to the person responsible for the document). According to Sandia Labs, this seems to only work if "made" is the only relationship in that **<LINK>** element — contrary to the specification of the HTML standard.

RELATED HTML TAGS

| <A> | Anchor. |
| <BASE> | The base URL address. |

<LISTING ... > *str* </LISTING>

(*Obsolete*) Displays enclosed text in its original form with no formatting.

SAMPLE MARKUP

■ To display test in LISTING format:

```
2. When the <I> Command: </I> prompt appears, type the following
on the keyboard:
<LISTING>
  Command: <B>(+ 9 7) [Enter] </B>
  16
  Command:
</LISTING>
```

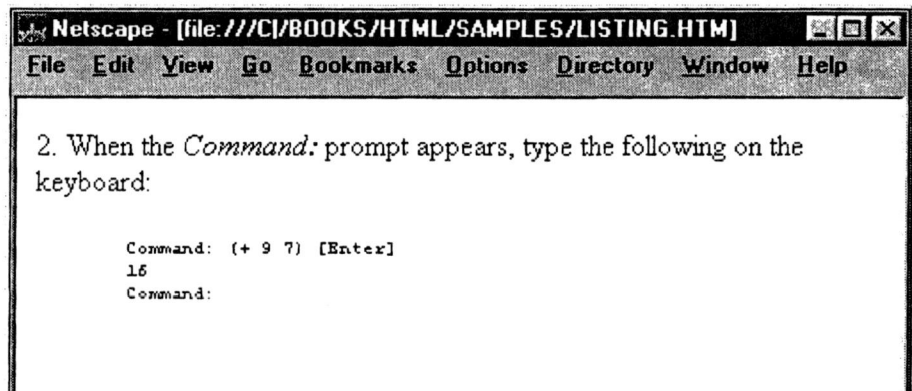

OPTIONAL ATTRIBUTE

WIDTH   The width of text, in characters.

TIPS

■ This tag has been replaced in practice by the **<PRE>** tag and was removed from the HTML v3.2 specification.

■ The HTML specification calls for browsers to use a font that allows **<LISTING>** text to display 132 columns wide.

RELATED HTML TAG

<PRE>   Displays text in a fixed-width font.

<MAP NAME ... > ... </MAP>

Map hotzones in the document; names and describes the client-side map.

REQUIRED ATTRIBUTE

NAME   Defines the map name used in the **<IMG>** element's USEMAP attribute.

EXAMPLE MARKUP

■ To create an image map with two "hot spots":

```
<MAP NAME="welcomemap">
  <AREA SHAPE="rect" coord="0,0,10,10" HREF="url-1.htm">
  <AREA SHAPE="rect" coord="10,10,20,20" HREF="url-2.htm">
</MAP>
```

OPTIONAL ATTRIBUTES

CORDS   (*Netscape v2.0*) Coordinates of the hotzone's location in the image.

HREF   (*Netscape v2.0*) Source of the hotzone specified by URL.

NAME   (*Netscape v2.0*) Filename of the image embedded by the **<IMG>** tag.

NOHREF   (*Netscape v2.0*) Hotzone performs no action.

SHAPE   (*Netscape v2.0*) Shape of the hotzone; default value is "rect", which defines a rectangle.

TIPS

■ This tag must be used with the **<AREA>** tag.

■ A "map" is a rectangular area defined on an image that is selected to make a hyperlink.

RELATED HTML TAGS

<AREA>   Defines a clickable hot spot.

<FIG>   Displays an image with any shape map.

<IMG>   Displays an image with integrated, rectangular maps.

HTML M

<MARQUEE ... > ... </MARQUEE>

Microsoft
Extension

Creates an independent area of scrolling text.

OPTIONAL ATTRIBUTES

ALIGN — Alignment of text within the marquee.

Align	Meaning
top	Align text to top of marquee.
middle	Center text in the middle of the marquee.
bottom	Align text to bottom of marquee.

BEHAVIOR — Determines behavior of text during scrolling.

Behavior	Meaning
scroll	Scroll off the side (default).
slide	Slide in and stay.
alternate	Bounce between alternate sides.

BGCOLOR — Background color of the marquee.

BgColor	Meaning
#rrggbb	Hexadecimal notation.
colorname	One of the following named colors: Black, Maroon, Green, Olive, Navy, Purple, Teal, Gray, Silver, Red, Lime, Yellow, Blue, White, Aqua, Fuchsia

DIRECTION — Text flow direction.

Direction	Meaning
left	Left to right (default)
right	Right to left.

HEIGHT — Height of the marquee.

Height	Meaning
n	Absolute height, in pixels.
n%	Relative height, in percent of screen height.

HSPACE — The horizontal margin distance between marquee and text, in pixels.

LOOP — Number of times the text loops.

Loop	Meaning
n	Loop n times.
INFINITE	An infinite number of times.
-1	An infinite number of times.

SCROLLAMOUNT — Number of pixels the text scrolls by.

SCROLLDELAY — Number of milliseconds of delay between each scroll.

VSPACE — The vertical margin distance between marquee and text, in pixels.

<MENU ... > *str* </MENU>

(*Obsolete*) Defines a list of multi-line elements.

SAMPLE MARKUP
- A menu list looks like an unordered list:

```
The following is a menu list:
<MENU>
  <LH> This is the heading.
  <LI> The first item.
  <LI TYPE="circle"> The second item.
  <LI TYPE="square"> The third item.
</MENU>
```

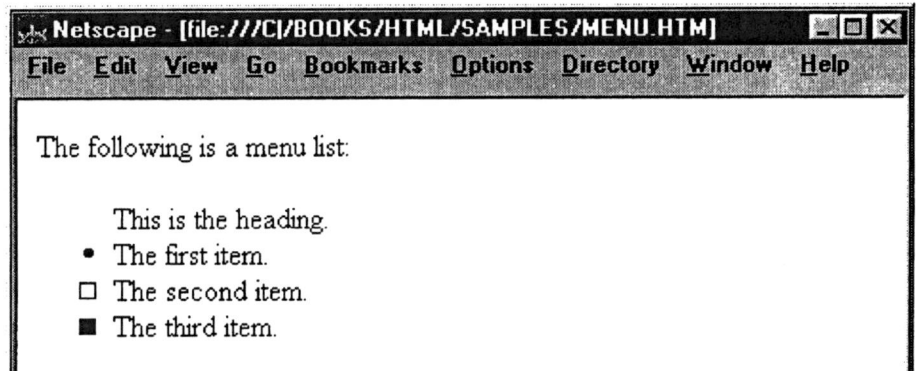

OPTIONAL ATTRIBUTE

COMPACT   Encourages the browser to display the list compactly.

TIPS
- This tag always uses </LI> is to indicate list items.

- This tag look identical to the <UL> tag but some browsers might display the text in a more compact manner.

- This tag has been removed from the HTML v3.2 specification.

RELATED HTML TAGS

<DL>   Directory list (no bullets or numbers).

<LI>   List item.

<OL>   Ordered list (numbers).

<UL>   Unordered list (bullets).

<META CONTENT ... >

Allows use of information in the **<HEAD>** section not recognized by HTML.

REQUIRED ATTRIBUTES
CONTENT   Assigns the content with the **<META>** element.

- *Either HTTP-EQUIV or NAME must be included:*

HTTP-EQUIV   Data to be parsed by the HTTP server; the alternative to **NAME**.

NAME   Specifies the meta-information name in a format understood by the browser; the alternative to **HTTP-EQUIV**.

SAMPLE MARKUP
- To indicate words appropriate for indexing:

  ```
  <META NAME="indexable" CONTENT="sphere box wedge torus">
  ```

OPTIONAL ATTRIBUTE
URL   *(Netscape v1.1)* URL used by Netscape servers for client-pull browser animation.

TIPS
- This tag can only be used in the **<HEAD>** section.

- This tag is useful to provide indexing words appropriate for the document.

RELATED HTML TAGS
<EMBED>   Embed an object unknown to the browser.

<IMG>   Display an image.

<NEXTID N>

(Obsolete) Next identifier available for use by automatic hypertext editors.

REQUIRED ATTRIBUTE
N   Specifies the next available identifier.

EXAMPLE MARKUP
■ To use this tag:
```
<NEXTID N="A">
```

OPTIONAL ATTRIBUTES
none

TIPS
■ The HTML spec recommends this tag not be used when creating an HTML document by hand; it was designed for use by software programs.

■ This tag has been removed from the HTML v3.2 specification.

RELATED HTML TAGS
none

<NOBR> *str* </NOBR>

Text within this elements cannot have a line break inserted (*short for NO BReak.*

SAMPLE MARKUP

■ To prevent the browser from wrapping text to fit the window:

```
<NOBR> The Netscape extension, NOBR, short for "NO BReak,"
means that the browser cannot wrap the text at any point
within the section of text enclosed in the NOBR tag pair.
</NOBR>
```

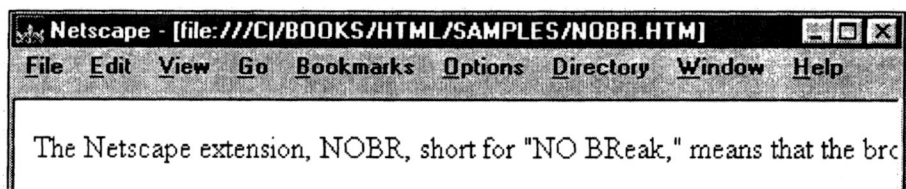

OPTIONAL ATTRIBUTES

none

TIPS

■ This tag prevents the browser from wrapping the text at any point within the section of text enclosed in the **<NOBR>** tag pair.

■ This tag is useful when two or three words should not be separated by an end of line, such as proper names. For example,

```
<NBR> XYZ Publishing, Ltd. <NBR>
```

looks better than

```
XYZ Publishing,
Ltd.
```

■ However, using **<NOBR>** on entire paragraphs means the user must scroll to read all the text.

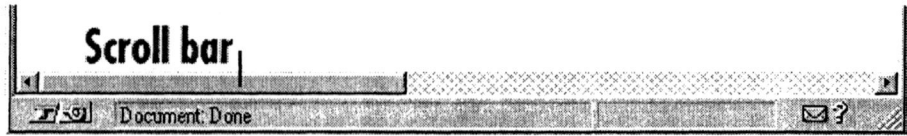

■ Use the **<WBR>** tag to allow line breaks in text treated by the **<NOBR>** element.

RELATED HTML TAGS

<P>	End of paragraph marker.
<WBR>	Word break.

<NOEMBED> ... </NOEMBED>

Displays information that should be ignored by browsers capable of handling the <EMBED> tag.

SAMPLE MARKUP

■ Use the <EMBED> and <NOEMBED> tags together:

```
<EMBED SRC="hrl.htm">
  <NOEMBED> This image viewable with the appropriate plug-in.
  </NOEMBED>
</EMBED>
```

OPTIONAL ATTRIBUTES

none

TIPS

■ This tag must be used within the <EMBED> tag.

■ This tag was designed by Netscape for those browsers that cannot use Navigator plug-ins to display nonstandard file formats, such as VRML, AutoCAD DWG, and Adobe PDF.

■ Browsers that understand the <EMBED> tag, such as Navigator, ignore this tag.

RELATED HTML TAG

<EMBED>   Causes the browser to launch a plug-in to display the file.

<NOFRAMES> ... </NOFRAMES>

Displays information that should be ignored by browsers capable of handling the <FRAMESET> and <FRAME> tags.

SAMPLE MARKUP

■ Use the <FRAMESET> and <NOFRAMES> tags together:

```
<FRAMESET>
  <NOFRAME> This frame viewable with the appropriate browser.
  </NOFRAME>
  <FRAME ...>
  ...
</FRAMESET>
```

OPTIONAL ATTRIBUTES

none

TIP

■ This tag must be used within the <FRAMESET> tag.

■ This tag was designed by Netscape for those browsers that cannot display frames.

■ Browsers that understand the <FRAME> and <FRAMESET> tags, such as Navigator, ignore this tag.

RELATED HTML TAGS

<FRAME>   Defines a frame.

<FRAMESET>   Defines a set of frames.

<OL ... > ... </OL>

A list prefixed by consecutive alphanumerics (*short for Ordered List*).

EXAMPLE MARKUPS

- The TYPE attribute in the **<LI>** tag specifies the type of prefix for this **<OL>** tag:

```
The ordered list uses numbers or letters:
<OL>
  <LH> This is the heading.
  <LI> The first item.
  <LI TYPE="A"> The second item.
  <LI TYPE="i"> The third item.
</OL>
```

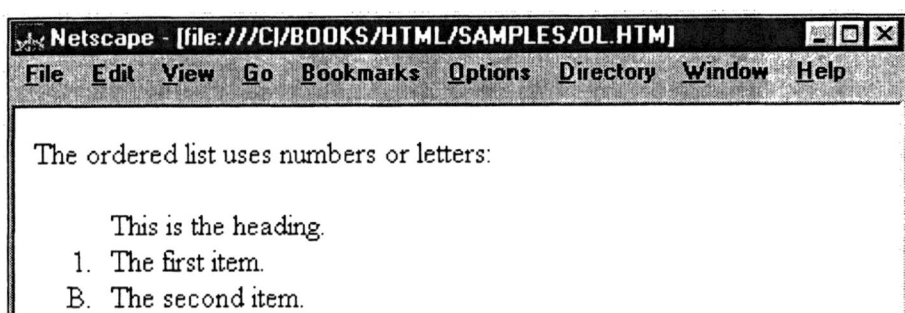

OPTIONAL ATTRIBUTES

COMPACT   *(Obsolete)* Display the list with a compact font.

START   *(Netscape v1.1; HTML v3.2)* Specify the first number in a the sequence of numbers.

TYPE   *(Netscape v1.1)* Specifies the type of list marking within an **<OL>** ordered list.

Example: **<LI TYPE="a">**

Type	Meaning
A	Uppercase alphabetical list (A, B, C, etc).
a	Lowercase alphabetical list (a, b, c, etc).
I	Uppercase Roman numeral list (I, II, III, etc).
i	Lowercase Roman numeral list (i, ii, iii, etc).
1	Numbered list (1, 2, 3, etc); default.

TIPS

■ Use the **START** attribute to start the list numbering with an alphanumeric other than A, a, I, i, or 1.

■ Since the **START** attribute is not recognized by most browsers, the numbering order will not appear correct.

RELATED HTML TAGS

\<LI\>	List item.
\<DL\>	Definition list.
\<MENU\>	Menu list.
\<UL\>	Unordered list.

\<OPTION ... > *str*

Identifies a choice in the **\<SELECT>** element; part of a **\<FORM>** element.

SAMPLE MARKUP

■ To display a selection with one or more options:

```
<FORM>
Chose up to three of the following solid primitives: <P>
  <SELECT NAME="solids" MULTIPLE SIZE=3>
    <OPTION SELECTED> Sphere
    <OPTION> Cylinder
    <OPTION> Cone
    <OPTION> Torus
  </SELECT>
</FORM>
```

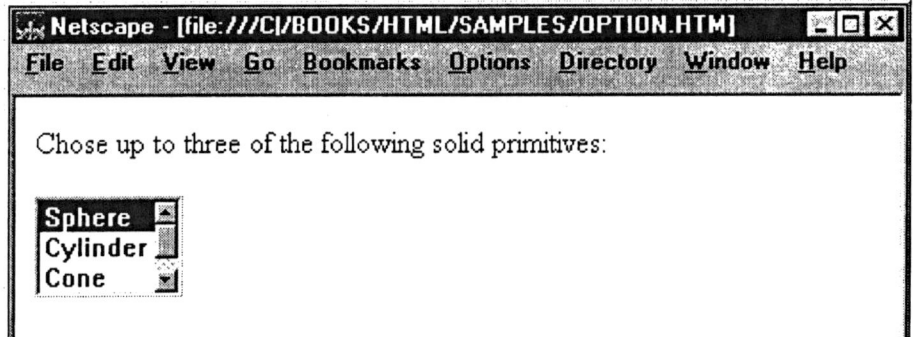

OPTIONAL ATTRIBUTES

SELECTED   Marks the **\<OPTION>** tag as selected, usually by highlighting.

Example: **\<OPTION SELECTED>**

VALUE   Specifies the value assigned to **\<OPTION>**.

ERROR   Displays an error message to the user when an incorrect option is selected.

TIPS

■ The **\</OPTION>** terminator is optional.

■ This tag must be inside the **\<SELECT>** element.

RELATED HTML TAGS

\<FORM>   Defines a form.

\<INPUT>   A variety of input methods for forms.

\<SELECT>   Sets up selections in a form.

<OVERLAY SRC ... >

Overlays one or more images on top of a **<FIG>** image.

REQUIRED ATTRIBUTE
SRC   The source filename of the image in URL format; see Appendix A.

SAMPLE MARKUP
- To specify an overlay:
```
<FIG SCR=img.gif>
  <OVERLAY SRC=url.jpg WIDTH=40 HEIGHT=60>
</FIG>
```

OPTIONAL ATTRIBUTES
UNITS   Measurement unit used by the **X**, **Y**, **WIDTH**, and **HEIGHT** attributes.

Units	Meaning
pixels	Screen pixels; the default.
en	Half character width of current font.

X   Horizontal offset relative to left edge of image, measured rightward.

Y   Vertical offset relative to top edge of image, measured downward.

WIDTH   Width of image.

HEIGHT   Height of image.

IMAGEMAP   The URL to which to send the click coordinates.

TIPS
- This tag must be used within the **<FIG>** tag.

- And, this tag must be the first tag used in the **<FIG>** tag.

- This tag was designed to take advantage of the browser's cache, which stores images and text in case there are needed a second time; this greatly increases the apparent speed of the browser. In this case, a series of similar images may only differ by one overlay.

RELATED HTML TAG
<FIG>   Displays an image.

str <P ... > *str*

Popularly used as the start of new paragraph marker (*short for Paragraph*).

EXAMPLE MARKUPS

■ Here is how this element is commonly used, with only the **<P>** tag at the end of each paragraph:

```
HTML is the primary reason for the sudden popularity of the
Internet in 1995, since it allows text, graphics, file
downloads, and multimedia -- all on a singe Web page.
<P>

Even Java and VRML can be thought of as extensions to HTML
since HTML is required to form the basis of the home page.
<P>
```

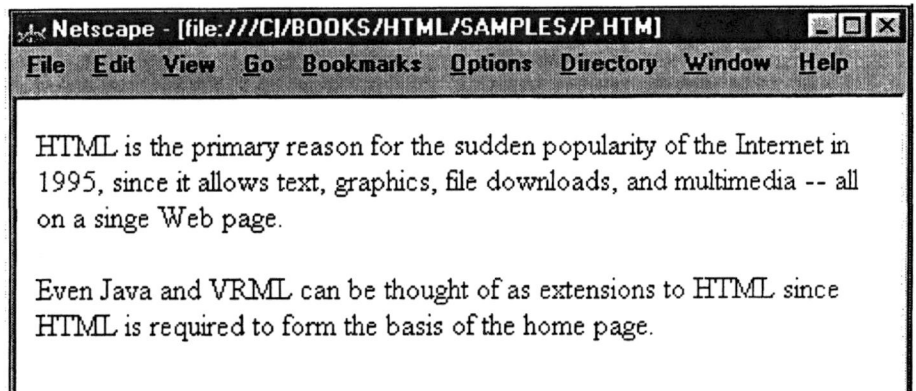

■ However, here is how the tag is used correctly, with **<P>** at the beginning and **</P>** at the end of each paragraph:

```
<P>HTML is the primary reason for the sudden popularity of
the Internet in 1995, since it allows text, graphics, file
downloads, and multimedia -- all on a singe Web page. </P>

<P> Even Java and VRML can be thought of as extensions to
HTML since HTML is required to form the basis of the home
page. </P>
```

OPTIONAL ELEMENT

</P>   Proper HTML procedure would require **<P>** at the start of a paragraph and **</P>** at the end of the paragraph.

OPTIONAL ATTRIBUTE

ALIGN   (*Netscape v2.0; HTML v3.2*) Alignment of text.

Align	Meaning
indent	Indent the text.
center	Center text between margins.
justify	Justify text.
left	Left align text.
right	Right align text.

TIPS

■ All HTML browsers ignore the [CR] [LF] used by DOS and Windows (or the [LF] used by Unix computers) to indicate the end of a paragraph.

■ Thus, you must place a <P> tag at the end of every paragraph — this is easily done with a text editor's search-and-replace feature.

■ If you want the HTML browser to respect the paragraph breaks and whitespace, use the <PRE> tag to keep text as originally formatted.

■ Traditionally, the <P> tag indicates the *end* of a paragraph.

■ However, the HTML convention is that </P> indicates the end of an element.

■ For this reason, it is proposed that paragraphs must be surrounded by a pair of <P> ... </P> tags.

■ The <P> is not always needed to mark the end of a paragraph of text; many other elements automatically create a paragraph break, such as the <H*n*> and <LI> tags.

RELATED HTML TAGS

                Line break (end of a paragraph without the blank line separator).

<NOBR>   Prevents a line break appearing in the enclosed text.

<PRE>   Obviates the need to format text with the <P> tag.

<WBR>   Permits a line break between two words enclosed by the <NOBR> tag.

<PARAM NAME VALUE>

Defines general purpose parameters passed to the **<APPLET>** application (*short for PARAMeters*).

REQUIRED ATTRIBUTES

NAME   Name of the parameters passed to the applet.

VALUE   Value obtained by the applet with the **getParameter()** method.

SAMPLE MARKUP

■ To pass parameters:

```
<PARAM NAME="joker" VALUE="24">
```

OPTIONAL ATTRIBUTES

none

TIPS

■ This tag is meant for Java applications.

■ This tag must be inside the **<APPLET>** element.

RELATED HTML TAG

<APPLET>   Executes a Java application.

<PLAINTEXT ... > *str* </PLAINTEXT>

(*Obsolete*) Displays all enclosed text literally, including all HTML tags, with the possible exception of </PLAINTEXT> ending tag.

SAMPLE MARKUP

■ The ending tag is not recognized by Navigator v2:

```
The specifications for this engine are: <PLAINTEXT>
Engine class: 2.4L, 4-cylinder
Engine type: DOHC balance shaft
Net power: 112kW, 150bhp @4000rpm
Net torque: 226 Nm, 167lb-ft @4000rpm
Fuel delivery: SMPI
</PLAINTEXT>
```

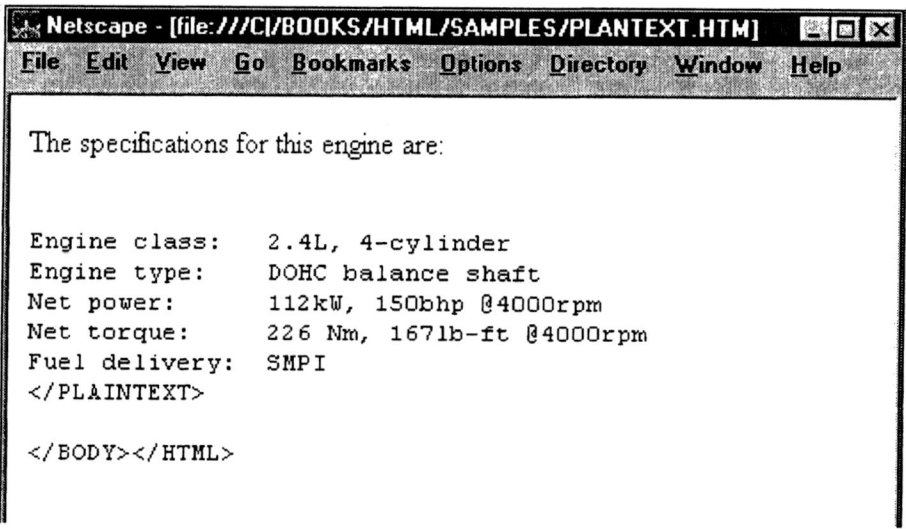

OPTIONAL ATTRIBUTE

WIDTH   Width of text lines, in characters.

TIPS

■ This tag has been removed from the HTML v3.2 specification.

■ Only the </PLAINTEXT> tag is recognized by some browsers to indicate the end of the plaintext section.

■ This tag has been replaced by the <PRE> and </PRE> tags.

RELATED HTML TAG

<PRE>   Displays text with no HTML formatting.

\<PRE ... > *str* \</PRE>

Displays enclosed text in a fixed font, preserving line breaks but removing multiple white spaces and line breaks (*short for PREformatted*).

SAMPLE MARKUP

- To use this tag:

```
The specifications for this engine are: <PRE>
Engine class: 2.4L, 4-cylinder
Engine type: DOHC balance shaft
Net power: 112kW, 150bhp @4000rpm
Net torque: 226 Nm, 167lb-ft @4000rpm
Fuel delivery: SMPI
</PRE>
```

```
Netscape - [file:///C|/BOOKS/HTML/SAMPLES/PRE.HTM]

File  Edit  View  Go  Bookmarks  Options  Directory  Window  Help


The specifications for this engine are:

Engine class:     2.4L, 4-cylinder
Engine type:      DOHC balance shaft
Net power:        112kW, 150bhp @4000rpm
Net torque:       226 Nm, 167lb-ft @4000rpm
Fuel delivery:    SMPI
```

OPTIONAL ATTRIBUTE

WIDTH   Maximum number of characters per line.

TIPS

- This tag display the enclosed text in a non-formatted manner.

- The **WIDTH** attribute might be removed for HTML v3 since most browsers ignore it.

RELATED HTML TAGS

\<CODE>   Displays a partial line of text in fixed width font.

\<KEYBOARD>   Displays text in fixed width font.

\<PLAINTEXT>   The precursor to \<PRE>.

\<XMP>   Another precursor to \<PRE>.

<SAMP> *str* </SAMP>

Displays text literally and strips out newline characters (carriage returns) and tabs (*short for SAMPle*).

SAMPLE MARKUP

- Notice how this tag strips out carriage returns and tabs:

```
The specifications for this engine are: <SAMP>
    Engine class:       2.4L, 4-cylinder
    Engine type:        DOHC balance shaft
    Net power:          112kW, 150bhp @4000rpm
    Net torque:         226 Nm, 167lb-ft @4000rpm
    Fuel delivery:      SMPI    </SAMP>
```

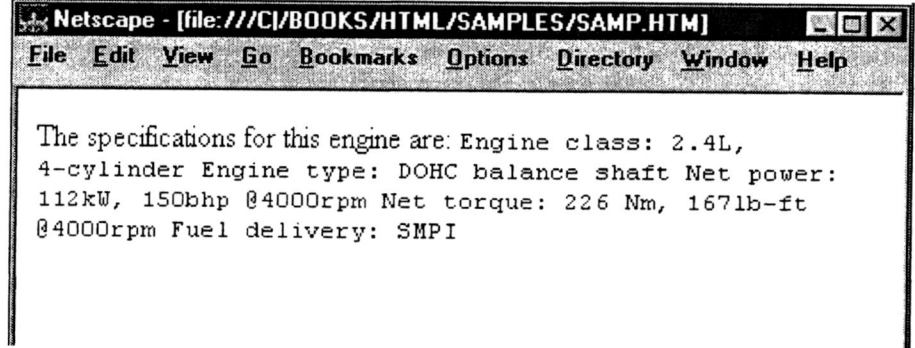

OPTIONAL ATTRIBUTES

none

TIP

- This tag displays text literally in a fixed-width font; this can be useful for displaying HTML code literally.

RELATED HTML TAG

<CODE>	Displays text as code in a fixed-width font.
<KBD>	Displays text as keyboard input in a fixed-width font.
<PRE>	Displays text unformatted.
<VAR>	Displays text as a programming variable name.

<SCRIPT ... > ... </SCRIPT>

Reserved for future use with scripting language.

EXAMPLE MARKUP

- To use this tag:

```
<SCRIPT LANGUAGE="JavaScript">
  <!-- Beginning of JavaScript Applet --
  /* JavaScript code goes here */
  // -- End of JavaScript Applet -->
</SCRIPT>
```

OPTIONAL ATTRIBUTE

LANGUAGE   Name of the scripting language; alerts the browser as to the kind of script to anticipate.

TIPS

- This tag must be located within the **<HEAD>** section of an HTML document.

- Currently, the only scripting language supported is JavaScript.

RELATED HTML TAGS

<HEAD>   Contains the document head.

<EMBED>   Embeds an object displayed by a plug-in.

HTML S

<SELECT NAME ... > ... </SELECT>

Defines a menu of multiple selections with the **<OPTION>** tag, nested within the **<FORM>** element.

REQUIRED ATTRIBUTE

NAME   A name assigned to the selection as an identifier.

SAMPLE MARKUP

■ To create a form displaying a scrollable list box with up to three choices:

```
<FORM>
  Chose up to three of the following solid primitives: <P>
  <SELECT NAME="solids" MULTIPLE SIZE=3>
    <OPTION SELECTED> Sphere
    <OPTION> Cylinder
    <OPTION> Cone
    <OPTION> Torus
  </SELECT>
</FORM>
```

■ To create a form displaying a drop box with a single choice:

```
<FORM>
  Chose one from the following surface shapes: <P>
  <SELECT NAME="surfaces">
    <OPTION SELECTED> Tabulated </OPTION>
    <OPTION> Revolved
    <OPTION> Edge
    <OPTION> Polyface
  </SELECT>
</FORM>
```

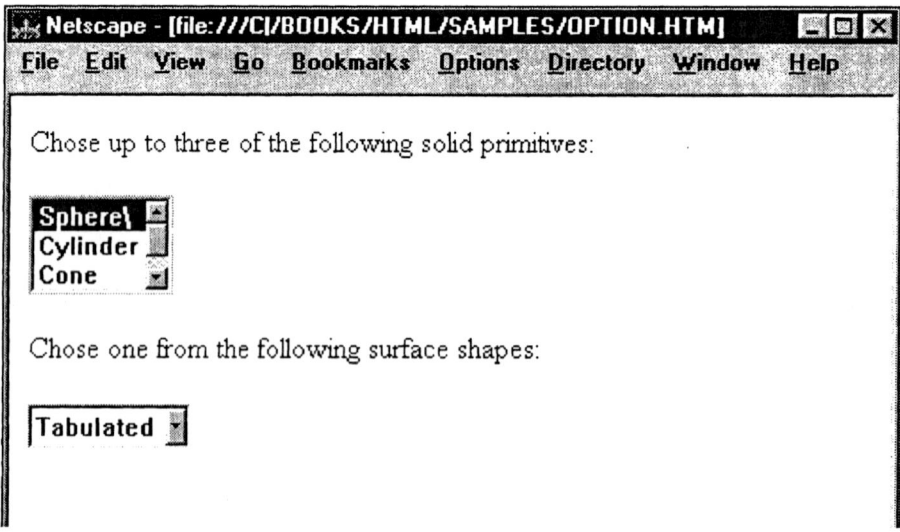

OPTIONAL ATTRIBUTES

SIZE   Specifies the number of option visible when the form is displayed; when size is less than the number of options, the browser displays a scrollbar or drop box.

NAME   Symbolic name of the field returned to the server.

MULTIPLE   Allows the user to make more than one selection.

TIPS

■ This tag must be used together with the <OPTION> tag; at least one <OPTION> element is expected within the contents of the <SELECT> element.

■ The elements <INPUT>, <SELECT>, and <TEXTAREA> elements are prohibited from being in the <SELECT> element.

RELATED HTML TAGS

<FORM>   Defines a form.

<OPTION>   Option statements within the <SELECT> tag.

HTML S

<SMALL> *str* </SMALL>

Changes the enclosed text to a smaller size than normal text.

SAMPLE MARKUP

■ To use this tag:

```
This is normal text and <SMALL> this is vertically-challenged
text. </SMALL>
```

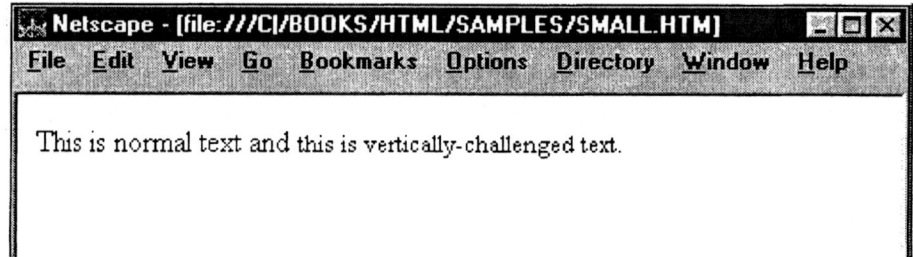

OPTIONAL ATTRIBUTES

none

TIPS

■ This tag display the enclosed text in a small size.

■ This tag is a Netscape extension and is proposed for HTML v3.

RELATED HTML TAG

<BIG>   Displays text in a larger size.

<BASEFONT>   Displays text in seven sizes.

<H*n*>   Displays text in six headline sizes, including smaller than normal text.

\<STRIKE\> *str* \</STRIKE\>

Displays text as ~~strike through text~~, usually with a horizontal line through (*short for STRIKE through*).

EXAMPLE MARKUPS

■ To use this tag:

```
This is normal text and <STRIKE> this text has been stricken
through </STRIKE>.
```

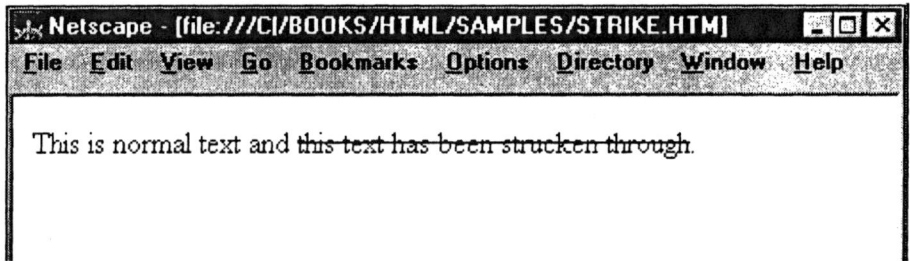

OPTIONAL ATTRIBUTES

none

TIPS

■ Strikethrough text is commonly used to indicated deleted text.

RELATED HTML TAGS

none

\<STRONG\> *str* \</STRONG\>

Changes the enclosed text to a stronger font, usually **boldface**.

SAMPLE MARKUP

■ To use this tag:

```
This is normal text but <STRONG> this is text is
strong </STRONG>.
```

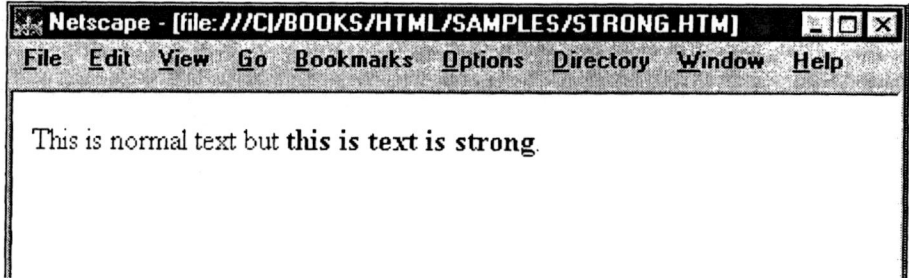

OPTIONAL ATTRIBUTES

none

TIP

■ This tag display the enclosed text in a stronger font different from **\<EM\>** emphasized text.

RELATED HTML TAGS

\<B\>	Displays text in a bold font.
\<EM\>	Displays text in an emphasized font.
\<I\>	Displays text in italics.

<SUB> *str* </SUB>

Displays text as ~subscript text~ (*short for SUBscript*).

EXAMPLE MARKUPS

■ Using the <SUB> tag:

```
This is normal text but <SUB> this is subscripted text</SUB>.
<BR> The chemical formula for water is: H<SUB>2</SUB>O
```

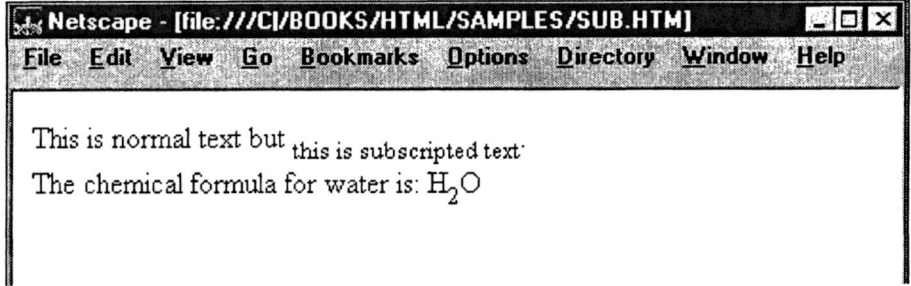

OPTIONAL ATTRIBUTES

none

TIPS

■ This tag displays the enclosed text with a lower baseline.

RELATED HTML TAGS

<SMALL>   Displays text smaller.

<SUP>   Displays text as superscript.

HTML S

<SUP> *str* </SUP>

Displays the enclosed text as ^{superscript text} (*short for SUPerscript*).

SAMPLE MARKUP

- To use this tag:

```
This is normal text but <SUP> this is superscripted text </
SUP>. <BR> The equation for a right-triangle is: x<SUP>2</
SUP> + y<SUP>2</SUP> = h<SUP>2</SUP>
```

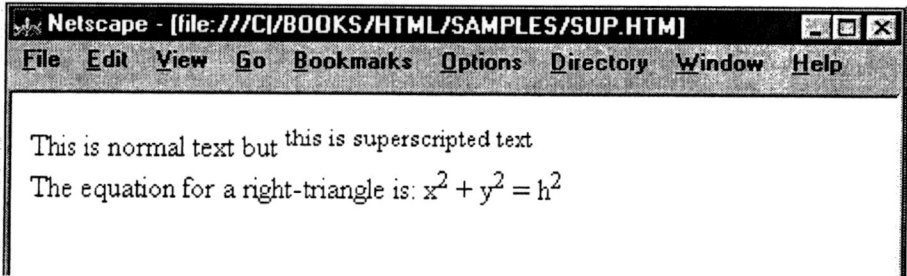

OPTIONAL ATTRIBUTES

none

TIP

- This tag display the enclosed text with a higher baseline.

RELATED HTML TAGS

<SMALL>   Displays text at a smaller size.

<SUB>   Displays text as subscript text.

\<STYLE\> ... \</STYLE\>

Reserved for future use with style sheets.

EXAMPLE MARKUP

■ To use this tag:

```
<HEAD>
  <TITLE>Document Title</TITLE>
  <STYLE>Style info goes here.</STYLE>
</HEAD>
```

OPTIONAL ATTRIBUTES

none

TIP

■ This tag must be located within the **\<HEAD\>** section of an HTML document.

RELATED HTML TAG

\<HEAD\>   Contains the document head.

HTML S

<TABLE ... > ... </TABLE>

Displays the enclosed text in a table format.

SAMPLE MARKUP

- A minimum two-row table following the HTML v3.2 spec looks like this:

```
<TABLE>    Start of table
 <TR>      Start of the first row.
   <TD>      The first cell of data.
   <TD>      The second cell in the row.
   . . .
   <TD>      The final cell in the row.
 </TR>     End of the first row.
 <TR>      Start of the second row.
   . . .
 </TR>       End of the second row.
</TABLE> End of the table.
```

- With some real data, the two-row table looks like this:

```
<TABLE>
 <TR><TD>2880<TD>113.3<TD>3030<TD>119.3</TR>
 <TR><TD>4730<TD>186.3<TD>5070<TD>199.6</TR>
</TABLE>
```

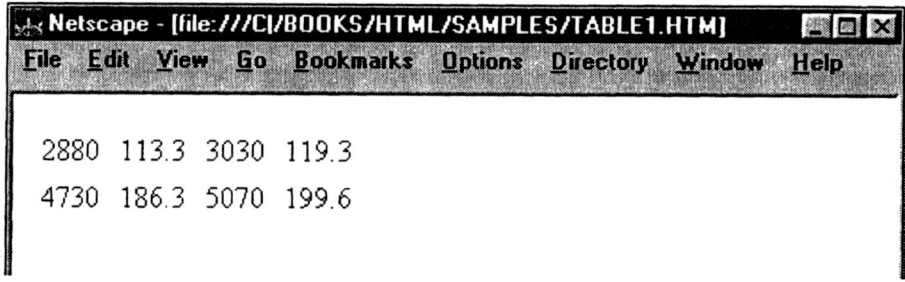

- To add headings for the columns (the <TH> tag creates the **boldface** look):

```
<TABLE>
 <TR><TH>MM<TH>Inches<TH>MM<TH>Inches</TR>
 <TR><TD>2880<TD>113.3<TD>3030<TD>119.3</TR>
 <TR><TD>4730<TD>186.3<TD>5070<TD>199.6</TR>
</TABLE>
```

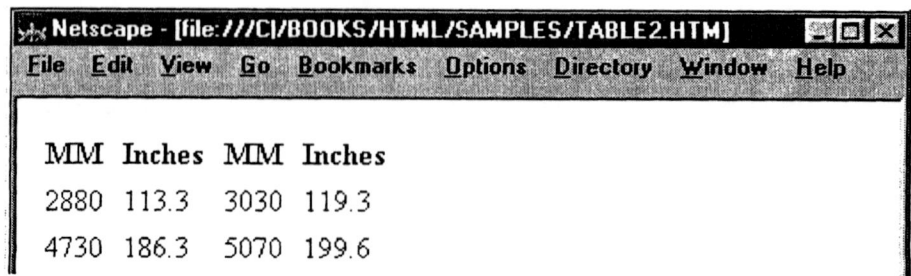

- To add a 1-pixel border:

```
<TABLE BORDER=1>
  <TR><TH>MM<TH>Inches<TH>MM<TH>Inches</TR>
  <TR><TD>2880<TD>113.3<TD>3030<TD>119.3</TR>
  <TR><TD>4730<TD>186.3<TD>5070<TD>199.6</TR>
</TABLE>
```

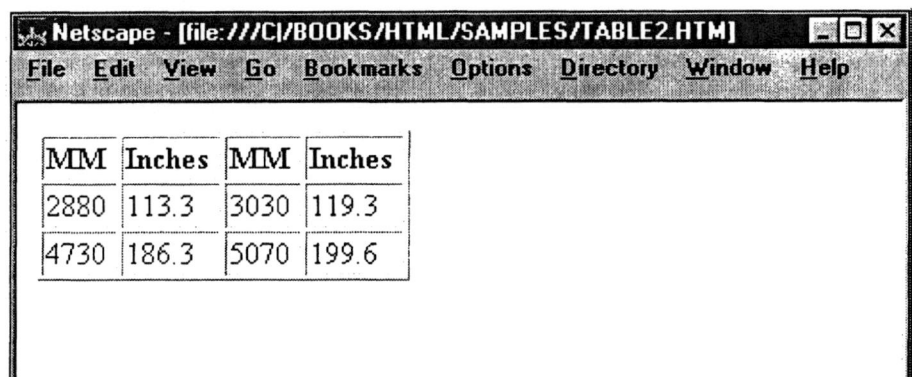

- To add headings for the rows (the **<TH>** tag creates the **boldface** look):

```
<TABLE BORDER=1>
  <TR><TH>Dimensions<TH>MM<TH>Inches<TH>MM<TH>Inches</TR>
  <TR><TH>Wheelbase<TD>2880<TD>113.3<TD>3030<TD>119.3</TR>
  <TR><TH>Overall Length<TD>4730<TD>186.3<TD>5070<TD>199.6</TR>
</TABLE>
```

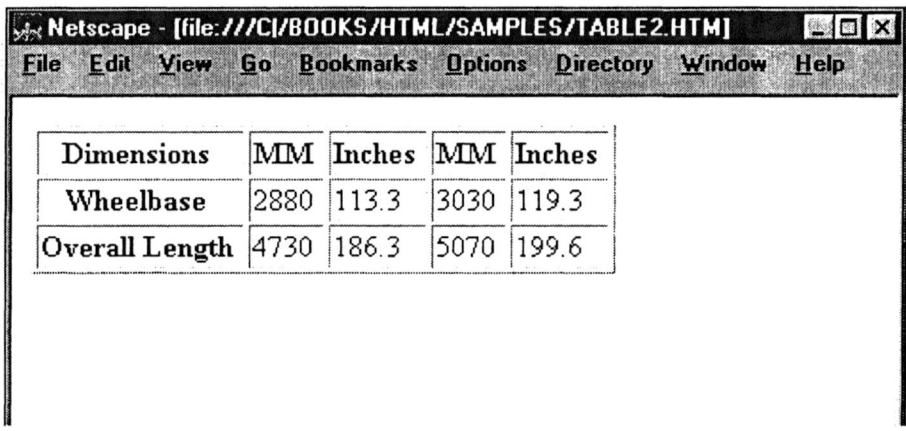

OPTIONAL ATTRIBUTES

ALIGN   Horizontal placement of the table.

Align	Meaning
bleedleft	Align table with window's left margin.
bleedright	Align table with window's right margin.
center	Center table within text left and right margins.
justify	Fill space between left and right text margins.
left	Align table with text's left margin (the default).
right	Align table with the text's right margin.

BORDER   Draw a border around the table. The value is the number of borders
                      (lines) you want around the table. Use a value of 0 to use the space
                      reserved for borders to expand the area of your table.

CELLPADDING Space between the border of a cell and the contents of the cell. The default
                      is 1.

CELLSPACING Space between individual cells in a table. The default is 2.

CLEAR   Start the table below or beside an image so that the table does not flow
                      around the image:

Clear	Meaning
all	Display table at next clear left & right margin.
left	Display table at the next clear left margin.
right	Display table at the next clear right margin.
n	Place table alongside the image at the specified distance, if there is enough space.

COLSPEC   Width and alignment of columns within the table. The units of
                      measurement are set by the **UNITS** or **DP** attributes.

Colspec	Meaning
C	Centers contents within cell.
DP	Aligns contents to the decimal point.
J	Justifies contents within cell.
L	Aligns contents with cell's left margin.
R	Aligns contents with cell's right margin.

DP   Character used by the **COLSPEC** attribute to represent a decimal point;
                      default is the period (.); European countries use the comma (,).

NOFLOW   Text lines are not wrapped around a table.

NOWRAP   Lines within a table cannot be broken.

UNITS   Units used by the **COLSPEC** attribute.

Width	Meaning
%	Percentage of width between left & right margins.
pt	Points (72 points per inch).
p	Picas (12 picas per inch).
in	Inches (25.4 mm per inch).
cm	Centimeters (100 cm per m).
mm	Millimeters (10 mm per cm).
em	Em units (**width of letter 'm' in current font**).
px	Screen pixels.

WIDTH   Width of the table; default = width of the page.

TIPS

■ Only the **<TABLE>**, **<TR>**, and **<TD>** tags are required.

■ This tag does not define the physical layout of a table; instead, **<TABLE>** defines the logical contents of table cells (and the location of their rows and columns).

■ When you don't have the correct number of cells in every row, the table is missing data and cell borders — but missing data is hard to spot in the HTML code:

```
<TABLE BORDER=1>
  <TR><TH>Dimensions<TH>MM<TH>Inches<TH>MM<TH>Inches</TR>
  <TR><TH>Wheelbase<TD>2880<TD>3030<TD>119.3</TR>
  <TR><TD>4730<TD>186.3<TD>5070<TD>199.6</TR>
</TABLE>
```

Netscape - [file:///C|/BOOKS/HTML/SAMPLES/TABLE3.HTM]

File   Edit   View   Go   Bookmarks   Options   Directory   Window   Help

Dimensions	MM	Inches	MM	Inches
Wheelbase	2880	3030	119.3	
4730		186.3	5070	199.6

RELATED HTML TAGS

<CAPTION>	Displays a caption for the table.
<TR>	Indicates the start of a row.
<TH>	Defines a header row or column.
<TD>	Specifies the table data in each cell.

<TD ... > str

The data in a single cell of the table (*short for Table Data*).

SAMPLE MARKUP

■ The **<TD>** tag simply displays the text in normal font:

```
<TABLE BORDER=1>
  <TR><TH>Dimensions<TH>MM<TH>Inches<TH>MM<TH>Inches</TR>
  <TR><TH>Wheelbase<TD>2880<TD>113.3<TD>3030<TD>119.3</TR>
  <TR><TH>Overall Length<TD>4730<TD>186.3<TD>5070<TD>199.6</TR>
</TABLE>
```

Netscape - [file:///C|/BOOKS/HTML/SAMPLES/TABLE2.HTM]

File Edit View Go Bookmarks Options Directory Window Help

Dimensions	MM	Inches	MM	Inches
Wheelbase	2880	113.3	3030	119.3
Overall Length	4730	186.3	5070	199.6

■ The **ROWSPAN** and **COLSPAN** attributes let you create a cell that spans two or more rows and columns:

```
<TABLE BORDER=1>
  <TR><TH ROWSPAN=2>Overall Dimensions<TH COLSPAN=2>Old Car
    Models<TH COLSPAN=2>New Car Models
  <TR><TH>MM<TH>Inches<TH>MM<TH>Inches</TR>
  <TR><TH>Wheelbase<TD>2880<TD>113.3<TD>  3030<TD>119.3</TR>
  <TR><TH>Overall Length<TD>4730<TD>186.3<TD>5070<TD>199.6</TR>
</TABLE>
```

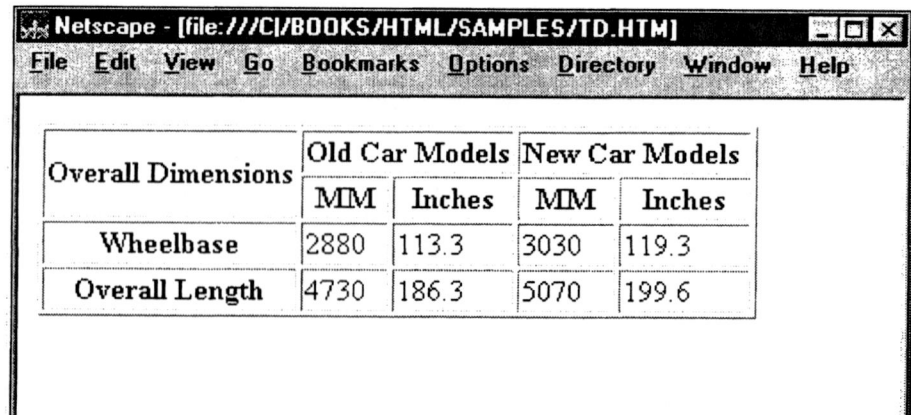

Netscape - [file:///C|/BOOKS/HTML/SAMPLES/TD.HTM]

File Edit View Go Bookmarks Options Directory Window Help

Overall Dimensions	Old Car Models		New Car Models	
	MM	Inches	MM	Inches
Wheelbase	2880	113.3	3030	119.3
Overall Length	4730	186.3	5070	199.6

OPTIONAL ATTRIBUTES

ROWSPAN   Cell spans this number of rows.

COLSPAN   Cell spans this number of columns (good for a title column).

ALIGN   (*HTML v3*) Describes where to align the contents of every cell.

Align	Meaning
left	Left justify data (the default).
center	Center justify data.
right	Right justify data.
justify	Full justify the data.
decimal	Align data with the decimal point.
char	Justify to a character specified by CHAR.

TIPS

■ This tag has no **</TD>** ending; thus, the current cell ends with the next **<TD>** tag or other table-related tag.

■ The **WIDTH** attribute accepts the following units of measurement:

■ A value of zero for **ROWSPAN**=0 and **COLSPAN**=0 causes the cell to span from the current cell to the end of the table.

■ Be careful that you don't mix up the purpose of **ROWSPAN** and **COLSPAN**; the table might not make any sense. In the following example, the **COLSPAN** and **ROWSPAN** attributes have been reversed:

```
<TABLE BORDER=1>
<TR><TH  COLSPAN=2>Overall  Dimensions<TH  ROWSPAN=2>Old  Car
Models<TH COLSPAN=2>New Car Models
  <TR><TH>MM<TH>Inches<TH>MM<TH>Inches</TR>
  <TR><TH>Wheelbase<TD>2880<TD>113.3<TD>  3030<TD>119.3</TR>
  <TR><TH>Overall Length<TD>4730<TD>186.3<TD>5070<TD>199.6</TR>
</TABLE>
```

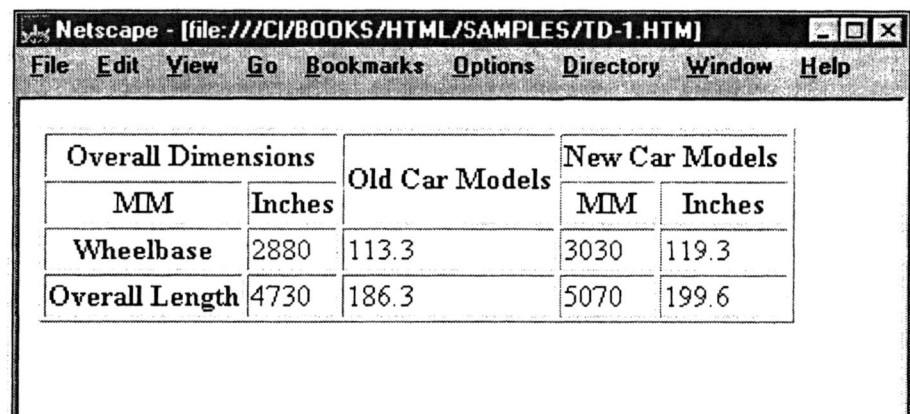

RELATED HTML TAGS

\<TABLE\>	Creates a table.
\<CAPTION\>	Displays a caption for the table.
\<TR\>	Indicates the start of a row.
\<TH\>	Defines a header row or column.

<TEXTAREA NAME COLS ROWS ... > ... </TEXTAREA>

Specifies a multiline text input field within a **<FORM>** element; only ASCII text is allowed as input by the user.

REQUIRED ATTRIBUTES

NAME   The default data entry text.

COLS   Size of the text area, in number of columns of text characters.

ROWS   Size of the text area, in number of rows of text lines.

SAMPLE MARKUP

■ To create a text input area in a form:

```
<FORM>
  Type your request here: <P>
  <TEXTAREA NAME="comment" COLS=40 ROWS=4>
  </TEXTAREA>
</FORM>
```

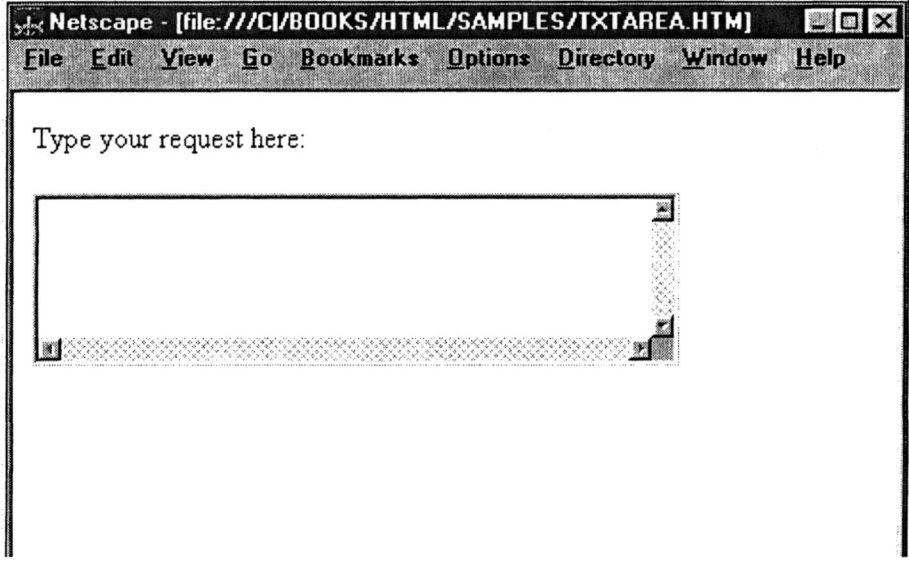

OPTIONAL ATTRIBUTES

DISABLED   Disables the text entry box; prevents user from typing text.

ERROR   Displays an error message when user makes a mistake.

TIPS

■ This tag only accepts ASCII characters, plus the newline (carriage return).

■ The text between the opening **<TEXTAREA>** and closing **</TEXTAREA>** tags defines the text displayed initially in the textarea.

RELATED HTML TAGS

<FORM>   Defines a form in the document.

<INPUT>   Defines the user input section in a form.

<OPTION>   Defines the options in multiple selections.

<SELECT>   Defines the multiple selections section of a form.

<TH ... > *str* </TH>

Defines a header cell at the beginning of a row (*short for Table Header*).

SAMPLE MARKUP

■ To add a heading for every row (the **<TH>** tag creates the **boldface** look):

```
<TABLE BORDER=1>
  <TR><TH>Dimensions<TH>MM<TH>Inches<TH>MM<TH>Inches</TR>
  <TR><TH>Wheelbase<TD>2880<TD>113.3<TD>3030<TD>119.3</TR>
  <TR><TH>Overall Length<TD>4730<TD>186.3<TD>5070<TD>199.6</TR>
</TABLE>
```

Dimensions	MM	Inches	MM	Inches
Wheelbase	2880	113.3	3030	119.3
Overall Length	4730	186.3	5070	199.6

OPTIONAL ATTRIBUTES

NOWRAP Suppresses word wrap within a cell.

ROWSPAN Cell spans this number of rows.

COLSPAN Cell spans this number of columns (good for a title column).

ALIGN Describes where to align the contents of every cell.

Align	Meaning
left	Left justify data (the default).
center	Center justify data.
right	Right justify data.
justify	Full justify the data.
decimal	Align data with the decimal point.
char	Justify to a character specified by CHAR.

VALIGN Vertical alignment of cell contents.

Valign	Meaning
top	Top justify the data.
middle	Center the data in the cell.
bottom	Bottom justify the data.
baseline	Align data with text baseline.

WIDTH   Width of the table; default = 100% of document width.

Width	Meaning
%	Percentage of width between left & right margins.
pt	Points (72 points per inch).
p	Picas (12 picas per inch).
in	Inches (25.4 mm per inch).
cm	Centimeters (100 cm per m).
mm	Millimeters (10 mm per cm).
em	Em units (width of letter 'm' in current font).
px	Screen pixels.

TIPS

■ This tag displays the enclosed text in a font different from <TD> table data text — usually boldface.

■ This tag is assumed to end at the start of the next tag; thus the </TD> ending is optional.

RELATED HTML TAGS

<TABLE>   Creates a table.

<CAPTION>   Displays a caption for the table.

<TR>   Indicates the start of a row.

<TD>   Specifies the table data in each cell.

<TITLE> *str* </TITLE>

Defines a title for the document, typically displayed on the HTML browser's title bar.

EXAMPLE MARKUPS

■ To use this tag:

```
<TITLE>The Title of This Document </TITLE>
```

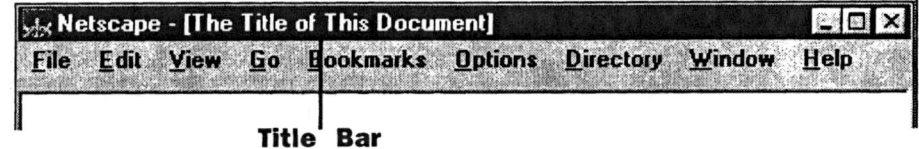

Title Bar

OPTIONAL ATTRIBUTES

none

TIPS

■ This tag is usually part of the <HEAD> section but can be located within the HTML document.

■ To fit on the browser's title bar, the text should be less than 64 characters long; otherwise, your title might get truncated.

■ When you don't use the <TITLE> tag in your document, the browser displays the HTML filename on the title bar:

RELATED HTML TAG

<HEAD>   Defines the content of the HTML document.

Indicates the start of a row of data in a table (*short for Table Row*).

EXAMPLE MARKUPS

■ This tag signals the start of a new row:

```
<TABLE>
  <TR><TD>2880<TD>113.3<TD>3030<TD>119.3
  <TR><TD>4730<TD>186.3<TD>5070<TD>199.6
</TABLE>
```

░░ Netscape - [file:///C|/BOOKS/HTML/SAMPLES/TABLE1.HTM] ▬□✕
File   Edit   View   Go   Bookmarks   Options   Directory   Window   Help
2880 113.3 3030 119.3
4730 186.3 5070 199.6

OPTIONAL ATTRIBUTES

ALIGN   (*HTML v3*) Describes where to align the contents of every cell.

Align	Meaning
left	Left justify data (the default).
center	Center justify data.
right	Right justify data.
justify	Full justify the data.

VALIGN   Vertical alignment of cell contents.

Valign	Meaning
top	Top justify the data.
middle	Center the data in the cell.
bottom	Bottom justify the data.
baseline	Align data with text baseline.

TIPS

■ This tag does not have an ending tag.

■ This tag is used in the **<THEAD>**, **<TFOOT>**, and **<TBODY>** sections.

■ This tag requires at least one **<TH>** or **<TD>** element.

RELATED HTML TAGS

<TABLE>   Creates a table.

<CAPTION>   Displays a caption for the table.

<TH>   Defines a header row or column.

<TD>   Specifies the table data in each cell.

`<TT>` *str* `</TT>`

Displays the enclosed text in a fixed-width font (*short for TeleType*).

EXAMPLE MARKUPS

■ To use this tag:

```
<BASEFONT SIZE=5>
This is normal text and <TT> this is teletype text. </TT>
```

OPTIONAL ATTRIBUTES

none

TIP

■ This tag displays text in a teletype font; if the browser is unable to do that, it uses a fixed-width font.

RELATED HTML TAGS

`<KBD>`	Displays text to be entered at the keyboard.
`<CODE>`	Display text as computer code.
`<VAR>`	Displays text as a programming variable name.

<U> str </U>

<u>Underlines</u> the enclosed text (*short for Underline*).

EXAMPLE MARKUPS

■ To use this tag:

```
It is easy to confuse <U> underlined text </U> with <A HREF=
"url.html">anchor text</A>.
```

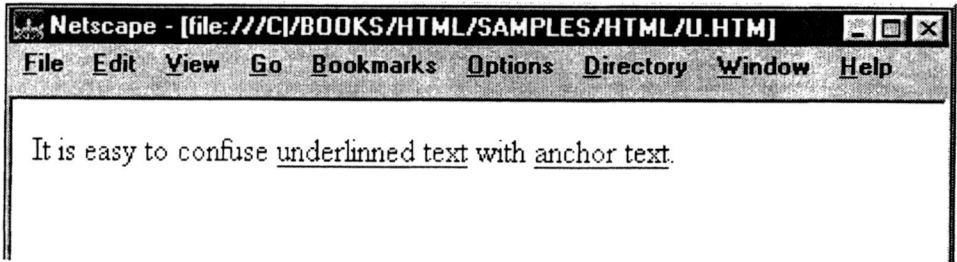

OPTIONAL ATTRIBUTES

none

TIPS

■ Don't use this tag since it can be confused with an **<A>** element, which is also underlined.

■ Some browsers display the enclosed text in italics instead of underlined.

RELATED HTML TAG

<B>	Boldface text.
<I>	Italic text.

<UL ... > ... </UL>

Defines an unordered list, one that uses bullets (*short for Unordered List*).

SAMPLE MARKUP

■ The <UL> tag prefixes each line with a bullet:

```
The following is an unordered list: <UL>
  <LH> This is the heading.
  <LI> The first item.
  <LI TYPE="circle"> The second item.
  <LI TYPE="square"> The third item.
</UL>
```

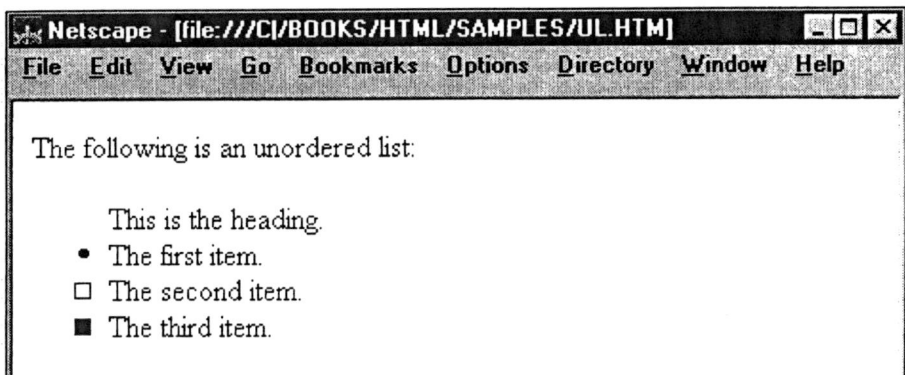

OPTIONAL ATTRIBUTES

COMPACT   (*Obsolete*) Display the list with a compact font.

TYPE   (*Netscape v1.1; HTML v3.2*) Specifies the type of bullet within an <UL> ordered list.

Example: `<LI TYPE="square">`

Type	Meaning
disk	A solid round bullet; the default.
circle	An open round bullet.
square	A square bullet.

TIPS

■ This tag requires the <LI> tag to indicate list items.

■ Nested <UL> lists are progressively indented.

RELATED HTML TAGS

<DL>   Directory list (no bullets or numbers).

<OL>   Ordered list (numbers).

<LI>   An item in a list.

<VAR> *str* </VAR>

Displays the enclosed text as a programming variable (*short for VARiable*).

EXAMPLE MARKUPS

- To use this tag:

```
These variables are used by function <VAR>Sdtopt.C</VAR>
three times.
```

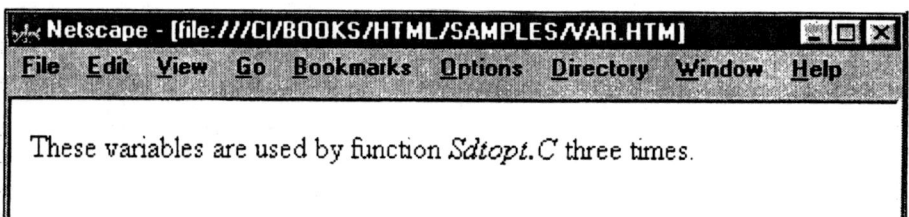

OPTIONAL ATTRIBUTES

none

TIP

- Browsers tend to display the enclosed text in italics.

RELATED HTML TAGS

<CODE>   Programming code within a paragraph.

<PRE>   Programming code as a paragraph.

Permits a break — such as a newline or text wrap — between two words in a <NBR> section of text (*short for Word BReak*).

EXAMPLE MARKUP

- To use this tag:

```
<NBR> This is a line of text where no break should occur,
except right <WBR> here. </NBR>
```

OPTIONAL ATTRIBUTES

none

RELATED HTML TAGS

 	Forces a line break.
<NBR>	Prevents a line break.
<P>	Forces a paragraph break with a blank separation line.

HTML U-X

<XMP> *str* </XMP>

(*Obsolete*) Displays a paragraph of text as it exists in the source document, including the same line breaks (*short for eXactly Marked Paragraph*).

EXAMPLE MARKUPS

■ To use this tag:

```
The specifications for this engine are: <XMP>
Engine class:  2.4L, 4-cylinder
Engine type:   DOHC balance shaft
Net power:     112kW, 150bhp @4000rpm
Net torque:    226 Nm, 167lb-ft @4000rpm
Fuel delivery: SMPI
</XMP>
```

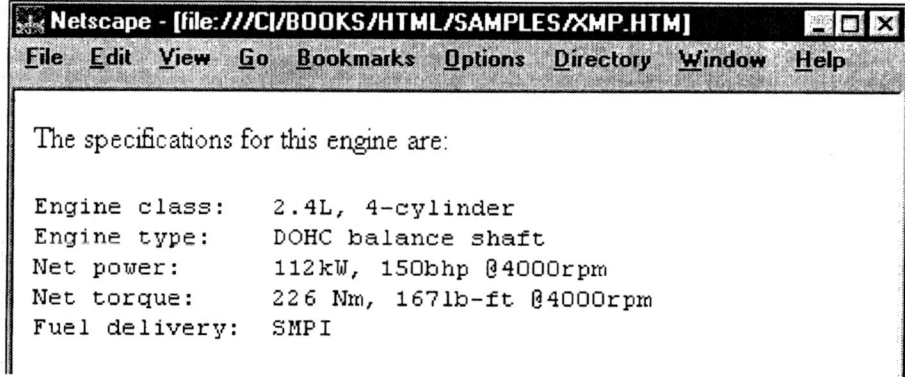

OPTIONAL ATTRIBUTES

none

TIP

■ This tag has been removed from the HTML v3.2 specification and replaced by the <PRE> tag.

■ The only tag recognized is the </XMP> ending tag.

RELATED HTML TAG

<PRE>   Displays text unformatted.

VRML

VRML is the three-dimensional interface to the World Wide Web (*short for virtual reality modeling language*); the file extension is WRL (*short for WoRLd*).

SAMPLE WRL FILE

■ VRML files are made up of *nodes*, shown in **boldface** below:

```
#VRML V1.0 ascii
Separator {
  Texture2 {
    filename "/textures/filename.jpg"
  }
  Cube {
    width  1
    depth  4
    height 9
  }
}
```

■ When a node is empty, such as **Cube {}**, it assumes default values; in the case of the Cube node, the default values are **Cube { width 1 depth 1 height 1}**.

■ The **Separator** node, in VRML v1.0, ties nodes together; in the code above, the **Texture2** node applies a texture map to the **Cube** node.

■ The header for VRML v1.0 files is **#VRMLV1.0 ascii**.

■ The header for VRML v2.0 files is **#VRML V2.0 utf8**.

VRML 1 SYNTAX

This book is based on the VRML v2.0 Draft #3 specification; the equivalent VRML v1.0c syntax is included, when appropriate. These v1.0 nodes changed in v2.0:

Node	Meaning
AsciiText	Renamed the **Text** node.
Coordinate3	Renamed the **Coordinate** node.
Cube	Renamed the **Box** node.
Info	Replaced by the **WorldInfo** node.
MaterialBinding	Replaced by the **Material** node.
MatrixTransform	Handled by the **Transform** node.
NormalBinding	Replaced by the **Normal** node.
OrthographicCamera	Handled by the browser.
PerspectiveCamera	Replaced by the **Viewpoint** node.
Rotation	Handled by the **Transform** node.
Scale	Handled by the **Transform** node.
Separator	Handled by the **Transform** node.
Texture2	Replaced by **TextureTransform** node.
Texture2Transform	Renamed the **TextureTransform** node.
TextureCoordinate2	Renamed the **TextureCoordinate** node.
Translation	Handled by the **Transform** node.
WWWAnchor	Renamed the **Anchor** node.
WWWLinline	Renamed the **Inline** node.

VRML

TIPS

■ VRML was first thought up by Mark Pesce and originally stood for virtual reality markup language.

■ Gavin Bell, of Silicon Graphics, first implemented VRML v1.0 in 1994, basing the file format on SGI's Open Inventor, an ASCII format for 3D worlds.

■ VRML v2 is based on SGI's "Moving Worlds" proposal and Apple's "Out of This World" proposal. The primary architects are Gavin Bell <gavin@acm.org>, Rikk Carey <rikk@best.com>, and Chris Marrin <cmarrin@sgi.com>, with input from the VAG and members of the www-vrml mailing list.

■ To join the www-vrml mailing list, send the following message (with a blank subject line) to majordomo@wired.com:

```
subscribe www-vrml your-email-address
```

■ To obtain the most up to date version of the VRML specification, visit the VAG (VRML Advisory Group) Web site at **http://vag.vrml.org**.

Anchor { }

Displays a file retrieved from a URL, when a child is selected (*formerly WWWAnchor; a Grouping node*).

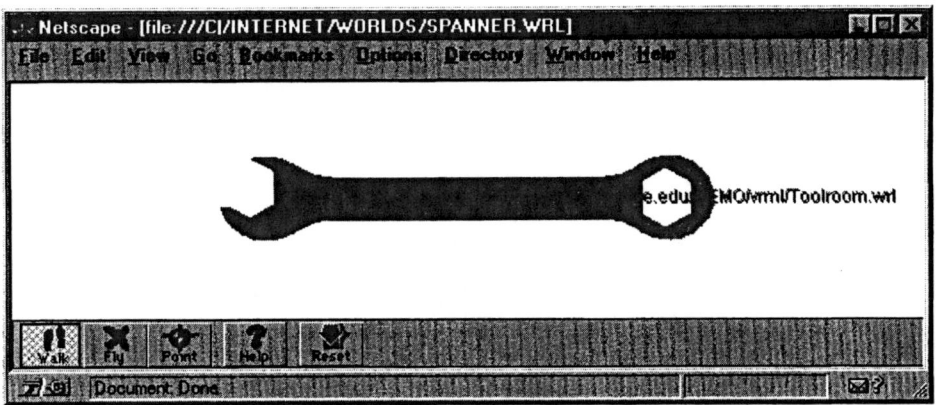

*This model of a wrench uses the **Anchor** node to specify a hyperlink.*
Spanner.Wrl reproduced by permission of Jeff Sonstein.

VRML 2 SYNTAX

```
Anchor {
  addChildren
  removeChildren
  children      [ ]
  description   " "
  parameter     [ ]
  url           [ ]
  bboxCenter    0 0 0
  bboxSize      -1 -1 -1
}
```

Field	Type	Name	Default	Meaning
eventIn	MFNode	addChildren		Adds nodes from children
eventIn	MFNode	removeChildren		Remove nodes from children
exposedField	MFNode	children	[ ]	Anchor attached to object
exposedField	SFString	description	" "	Description of URL
exposedField	MFString	parameter	[ ]	Additional file info
exposedField	MFString	url	[ ]	Uniform resource locator
field	SFVec3f	bboxCenter	0 0 0	Bounding box center point
field	SFVec3f	bboxSize	-1 -1 -1	Bounding box size.

VRML A

VRML 1 SYNTAX

```
WWWAnchor {
  name        "url"
  description ""
  map         NONE
}
```

■ Where **map** has one of two values:

NONE   Don't add mapping information to the URL.

POINT   Add coordinate mapping to the URL.

NODE GEOMETRY

■ The **addChildren** node adds the nodes passed in to the group's **children** field.

■ The **removeChildren** node removes added nodes.

■ The **children** node defines the children of the **Anchor** node.

■ The **description** node causes the browser to display a prompt other than the URL.

■ The **parameter** node contains additional information useful to the browser, in the format of `keyword=value`.

■ The **url** node is a list of one or more URLs.

■ The **bboxCenter** node specifies the center coordinates of the maximum possible bounding box, which should be large to contain all nodes.

■ The **bboxSize** node specifies the size of the bounding box.

TIPS

■ It is up to the VRML browser to handle that data returned by the **url** field.

■ A VRML browser typically displays a message when the cursor passes over an **Anchor** node; this message is held by the **description** field.

■ This node is usually attached to an object in the VRML scene using the **children** field

■ The **Sphere** node is popularly used to represent a planet floating in space:

```
Anchor {
  url "http://www.url/vrml.wrl#Surface"
  description "Click here to land on the surface of the planet."
  children [
    Sphere { }
  ]
}
```

■ Here is what the above code causes:

1. As the cursor passes over the sphere, the VRML browser displays the message, "Click here to land on the surface of the planet."

2. When the user clicks on the sphere, the browser loads the Vrml.Wrl file located at http://www.url.

---

3. After loading the WRL file, the browser displays the viewpoint specified by the **Viewpoint** node named "Surface" in that Vrml.Wrl file.

4. If the programmer did not provide a way to get back to the original world, simply click on the browser's **Back** button to return.

■ You can specify a specific viewpoint by adding the suffix *#viewpointName* to the URL, which is the name of a **Viewpoint** node defined in the world located at URL.

■ You can use the **Anchor** node to jump to a new viewpoint within the current world:

```
Anchor {
  url "#Surface"
  children [ Sphere { } ]
}
```

would take you to the **Viewpoint** node named "Surface" when you click on the sphere.

RELATED NODES

Billboard	Rotates a group about an axis to always faces the camera.
Collision	Prevents navigation through an object.
Group	Groups nodes together without performing a transformation.
Inline	Groups nodes together from around the World Wide Web.
LOD	Level of detail.
Switch	Switches between zero or more children.
Transform	Transforms the coordinate system of a group of nodes.

VRML A

Appearance { }

Specifies the appearance of a **Shape**; occurs only within the **appearance** field of a Shape node (*an Appearance node*).

VRML 2 SYNTAX

```
Appearance {
  material           NULL
  texture            NULL
  textureTransform   NULL
}
```

Field	Type	Name	Default	Meaning
exposedField	SFNode	material	NULL	Contains **Material** node.
exposedField	SFNode	texture	NULL	Contains texture nodes.
exposedField	SFNode	textureTransform	NULL	Contains **TextureTransform**.

VRML 1 SYNTAX
Node is new to VRML v2.0.

NODE GEOMETRY

■ The **material** field must contain the **Material** node.

■ The **texture** field must contain the **ImageTexture, MovieTexture,** or **PixelTexture** node.

■ The **textureTransform** field must contain a **TextureTransform** node.

TIPS

■ This node occurs only within the **appearance** field of the **Shape** node.

■ Any or all of the fields can be set to **NULL**.

RELATED NODES

Shape   Defines a shape.

ImageTexture   Defines a texture map and its parameters.

Material   Assigns a material to an object.

MovieTexture   Defines an animated movie map and its parameters.

PixelTexture   Defines a repetitive pixel map and its parameters.

TextureTransform

            Applies a 2D transformation to a texture.

AudioClip { }

Plays a pre-loaded audio clip (*a Media Property node*).

VRML 2 SYNTAX
```
AudioClip {
  url                  [ ]
  description          " "
  loop                 FALSE
  startTime            0
  stopTime             0
  pitch                1.0
  duration_changed     0
  isActive             FALSE
}
```

Field	Type	Name	Default	Meaning
exposedField	MFString	url	[ ]	URL of the audio file.
exposedField	SFString	description	" "	Text description.
exposedField	SFBool	loop	FALSE	Repeat audio file.
exposedField	SFTime	startTime	0	Time to start playing.
exposedField	SFTime	stopTime	0	Time to stop playing.
exposedField	SFFloat	pitch	1.0	Pitch to play back at.
eventOut	SFTime	duration_changed		Duration of file.
eventOut	SFBool	isActive		Is audio playing back?

VRML 1 SYNTAX
Node is new to VRML v2.0.

NODE GEOMETRY
- The **url** field is the source filename for the audio file in URL format; see Appendix A.
- The **description** field describes the audio.
- The **loop** field repeats the audio over and over:

loop	Meaning
FALSE	Audio file is played once; the default.
TRUE	Audio file is played over and over.

- The **startTime** field is the time to begin playing the audio file.
- The **stopTime** field is the time to stop the audio file.
- The **pitch** field specifies the pitch to playback the audio file:

pitch	Meaning
0.5	Play audio file one octave lower.
1.0	Play audio file normally; the default.
2.0	Play audio file one octave higher.

- The **duration_changed** field reports the length of the time to play the audio file, in seconds.

- The **isActive** field reports whether the audio file is being played.

TIPS

- The audio file should load when the **Sound** node is loaded so that it is ready to play at any time.

- The **url** field can specify more than one URL so that the browser can choose the audio file that best suits its own capabilities.

- The browser should support any MIME type for a sound file.

- At the minimum, the browser should support uncompressed PCM format; one level higher, the browser should support the MIDI type 1 and use the General MIDI patch set.

- The value of **duration** is only valid when **pitch** is set to **1.0**, otherwise the value must be adjusted. For example, if **pitch** is set to **2.0**, then **duration** is half as long.

- The **isActive** field reports to other nodes whether the audio file is currently being played by the **Sound** node.

RELATED NODES

Sound   Indicates the source point of a sound.

MovieTexture   Defines an animated movie map and its parameters.

Background { }

Creates a color-ramped backdrop to simulate the ground and sky (*a Bindable Leaf node*).

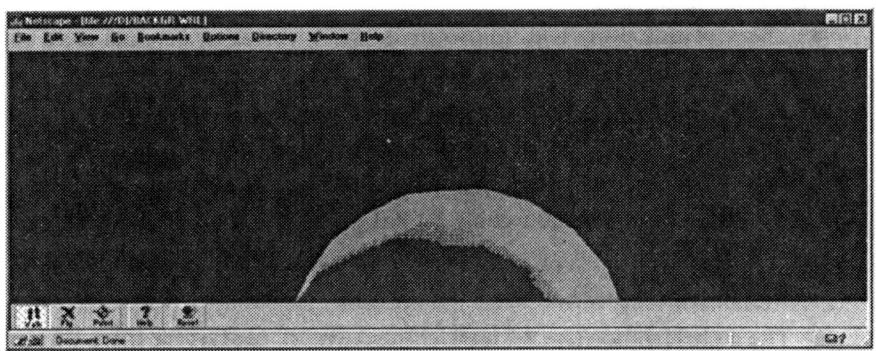

A starry background in Netscape.Wrl, a VRML file provided with Live3D.

VRML 2 SYNTAX

```
Background {
    groundColor   [ ]
    groundAngle   [ ]
    skyColor      [ 0 0 0 ]
    skyAngle      [ ]
    rightUrl      [ ]
    leftUrl       [ ]
    topUrl        [ ]
    frontUrl      [ ]
    backUrl       [ ]
    negZ          [ ]
    set_bind
    is Bound
}
```

Field	Type	Name	Default	Meaning
exposedfield	MFColor	groundColor	[ ]	Ramped ground color.
exposedField	MFFloat	groundAngle	[ ]	Start of horizon.
exposedField	MFColor	skyColor	[0 0 0]	Ramped sky color.
exposedField	MFFloat	skyAngle	[ ]	Horizon.
exposedField	MFString	rightUrl	[ ]	Right side panorama.
exposedField	MFString	leftUrl	[ ]	Left side panorama.
exposedField	MFString	topUrl	[ ]	Top panorama.
exposedField	MFString	bottomUrl	[ ]	Bottom panorama.
exposedField	MFString	frontUrl	[ ]	Front panorama.
exposedField	MFString	backUrl	[ ]	Back panorama.
eventIn	SFBool	set_bind		Bind **Background** to browser.
eventOut	SFBool	isBound		Bind status has changed.

VRML 1 SYNTAX
Node is new to VRML v2.0.

NODE GEOMETRY

■ The **groundColor** field holds one or more colors in decimal RGB notation describing the color of the ground.

■ The **groundAngle** field specifies, in radians, the cutoff angle for the **groundColor** field; default initial value is 0.0 radians (south pole) and moves upward to *pi* radians (north pole).

■ The **skyColor** field holds one or more colors in decimal RGB notation describing the color of the sky; the default color [0 0 0] is black.

■ The **skyAngle** field starts at 0.0 radians at the north pole and moves to the final value of *pi* radians (south pole).

■ The **rightUrl** (positive X), **leftUrl** (negative X), **topUrl** (positive Y), **bottomUrl** (negative Y), **frontUrl** (positive Z), and **backUrl** (negative Z) fields defines the size sides of a cube, called the panorama, which can be used to paste six background images, such as mountains or a cityscape.

■ The **set_bind** field attaches the Background node to the browser's view:

set_bind	Meaning
TRUE	Push the Background to top of stack.
FALSE	Pop the Background from the stack.

■ The **isBound** field reports changes in binding the **Background** to the browser.

TIPS

■ The **Background** node is like being inside a sphere of infinite radius painted with a smooth gradation of ground and sky colors.

■ By default, the ground color ramps from light green to dark green; the sky color ramps from twilight blue to light blue.

■ Depending on the capability of the browser, the background colors might appear as a smooth gradation or as banded colors; some browsers might implement this node as a cube, rather than a sphere.

■ The **groundAngle** field can contain a list of radian values to indicate the cutoff for each **groundColor** field.

■ When **groundColor** is set to **NULL**, no ground color is displayed.

■ By default, there is no panorama.

■ To display the ground and sky gradations, keep the **topUrl** and **bottomUrl** fields blank.

RELATED NODES

Billboard	Keeps one of more shapes always facing the camera.
Fog	Creates the appearance of fog or smog in the background.
LOD	Changes the level of detail, according to the distance from object.

Billboard { }

Automatically rotates nodes about an axis to always face the camera (*a Group node*).

VRML 2 SYNTAX

```
Billboard {
  addChildren
  removeChildren
  axisOfRotation     0 1 0
  children           [ ]
  bboxCenter         0 0 0
  bboxSize           -1 -1 -1
}
```

Field	Type	Name	Default	Meaning
eventIn	MFNode	addChildren		Add children
eventIn	MFNode	removeChildren		Remove children
exposedField	MFNode	children	[ ]	List of objects
exposedField	SFVec3f	axisOfRotation	0 1 0	Axis about which to rotate
field	SFVec3f	bboxCenter	0 0 0	Center of bounding box
field	SFVec3f	bboxSize	-1 -1 -1	Size of bounding box

VRML 1 SYNTAX

Node is new to VRML v2.0.

NODE GEOMETRY

■ The **addChildren** node adds the nodes passed in to the group's **children** field.

■ The **removeChildren** node removes added nodes.

■ You specify which axis to rotate the object with the **axisOfRotation** field (the axis is defined using the local billboard node coordinates.)

■ *Special case*: To cause an object to always face the camera — no matter how the camera moves — set **axisOfRotation** to **0 0 0**.

■ *Special case*: The object cannot rotate when the axis specified by **axisOfRotation** aligns with the camera's axis.

■ This node is usually attached to one or more objects in the VRML scene using the **children** field.

■ The **bboxCenter** node specifies the center coordinates of the maximum possible bounding box, which should be large to contain all nodes.

■ The **bboxSize** node specifies the size of the bounding box.

TIPS

■ The **Billboard** node automatically modifies its coordinate system so that children nodes turn to point at the camera.

■ The default **axisOfRotation** value of **0 1 0** is useful for rotating 2D trees and people to always face the camera and hence look "3D."

■ For objects located at an angle, such as roof of a house, you will have to employ the other one or two axes of rotation.

■ Any geometry can be billboarded.

RELATED NODES

Anchor	Loads another world or viewpoint.
Collision	Prevents navigation through an object.
Group	Groups nodes together without performing a transformation.
Inline	Groups nodes together from around the World Wide Web.
LOD	Level of detail.
Switch	Switches between zero or more children.
Transform	Transforms the coordinate system of a group of nodes.

Box { }

Creates a 3D box *(formerly the **Cube** node in VRML v1; a Geometry node).*

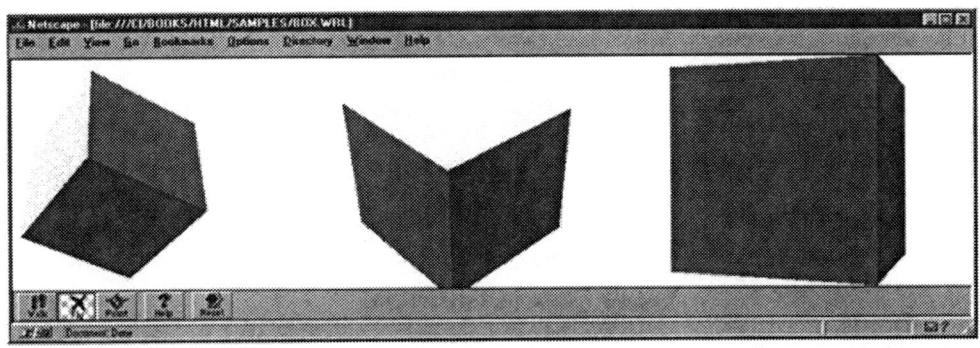

VRML 2 SYNTAX
```
Box {
  size 2 2 2
}
```

Field	Type	Name	Default	Meaning
field	SFVec3f	size	2 2 2	Size of three sides

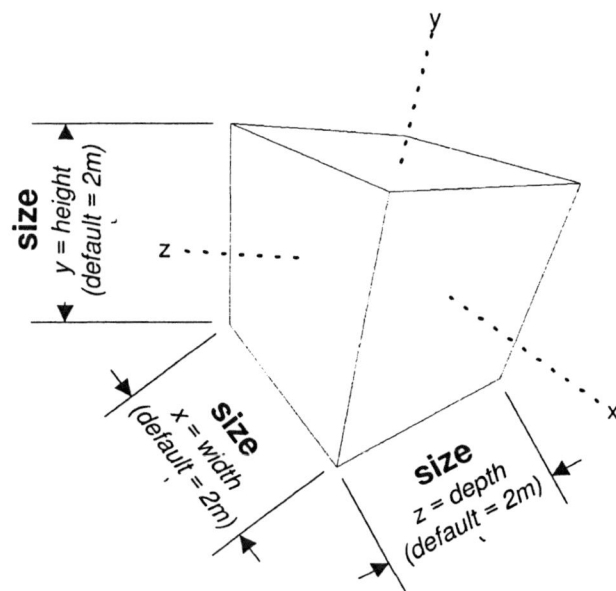

VRML 1 SYNTAX

```
Cube {
  width   2
  height  2
  depth   2
}
```

- Where the **Cube** node is centered on the origin (0,0,0):

width   Size of **Cube** in x-direction.

height   Size of **Cube** in y-direction.

depth   Size of **Cube** in z-direction.

NODE GEOMETRY

- The box is aligned with the coordinate axes: (1) width along x-axis; (2) height along the y-axis; and (3) depth along the z-axis.

- The default box is centered at (0,0,0) with a size of -1 to +1 in the x,y,z-directions.

- The default box has square sides, each two units long.

- A box has a single part: the six sides; unlike the cone or cylinder, you cannot turn off some of the sides.

RELATED EQUATIONS

Area of front or back side

= **width** * **height**

Area of left or right side

= **depth** * **height**

Area of top or bottom side

= **width** * **depth**

Total surface area of a rectangular box

= (2 * **width** * **height**) + (2 * **width** * **depth**) + (2 * **height** * **depth**)

Surface area of a cube

= 6 * (**width**)^2

Volume

= **width** * **height** * **depth**

TEXTURE MAPPING
- **Front, back, left, and right sides:** texture is applied right side up.
- **Top:** texture appears rightside up when top of box tilts toward viewer.
- **Bottom:** texture appears rightside up when the top of the box tilts toward the -z-axis.

*The texture map (upper left) applied to the **Box** node.*

TIPS
- The **Box** node is the basis for creating buildings in a VRML scene; apply texture maps to create the front and sides of the building.

- Use thin boxes to create walls; for example, to create a standard 8'-high exterior wall, ten feet long, set **size** to 3.048 2.438 0.152 (units in meters, meaning 10 feet long, 8 feet high, and 6 inches thick).

- To create a flat square, set **size** to **2 2 0**.

- A texture map is applied individually to each face of the box; the entire texture goes on each face.
- This **Box** node was known as the **Cube** node in VRML v1.

RELATED NODES

Cone	Creates a 3D cone.
Cylinder	Creates a 3D cylinder.
ElevationGrid	Creates a 3D terrain-like surface.
Extrusion	Extrudes a 2D shape along a 3D spine.
IndexedFaceSet	Creates a 3D surface from multiple polyfaces.
IndexedLineSet	Creates a 3D shape from multiple polylines.
PointSet	Creates a 3D space from multiple dots.
Sphere	Creates a 3D sphere or ball.
Text	Creates 3D text; formerly the **AsciiText** node.

Collision { }

Prevents the camera from going through an object (*a Groups node*).

VRML 2 SYNTAX

```
Collision {
    addChildren
    removeChildren
    children              [ ]
    collide               TRUE
    bboxCenter            0 0 0
    bboxSize              -1 -1 -1
    proxy                 NULL
    collideTime
}
```

Field	Type	Name	Default	Meaning
eventIn	MFNode	addChildren		Children added
eventIn	MFNode	removeChildren		Children removed
exposedField	MFNode	children	[ ]	Collision-proofed objects
exposedField	SFBool	collide	TRUE	Toggle collision detection
field	SFVec3f	bboxCenter	0 0 0	Bounding box center
field	SFVec3f	bboxSize	-1 -1 -1	Bounding box size
field	SFNode	proxy	NULL	Alternate geometry
eventOut	SFTime	collideTime		Time of collision

VRML 1 SYNTAX

Node is new to VRML v2.0.

NODE GEOMETRY

■ The **addChildren** node adds the nodes passed in to the group's **children** field.

■ The **removeChildren** node removes added nodes.

■ The objects listed the **children** field are the ones that create a collision.

■ The **collideTime** eventOut estimates the time when the user intersected the collision node.

■ The **bboxCenter** node specifies the center coordinates of the maximum possible bounding box, which should be large to contain all nodes.

■ The **bboxSize** node specifies the size of the bounding box.

■ The **proxy** field lets you define a box, sphere or polyhedron that acts as a simpler representation of the anticollision field (the **proxy** field should contain a group or leaf node).

- By default, the **collision** field has detection turned on:

collideTime	Meaning
TRUE	Collision detection is turned on; default.
FALSE	Collision detection is turned off.

TIPS

- This node keep you from flying through the walls of a building, although some users may not find that useful at all.

- Turning off collision detection (set **collide** to **FALSE**) means you can pass through the objects.

- It is up to the browser to handle the collision. The response may be to stop moving or to bounce.

- Since collision detection can take up a lot of CPU cycles, it is useful to approximate a complex set of objects (such as an automobile or ferris wheel) with a simpler representation (such as a **Box** or **Cylinder** node) via the **proxy** field.

- By having no **children** but defining a **proxy** field, you create a collision with an invisible object.

RELATED NODES

Anchor	Loads another world or viewpoint.
Billboard	Rotates a group about an axis to always faces the camera.
Group	Groups nodes together without performing a transformation.
Inline	Groups nodes together from around the World Wide Web.
LOD	Level of detail.
Switch	Switches between zero or more children.
Transform	Transforms the coordinate system of a group of nodes.

Color { }

Defines the RGB colors used in the **color** field of the **IndexedFaceSet, Indexed-LineSet,** and **PointSet** nodes (*a Geometric Property node*).

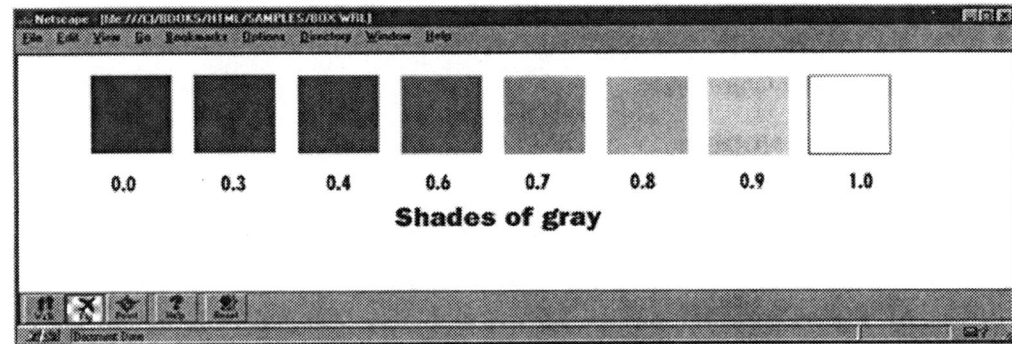

Eight shades of gray, such as 0.7 0.7 0.7, ranging from black (0 0 0) to white (1 1 1).

VRML 2 SYNTAX

```
Color {
  color      [ ]
}
```

Field	Type	Name	Default	Meaning
exposedField	MFColor	*color*	[ ]	Color in RGB format.

VRML 1 SYNTAX

Node is new to VRML v2.0.

NODE GEOMETRY

■ The **color** field in decimal notation. For example:

color	Meaning
1 1 1	White color (#FFFFFF in hex notation).
.5 .5 .5	Medium gray color.
.75 .75 .75	Dialogue box gray.
0 0 0	Black color.
1 0 0	Red color.
1 1 0	Yellow color.
0 1 0	Green color.
0 1 1	Cyan color.
0 0 1	Blue color.

■ The **rgb** field can hold one or more colors.

■ The **Color** node should only be used to specify multiple colors for each face or vertex of the **IndexedFaceSet, IndexedLineSet,** and **PointSet** nodes.

■ The **Color** node replaces the **Material** node (if present); a texture node (if present) replaces the **Color** node.

RELATED NODES

Material   Defines a surface material look.

Coordinate   Specifies the 3D x,y,z-coordinates of points, lines, and faces.

Normal   Specifies the normals for faces and grids.

TextureCoordinate

                 Specifies the 2D texture coordinates for faces and grids.

IndexedFaceSet   Creates a complex object from 3D faces.

IndexedLineSet   Creates a complex object from 3D lines.

PointSet   Creates a 3D point cloud.

ColorInterpolator { }

Interpolates between a set of colors in **MFColor** format to create an **SFColor** event (*an Interpolator node*).

VRML 2 SYNTAX

```
ColorInterpolator {
  key            [ ]
  keyValue       [ ]
  set_fraction
  value_changed
}
```

Field	Type	Name	Default	Meaning
exposedField	MFFloat	key	[ ]	Parameterized time.
exposedField	MFColor	keyVvalue	[ ]	Color values.
eventIn	SFFloat	set_fraction		Input trigger.
eventOut	SFColor	value_changed		Output value.

VRML 1 SYNTAX
Node is new to VRML v2.0.

NODE GEOMETRY
- The **key** field holds parameterized time values from 0.0 to 1.0.
- The **keyValue** field holds the color values in **MFColor** format.
- The **set_fraction** field causes the interpolator function to operate.
- The **value_changed** field returns the interpolated color value in **SFColor** format.

TIPS
- This node can be used to create color cycling.
- These interpolator nodes are meant to be used to create linear, keyframed animation.
- Values in the **key** field must increase and cannot repeat.
- The number of colors in the **keyValue** field must have the same number of colors as the keyframe times in the **key** field.

RELATED NODES
CoordinateInterpolator	Linearly interpolates along a set of **MFVec3f** values.
NormalInterpolator	Interpolates along a set of multivalue **Vec3f** values.
OrientationInterpolator	Interpolates along a set of **SFRotation** values.
PositionInterpolator	Linearly interpolates along a set of **SFVec3f** values.
ScalarInterpolator	Linearly interpolates along a set of **SFFloat** values.

VRML C

Cone { }

Creates a cone (*a Geometry node*).

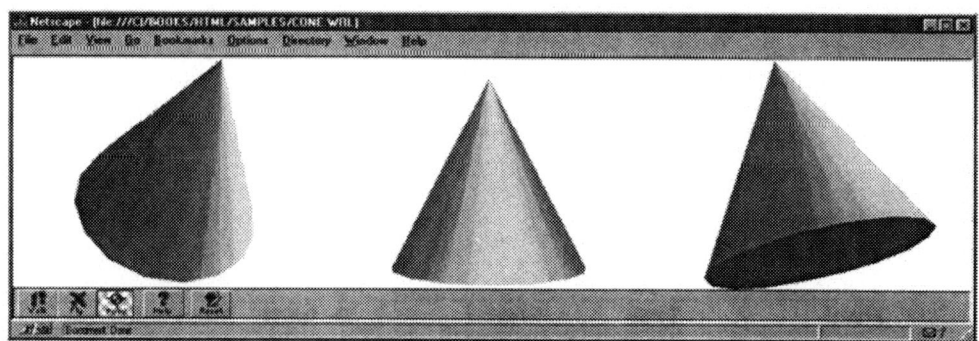

VRML 2 SYNTAX

```
Cone {
  bottomRadius 1
  height       2
  side         TRUE
  bottom       TRUE
}
```

Field	Type	Name	Default	Meaning
field	SFFloat	bottomRadius	1	Radius of cone's base.
field	SFFloat	height	2	Height of cone.
field	SFBool	side	TRUE	Cone has sides.
field	SFBool	bottom	TRUE	Cone has bottom.

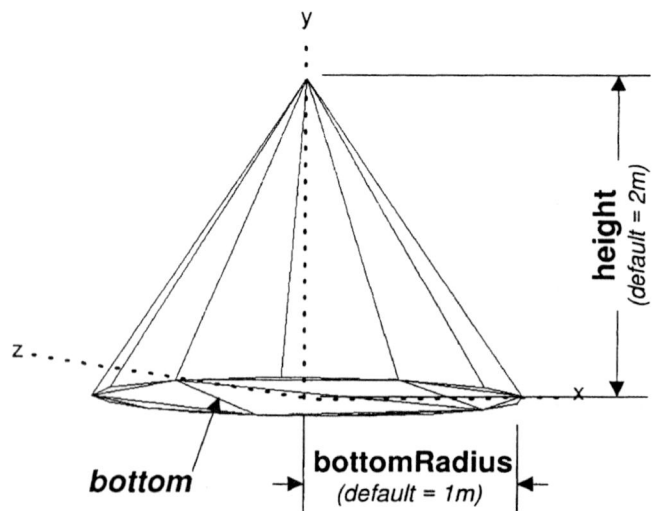

VRML 1 SYNTAX

```
Cone {
  parts         ALL
  bottomRadius  1
  height        2
  }
```

- Where **parts** is one of:

  SIDES   The cone.

  BOTTOM   The bottom face.

  ALL   Both parts.

NODE GEOMETRY

- The cone has its central axis aligned with the y-axis.

- The default cone is centered at **0 0 0** with a size of -1 to +1 in the x,y,z-directions.

- The default cone has a base radius of 1, with the base located at y = -1; the cone's height is 2, with the apex located at y = +1.

- A cone has two parts: (1) the side; and (2) the bottom; the **SFBool** field specifies whether each part is visible (set **SfBool** to TRUE) or invisible, **FALSE**.

RELATED EQUATIONS

pi = 3.141

Area of base

$\quad = pi *$ (**bottomRadius**)^2

Circumference of base

$\quad = 2 * pi *$ **bottomRadius**

Total surface area

$\quad = pi *$ **bottomRadius** $*$ sqrt(**bottomRadius**^{2} + **height**^{2})

Volume of cone

$\quad = {}^1/_3 * pi *$ (**bottomRadius**)$^2 *$ **height**

TEXTURE MAPPING

- **Side:** wraps counterclockwise (looking from above) starting at the back of the cone, with a vertical seam down the back.

- **Bottom:** a disc is cut out of the texture square and applied to the cone's base, which maps the texture to appear flipped over.

Vertical seam

*The texture map (upper left) applied to the **Cone** node.*

TIPS

■ To create a flat disc, set **height** to **0**.

■ To create an open cone, such as an ice cream cone, set **bottom** to **FALSE** and rotate the cone toward the -z-axis.

RELATED NODES

Box	Creates a 3D box; formerly the **Cube** node.
Cylinder	Creates a 3D cylinder.
ElevationGrid	Creates a 3D terrain-like surface.
Extrusion	Extrudes a 2D shape along a 3D spine.
IndexedFaceSet	Creates a 3D surface from multiple polyfaces.
IndexedLineSet	Creates a 3D shape from multiple polylines.
PointSet	Creates a 3D space from multiple dots.
Sphere	Creates a 3D sphere or ball.
Text	Creates 3D text; formerly the **AsciiText** node.

VRML C

Coordinate { }

Contains a list of 3D coordinates for use by other nodes (*formerly **Coordinate3**; a Geometric Property node*).

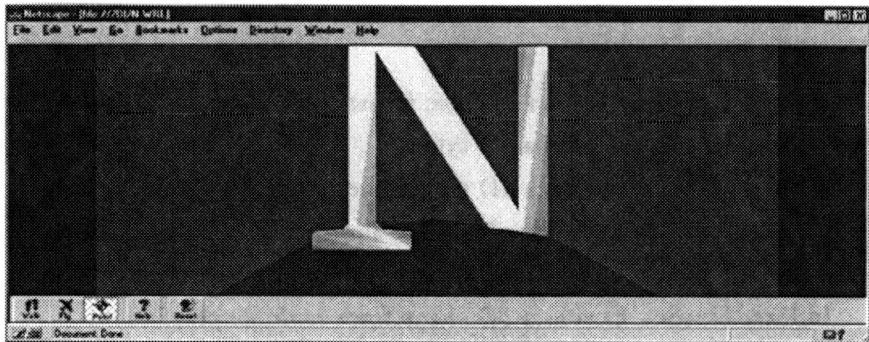

*The "N" of the Netscape logo was created using a **Coordinate** node, followed by an **IndexedFaceSet** node. Netscape.Wrl provided with Live3D.*

VRML 2 SYNTAX

```
Coordinate {
  point     [ ]
}
```

Field	Type	Name	Default	Meaning
exposedField	MFVec3f	point	[ ]	X,y,z-coordinate list.

VRML 1 SYNTAX

```
Coordinate3 {
  point [ 0.0 0.0 0.0 ]
}
```

■ Where **point** is a list of x,y,z distances from the origin that define the vertices of a shape. Each set of x,y,z-distances is separated by a comma.

NODE GEOMETRY

■ The **point** field holds one or more 3D x,y,z-coordinates, each set separated by a comma.

TIPS

■ The large "N" in the Netscape.Wrl file, shown above, was created with the **Coordinate** and **IndexedFaceSet** nodes. (The sphere was created with the **Sphere** node.)

■ The **Coordinate** node is used with the **IndexedFaceSet, IndexedLineSet,** and **PointSet** nodes.

■ Each number in the **IndexedFaceSet** (or **IndexedLineSet** or **PointSet**) node matches a coordinate triple in the **Coordinate** node.

- For example, here the **Coordinate** node is used with the **IndexedFaceSet** node:

```
Coordinate {
  point [ -1.223653  2.402087  -2.128398,
          -1.028676  2.400000  -2.728398,
          -1.642742  2.152785  -2.483273,
          . . .
          0.333486  1.686486  -0.231100,
          1.457810  0.562162  -0.231100 ]
}
IndexedFaceSet {
  coordIndex [ 0, 1, 2, -1, 3, ... 119, -1 ]
}
```

RELATED NODES

Color   Specifies the RGB colors of points, lines, and faces.

Normal   Specifies the normals for faces and grids.

TextureCoordinate

    Specifies the 2D texture coordinates for faces and grids.

IndexedFaceSet Creates a complex object from 3D faces.

IndexedLineSet Creates a complex object from 3D lines.

PointSet   Creates a 3D point cloud.

VRML C

CoordinateInterpolator { }

Interpolates a set of MFVec3f values, such as vertex positions (*an Interpolator node*).

VRML 2 SYNTAX

```
CoordinateInterpolator {
  key              [ ]
  keyValue         [ ]
  set_fraction
  value_changed
}
```

Field	Type	Name	Default	Meaning
exposedField	MFFloat	key	[ ]	Parameterized coordinates.
exposedField	MFVec3f	keyValue	[ ]	Coordinate values.
eventIn	SFFloat	set_fraction		Triggers interpolator.
eventOut	MFVec3f	value_changed		Returns results.

VRML 1 SYNTAX

Node is new to VRML v2.0.

NODE GEOMETRY

- The **key** field holds parameterized coordinate values from **0.0** to **1.0**.

- The **keyValue** field holds the coordinate values in **MFVect3f** format.

- The **set_fraction** field causes the interpolator function to operate.

- The **value_changed** field returns the interpolated color value in **MFVec3f** format.

TIPS

- This node can be used to create a morphing action via geometric interpolation.

- These interpolator nodes are meant to be used to create linear, keyframed animation.

- Values in the **key** field must increase and cannot repeat.

- The number of coordinates in the **keyValue** field must have the same **number of** coordinates as the keyframe times in the **key** field.

RELATED NODES

ColorInterpolator	Linearly interpolates along a set of **MFColor** values.
NormalInterpolator	Interpolates along a set of multivalue **Vec3f** values.
OrientationInterpolator	Interpolates along a set of **SFRotation** values.
PositionInterpolator	Linearly interpolates along a set of **SFVec3f** values.
ScalarInterpolator	Linearly interpolates along a set of **SFFloat** values.

Cylinder { }

Creates a cylinder (*a Geometry node*).

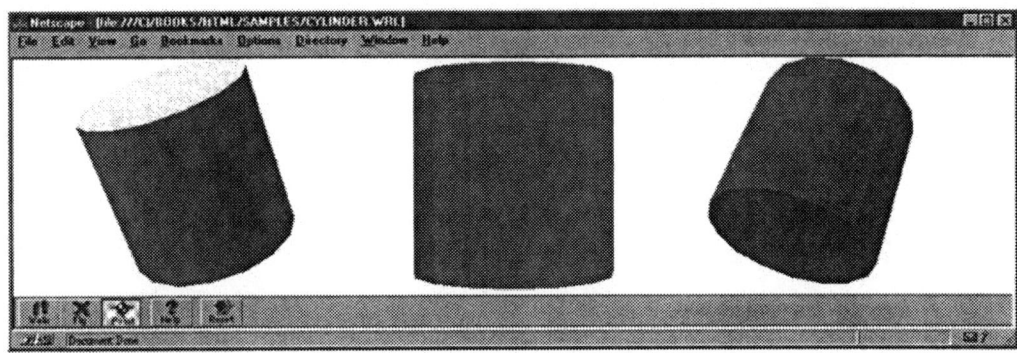

VRML 2 SYNTAX

```
Cylinder {
   radius   1
   height   2
   side     TRUE
   top      TRUE
   bottom   TRUE
}
```

Field	Type	Name	Default	Meaning
field	SFFloat	radius	1	Radius of circular base
field	SFFloat	height	2	Height of the tube
field	SFBool	side	TRUE	Cylinder has sides
field	SFBool	top	TRUE	Cylinder has a top
field	SFBool	bottom	TRUE	Cylinder has a bottom

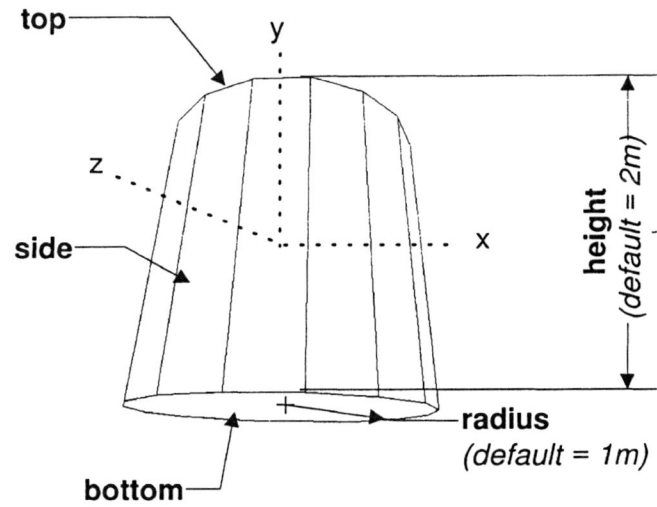

VRML 1 SYNTAX

```
Cylinder {
   height   2
   radius   1
   parts    ALL
}
```

Where the **parts** options are:

SIDES   The tube.

TOP   Top disc.

BOTTOM   Bottom disc.

NODE GEOMETRY

■ The cylinder is aligned with the coordinate axes: (1) radius in the x- and z-axes; and (2) height in the y-axis.

■ The default cylinder is centered at **0 0 0** with a size of -1 to +1 in the x,y,z-directions.

■ The default cylinder is "square", with a height of 2 units and a diameter of two units.

■ The cylinder has three parts, each of which can be turned on and off: (1) the **top** at y = +1; (2) the **side**; and (3) the **bottom** at y = -1.

RELATED EQUATIONS

pi = 3.141

Diameter of base

= 2 * **radius**

Circumference of base

= 2 * *pi* * **radius**

Surface area of top or bottom

= *pi* * **radius**^{2}

Surface area of side

= 2 * *pi* * **radius** * **height**

Total surface area

= 2 * *pi* * (**radius**^{2} + (**radius** * **height**))

Volume of cylinder

= *pi* * (**radius**)^2 * **height**

TEXTURE MAPPING

■ **Side:** texture wraps counterclockwise looking from above, starting at the back of the cylinder, which means the texture has a vertical seam at the back.

■ **Top and bottom:** a disc is cut from the texture square and applied to the top and bottom.

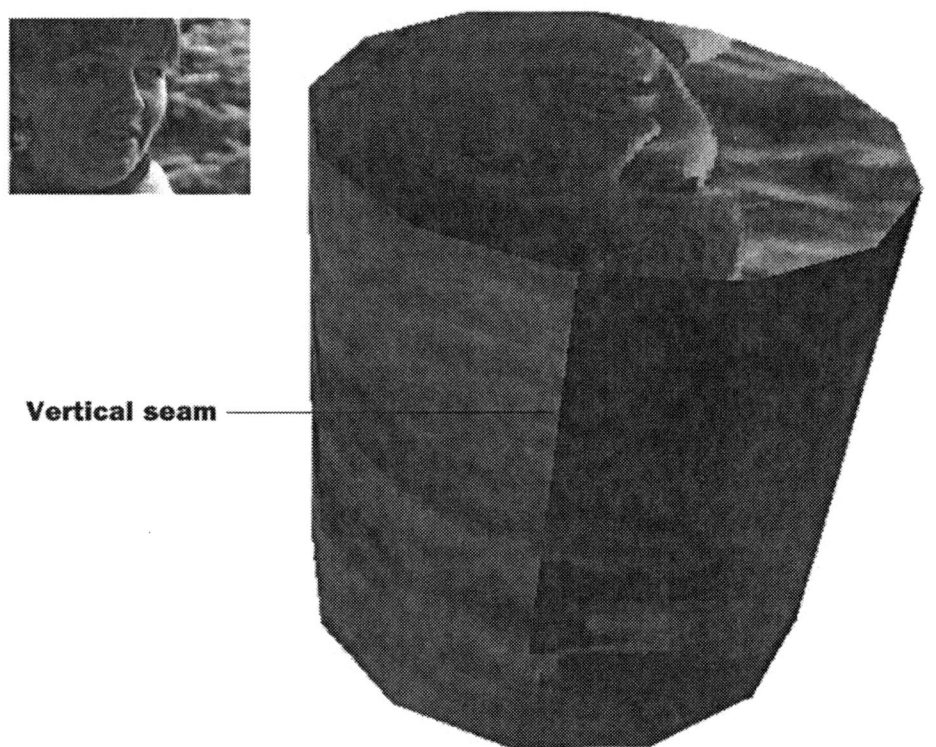

Vertical seam

The texture map (upper left) applied to the Cylinder node.

TIPS

■ The **Box** node is the basis for creating buildings in a VRML scene; apply texture maps to create the front and sides of the building.

■ To create a tube, set **top** and **bottom** to **FALSE**.

■ To create a disc, set **height** to **0**; to help make the disc more visible, set **height** to **0.01**, which gives it a tiny amount of thickness.

■ The top texture map appears rightside up when cylinder's top is tilted toward the viewer; the bottom texture appears rightside up when the top is tilted away from viewer.

RELATED NODES

Box	Creates a 3D box; formerly the **Cube** node.
Cone	Creates a 3D cone.
ElevationGrid	Creates a 3D terrain-like surface.
Extrusion	Extrudes a 2D shape along a 3D spine.
IndexedFaceSet	Creates a 3D surface from multiple polyfaces.
IndexedLineSet	Creates a 3D shape from multiple polylines.
PointSet	Creates a 3D space from multiple dots.
Sphere	Creates a 3D sphere or ball.
Text	Creates 3D text; formerly the **AsciiText** node.

CylinderSensor { }

Maps dragging motion about the y-axis in a cylinder-like envelope (*a Sensor node*).

VRML 2 SYNTAX

```
CylinderSensor  {
  minAngle              0
  maxAngle              -1
  diskAngle             0.262
  enabled               TRUE
  offset                0 1 0 0
  autoOffset            TRUE
  isActive
  trackPoint_changed
  rotation_changed
}
```

Field	Type	Name	Default	Meaning
exposedField	SFFloat	minAngle	0	Starting angle (radians).
exposedField	SFFloat	maxAngle	-1	Ending angle (radians).
exposedField	SFFloat	diskAngle	0.262	Disk-shaped sensor.
exposedField	SFBool	enabled	TRUE	Toggle on and off.
exposedField	SFRotation	offset	0 1 0 0	Offset added to output.
exposedField	SFBool	autoOffset	TRUE	Send to last output value.
eventOut	SFBool	isActive		Reports sensor is active.
eventOut	SFVec3f	trackPoint_changed		Current cursor position.
eventOut	SFRotation	rotation_changed		Current rotation angle.

VRML 1 SYNTAX
Node is new to VRML v2.0.

NODE GEOMETRY

■ The **minAngle** and **maxAngle** fields are the starting and ending angles (in radians) for an incomplete cylinder sensor; for example, set the angle values to **0** and **1.571** to create a half-cylinder sensor.

■ The **diskAngle** field determines if the sensor is like a cylinder or a disk.

■ The **enabled** field toggles the **CylinderSensor** on and off:

enabled	Meaning
FALSE	CylinderSensor is off.
TRUE	CylinderSensor is on; the default.

■ The **offset** is added to the output value **rotation_changed** when the **CylinderSensor** generates output in response to the pointer's motion.

- The **autoOffset** field determines if the **offset** is set when the pointing device button is released:

autoOffset	Meaning
FALSE	Don't send `offset`.
TRUE	Send `offset` when button is released; default

- The **isActive** field reports to other nodes that the **CylinderSensor** is active.

- The **trackPoint_changed** field reports the cursor's current position on the surface of the cylinder.

- The **rotation_changed** field reports the angle of rotation between **minAngle** and **maxAngle**.

TIPS

- This node determines if a hit occurs with all geometry contained by its parent node.

- The **rotation_changed** event is not clamped when **minAngle** is greater than **maxAngle**.

RELATED NODES

PlaneSensor	Maps dragging motion into the x,y-plane.
SphereSensor	Maps dragging motion into free rotation about its center.
ProximitySensor	Generates events when camera enters, moves inside, and exits 3D space.
TimeSensor	Generate events as time passes.
TouchSensor	Generates events as the cursor passes over child geometry nodes.
VisibilitySensor	Generates events when a bounding box enters and leaves the viewing frustum.

DEF, USE

Defines (DEF) and employs (USE) an instance multiple times.

Temple.Wrl uses the DEF and USE keywords to define the eight columns and 16 square pads.

VRML 2 SYNTAX
```
DEF   nodename   node
USE   nodename
```

VRML 1 SYNTAX
```
DEF   nodename node
USE   nodename
```

TIPS

■ The DEF/USE pair allow you to create more efficient files. For example, if a scene has six columns (cylinders), define one **Cylinder** node as **aColumn**:

```
DEF aColumn Cylinder {
  bottom   TRUE
  side     TRUE
  top      TRUE
  radius   0.5
  height   3.0
}
```

■ Reuse the **aColumn** definition six times, together with the **Transform** node:

```
Transform { translation 2 0 0 children [USE aColumn] }
```

■ The **DEF** keyword gives a node a name and creates the node of that type.

■ The **USE** keyword inserts a reference to a **DEF**-named node in the scene graph.

RELATED KEYWORDS

EXTERNPROTO Allows the creation of user-definable nodes from an external file.

PROTO   Allows the creation of user-definable nodes.

ROUTE   eventOut value from one node and inputs it to eventIn of another node.

DirectionalLight { }

A light source with parallel light beams that only illuminates objects in its group (*a Leaf node*).

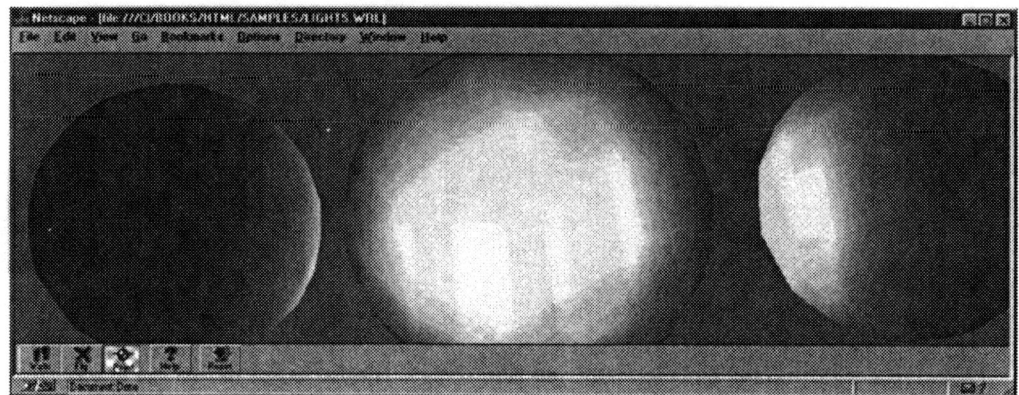

VRML 2 SYNTAX

```
DirectionalLight {
    on                    TRUE
    intensity             1
    ambientIntensity      0
    color                 1 1 1
    direction             0 0 -1
}
```

Field	Type	Name	Default	Meaning
exposedField	SFBool	on	TRUE	Toggles the light.
exposedField	SFFloat	intensity	1	Brightness of the light.
exposedField	SFFloat	ambientIntensity	0	Amount of ambient light.
exposedField	SFColor	color	1 1 1	Color of the light.
exposedField	SFVec3f	direction	0 0 -1	Direction the light faces

VRML 1 SYNTAX

```
DirectionalLight {
    on                    TRUE
    intensity             1
    color                 1 1 1
    direction             0 0 -1
}
```

NODE GEOMETRY

■ The **on** field switches the light

on	Meaning
TRUE	Light is turned on.
FALSE	Light is turned off.

■ The **intensity** field controls the brightness of the light:

intensity	Meaning
0.0	Light is off; no intensity.
1.0	Full intensity; default value.
> 1.0	Can create an overbright light.
< 0.0	Can add darkness; an anti-light.

■ The **ambientIntensity** field determines the amount of ambient light, light that is reflected off surfaces and creates an overall illumination.

■ The **color** field determines the color of the light using decimal RGB notation:

color	Meaning
1 1 1	White light; the default.
0 0 0	No light.
1 0 0	Red light.
0 1 0	Green light.
0 0 1	Blue light.

■ The **direction** field aims the light from the current origin in the x,y,z-direction; the default of **0 0 -1** aims the light into the scene (like a headlight).

TIPS

■ Since a directional light has parallel light beams, it needs no location, only a direction.

■ Shapes do no cast shadows in VRML since that is computational too intensive; you can simulate shadows with flat objects colored gray or black.

■ It can be tricky to set up lights appropriately; for this reason, you may want to install many lights, then turn off (set **on** to **FALSE**) the lights you don't want.

VRML D-E

- The **DirectionalLight** node illuminates only objects in its enclosing **Group**; for example, the light illuminates the objects in the preceding **Shape** node:

```
Group {
  children [
    Shape {
      ... shape data ...
    },
    DirectionalLight {
      ... light data ...
    }
  ]
}
```

- Some browsers cannot handle lighting limited to specific objects.

RELATED NODES

Fog	An axis-aligned, ellipsoid of colored atmosphere.
PointLight	An omnidirectional light source.
SpotLight	A cone-shaped, directional light source.

ElevationGrid { }

Creates a grid of elevations (*a Geometry node*).

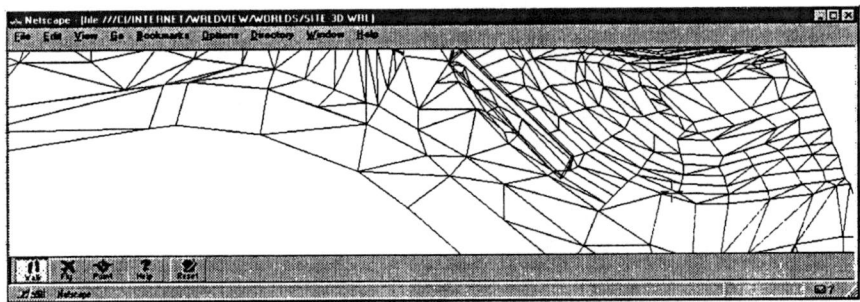

This elevation grid was created from an AutoCAD sample drawing, Site-3D.Dwg.
The original drawing was exported from AutoCAD Release 12 in DXF format,
imported into Caligari Fountain beta (now called Pioneer), then exported as a VRML file.

VRML 2 SYNTAX

```
ElevationGrid {
    set_height
    height                  [ ]
    color                   NULL
    colorPerVertex          TRUE
    normal                  NULL
    normalPerVertex         TRUE
    texCoord                NULL
    ccw                     TRUE
    solid                   TRUE
    creaseAngle             0
    xDimension              0
    xSpacing                0.0
    zDimension              0
    zSpacing                0.0
}
```

Field	Type	Name	Default	Meaning
eventIn	MFFloat	set_height		
field	MFFloat	height	[ ]	An array of heights.
exposedField	SFNode	color	NULL	Color of each node.
field	SFBool	colorPerVertex	TRUE	Colors applied vertices.
exposedField	SFNode	normal	NULL	Normals.
field	SFBool	normalPerVertex	TRUE	Normals applied to vertices.
exposedField	SFNode	texCoord	NULL	Apply texture coordinate.
field	SFBool	ccw	TRUE	Vertices in ccw direction.
field	SFBool	solid	TRUE	Shape encloses volume.
field	SFFloat	creaseAngle	0	Smoothing angle.
field	SFInt32	xDimension	0	Number of x grid.
field	SFFloat	xSpacing	0.0	Distance between x-vertices.
field	SFInt32	zDimension	0	Number of z grid.
field	SFFloat	zSpacing	0.0	Distance between z-vertices.

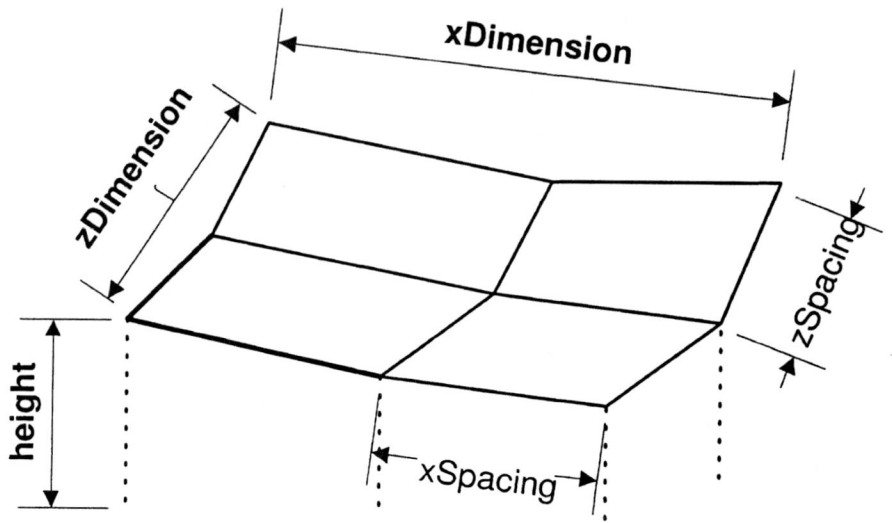

VRML 1 SYNTAX

Node is new to VRML v2.0.

NODE GEOMETRY

■ This node defines a grid of height values of the surface above each point of the grid.

■ The set_height field allows changes to the the **height** field, to create an animated ElevationGrids — can you imagine rolling fields of wheat?

■ The ccw field indicates vertex ordering when the shape is viewed from the outside:

ccw	Meaning
TRUE	Counterclockwise direction; the default.
FALSE	Clockwise or unknown direction.

■ The solid field indicates the type of shape:

solid	Meaning
TRUE	The shape encloses a volume; the default.
FALSE	Nothing is known about the shape.

■ The convex field indicates:

convex	Meaning
TRUE	All faces in the shape are convex; the default.
FALSE	Nothing is known about the faces.

■ The **creaseAngle** field determines which edges should be smoothly shaded and which have a sharp crease.

RELATED EQUATIONS

Total number of quadrilaterals

= **xDimension** * **zDimension**

= **height**

The vertex corresponding to a point, P[i, j], on the grid is placed at:

P[i,j].x = **xSpacing** * i

P[i,j].y = **height** [i + j * **zDimension**]

P[i,j].z = **zSpacing** * j

where 0 < i < **xDimension** and 0 < j < **zDimension**

TEXTURE MAPPING

■   The default texture coordinates start at **[0 0]** for the first vertex to **[1 1]** at the diagonal side.

■   The rendered look of the terrain depends on the **Color** nodes, along with the **Material** and **Texture** in the associated **Appearance** node.

■   If the material field of the **Appearance** node is set to **NULL**, then the elevation grid functions as an emissive surface (is unaffected by light sources).

■   When no color or texture is specified, the surface appears black (the default emissive color).

TIP

■   To enable backface culling (as it is, by default) set both the **ccw** and **solid** fields to TRUE.

RELATED NODES

Extrusion   Extrudes a 2D shape along a 3D spine.

IndexedFaceSet Creates a 3D surface from multiple polyfaces.

IndexedLineSet Creates a 3D shape from multiple polylines.

PointSet   Creates a 3D space from multiple dots.

Coordinate   Contains a list of 3D points; formerly the **Coordinate3** node.

Normal   Specifies the orientation of a face.

TextureCoordinate

Contains a 2D texture coordinate list.

VRML D-E

EXTERNPROTO

Defines a prototype node in an external file.

VRML 2 SYNTAX

```
EXTERNPROTO prototypename
  [
    eventIn    eventtypename    name
    eventOut   eventtypename    name
    field      fieldtypename
    ...
  ]
  [ "URL", "URL", ... ]
```

Field	Type	Name	Default	Meaning
field	...	fieldtypename		Parameters.
eventIn	...	eventtypename		Input.
eventOut	...	eventtypename		Output.
	...	URL		External file reference.

VRML 1 SYNTAX

Keyword is new to VRML v2.0.

TIPS

■ The implementation of an **EXTERNPROTO** is fetched from the URL.

■ The **EXTERNPROTO** does not contain default values for fields.

■ When the **EXTERNPROTO** references a file containing the prototype implementation, the file contains the default values for fields.

■ Prototype instances are named with **DEF**; the **DEF** keyword gives a node a name and creates the node of that type.

■ To use a prototype more than once, employ **USE**; the **USE** keyword inserts a reference to a **DEF**-named node in the scene graph.

RELATED KEYWORDS

DWF, USE   Creates an instance.

PROTO   Allows the creation of user-definable nodes.

ROUTE   Takes the eventOut value from one node and inputs it to the eventIn of another node.

Extrusion { }

Extrudes a 2D cross-section along a 3D spine path (*a Geometry node*).

VRML 2 SYNTAX

```
Extrusion {
  spine                [0 0 0, 0 1 0]
  set_spine
  crossSection         [1 1, 1 -1, -1 -1, -1 1, 1 1]
  set_crossSection
  scale                [ ]
  set_scale
  orientation          0 0 1 0
  set_orientation
  beginCap             TRUE
  endCap               TRUE
  ccw                  TRUE
  solid                TRUE
  convex               TRUE
  creaseAngle          0
}
```

Field	Type	Name	Default	Meaning
field	MFVec3f	spine	[0 0 0, 0 1 0]	A 3D linear curve that defines the path.
eventIn	MFVec3f	set_spine		Turns on **spine**.
field	MFVec2f	crossSection	[1 1,1 -1, -1 -1,-1 1, 1 1]	A 2D linear curve that defines the cross-sectional shape.
eventIn	MFVec2f	set_crossSection		Turns on **crossSection**.
field	MFVec2f	scale	[ ]	Scales the extrusion.
eventIn	MFVec2f	set_scale		Turns on **scale**.
field	MFRotation	orientation	0 0 1 0	Extrusion orientation.
eventIn	MFRotation	set_orientation		Turns on **orientation**.
field	SFBool	beginCap	TRUE	Create planar cap.
field	SFBool	endCap	TRUE	Create planar endcap.
field	SFBool	ccw	TRUE	Vertex order.
field	SFBool	solid	TRUE	Shape encloses volume.
field	SFBool	convex	TRUE	All faces are convex.
field	SFFloat	creaseAngle	0	Angle at which edges are rendered smoothly.

VRML D-E

VRML 1 SYNTAX
Node is new to VRML v2.0.

NODE GEOMETRY

■ The **Extrusion** node has three parts: (1) the side, extruded portion; (2) the **beginCap** surface at the starting point; and (3) the **endCap** surface at the endpoint.

■ Endcaps are always flat (planar); endcaps are available when the cross-section is not closed.

■ The **Extrusion** generates its own normals, orientated by the vertex ordering of the triangles generated by the **Extrusion**; the **crossSection** curve determines the vertex ordering.

■ When the **crossSection** is drawn counterclockwise, polygons have counterclockwise ordering when viewed from the outside of the extrusion.

■ The **ccw** field indicates vertex ordering when the shape is viewed from the outside:

ccw	Meaning
TRUE	Counterclockwise direction; the default.
FALSE	Clockwise or unknown direction.

■ The **solid** field indicates the type of shape:

solid	Meaning
TRUE	The shape encloses a volume; the default.
FALSE	Nothing is known about the shape.

■ The **convex** field indicates:

convex	Meaning
TRUE	All faces in the shape are convex; the default.
FALSE	Nothing is known about the faces.

■ The **creaseAngle** field determines which edges should be smoothly shaded and which have a sharp crease.

RELATED EQUATIONS

■ The crease angle is the angle between surface normals on adjacent polygons.

■ The tangent for the spine [i] is for points except the first and last: normalize the vector defined by **spine** [$i + 1$] - **spine** [$i - 1$]

■ When the spine curve is closed, the first and last points share the same tangent: use

spine [0] *for* **spine** [i]

spine [1] *for* **spine** [$i + 1$]

spine [$n - 2$] *for* **spine** [$i - 1$]

where:

spine [0]   is the first point on the curve;

spine [$n - 2$]   is the next to last point on the curve;

spine [$n - 1$]   is the last point in the curve and the same as the first point.

- When the spine curve is not closed, the tangent used for the:

first point is the direction from **spine** [0] to **spine** [1]

last point is the direction from **spine** [n - 2] to **spine** [n - 1]

- The z-axis

= (**spine** [i -1] - **spine** [i]) crossproduct (**spine** [i + 1] - **spine** [i])

- The y-axis

= the approximate tangent, as determined above.

- The x-axis

= y-axis crossproduct z-axis

TEXTURE MAPPING

- The texture coordinates are generated by the **Extrusion**.

- The texture is mapped like a label on a soup can.

- When the **crossSection** is closed, the texture shows a seam along the **crossSection** starting and endpoint.

- The texture square is applied to the begin and end caps.

TIPS

- To create a surface of revolution, start with a straight spine; the cross-section can have any shape.

- To create a 'cookie-cutter' extrusion, start with a straight spine and set the **scale** to [1, 1] ; the thickness of the extrusion is the length of the spine.

- To create an bending shape, start with a curved spine.

- To create a twisting shape, adjust the **orientation** parameters twist the cross-section around the spine.

- To create a tapered shape, set the **scale** parameters to scale about the spine.

- No check is made whether the extrusion intersects itself.

- A crease angle of 0.5 radians means an edge between two adjacent polyfaces is smooth shaded when the normals to the two faces form an angle less than 0.5 radians (about 29 degrees); when the angle is greater than 0.5 radians, it retains the facet.

RELATED NODES

ElevationGrid   Creates a 3D terrain-like surface.

IndexedFaceSet   Creates a 3D surface from multiple polyfaces.

IndexedLineSet   Creates a 3D shape from multiple polylines.

PointSet   Creates a 3D space from multiple dots.

Sphere   Creates a 3D sphere or ball.

VRML D-E

Fog { }

Defines an axis-aligned, ellipsoid of colored atmosphere to simulate fog, smog and other atmospheric conditions (*a Leaf node*).

VRML 2 SYNTAX

```
Fog {
    color              1 1 1
    fogType            "LINEAR"
    visibilityRange    1000
    set_bind
    isBound
}
```

Field	Type	Name	Default	Meaning
exposedField	SFColor	color	1 1 1	Color of fog.
exposedField	SFString	fogType	"LINEAR"	Fog attenuation.
exposedField	SFFloat	visibilityRange	1000	Point of obscurity.
eventIn	SFBool	set_bind		Toggles fog mode.
eventOut	SFBool	isBound		Reports fog binding.

VRML 1 SYNTAX

Node is new to VRML v2.0.

NODE GEOMETRY

■ The **fogType** field specifies attenuation of the fog effect:

fogType	Meaning
"LINEAR"	Fog effect increases with distance; default.
"EXPONENTIAL"	Exponential increase with distance.

■ The **visibilityRange** field specifies the distance (in meters) where objects are completely obscured by the fog effect:

visibilityRange	Meaning
1000	Default; 1,000 meters.
0.0	Fog effect turned off.

■ The **color** field specifies the color of the fog in RGB notation:

color	Meaning
1 1 1	White light; the default.
0 0 0	No light; depth cueing.
.5 .5 .5	Grey light; smog-like.
1 0 0	Red light.
0 1 0	Green light.
0 0 1	Blue light.

■ The set_bind field determines whether the **Fog** node is bound:

set_bind	Meaning
TRUE	`Fog` node is bound; default.
FALSE	`Fog` node is not bound.

■ The **isBound** field reports whether the **Fog** node is bound.

TIPS

■ The **Fog** node can be used to simulate fog, smog, and depth cueing (where slightly darker objects look further away than slightly brighter objects).

■ Use a **color** field of **1 1 1** to simulate fog; **.5 .5 .5** to simulate smog, and **0 0 0** to simulate depth cueing.

■ For more realistic fog, include a **Background** node with **skyColor** field set to the color of fog.

■ An *ellipsoid* is a 3D ellipse.

■ Different browsers will simulate fog in different ways, such as an exponential falloff.

RELATED NODES

Background	Creates a green-blue background to represent ground and sky.
DirectionalLight	A light source with parallel beams.
LOD	Changes the level of detail, depending on the distance from camera.
PointLight	An omnidirectional light source.
Shape	Holds **appearance** and **geometry** fields.
Sound	Position and spatial presentation of a sound.
SpotLight	A cone-shaped, directional light source.

VRML F-G

FontStyle { }

Defines the size, font family, text style, direction, and language rendering of text; used only within the **Text** node (*an Appearance node*).

VRML 2 SYNTAX

```
FontStyle {
  size          1.0
  family        "SERIF"
  style         " "
  horizontal    TRUE
  leftToRight   TRUE
  topToBottom   TRUE
  language      " "
  justify       "BEGIN"
  spacing       1.0
}
```

Field	Type	Name	Default	Meaning
field	SFFloat	size	1.0	Size of font.
field	SFString	family	"SERIF"	Font family.
field	SFString	style	" "	Font weight.
field	SFBool	horizontal	TRUE	Orientation.
field	SFBool	leftToRight	TRUE	Horizontal orientation.
field	SFBool	topToBottom	TRUE	Vertical orientation.
field	SFString	language	" "	Human language.
field	SFString	justify	"BEGIN"	Justification.
field	SFFloat	spacing	1.0	Line spacing.

VRML 1 SYNTAX

```
FontStyle {
  size      10
  family    SERIF
  style     NONE
}
```

NODE GEOMETRY

- The size field specifies the height of the text, in the current units.
- The **family** field specifies the font family:

family	Meaning
"SERIF"	A serif font, such as Times New Roman; the default.
"SANS"	A sans-serif font, such as Arial.
"TYPEWRITER"	A fixed-pitch font, such as Courier New.

■ The **style** field specifies the look of the font:

style	Meaning
" "	(empty string) Normal text; the default.
"BOLD"	Boldface text.
"ITALIC"	Italicized text.
"BOLD ITALIC"	Boldface italicized text.

■ The **horizontal** field specifies the orientation of the text:

horizontal	Meaning
FALSE	Text is printed vertical.
TRUE	Text is printed horizontal; the default.

■ The **leftToRight** field specifies the horizontal direction of the text characters:

leftToRight	Meaning
FALSE	Characters display right to left.
TRUE	Left to right; the default.

■ The **topToBottom** field specifies the vertical direction of text lines

topToBottom	Meaning
FALSE	Lines of text display from bottom to top.
TRUE	Top to bottom; the default.

■ The **language** field describes the human language, such as EN for English.

■ The **justify** field specifies how text is positioned in relative to the origin **0 0 0** of the object coordinate system:

justify	Meaning
"BEGIN"	Left-justified text; the default.
"MIDDLE"	Centered text.
"END"	Right-justified text.

■ The **spacing** field specifies the spacing between text strings:

spacing	Meaning
n	Next line of text is n units lower.
0	Next line of text overwrites first line.
-1	Next line of text is above the first line.

TIPS

■ The first line of text is positioned with its *baseline* (bottom of capital letters) at y = 0.

■ The next line of text is placed - (**size** * **spacing**) below the previous line of text.

■ This node is only used in the **fontStyle** field of the **Text** node.

VRML F-G

- Examples of serif, sans, and typewriter families:

| Serif | Sans | Typewriter |

- Examples of begin, middle, and end justifications:

Begin

Middle

End

- Examples of normal, bold, italic, and bold italic styles:

| Normal | **Bold** | *Italic* | ***Bold-Italic*** |

RELATED NODE

Text   Displays text in the scene.

Group { }

Creates a group of nodes (*a Group node*).

VRML 2 SYNTAX

```
Group {
  bboxCenter    0 0 0
  bboxSize      -1 -1 -1
  children      [ ]
  addChildren
  removeChildren
}
```

Field	Type	Name	Default	Meaning
field	SFVec3f	bboxCenter	0 0 0	Bounding box center.
field	SFVec3f	bboxSize	-1 -1 -1	Bounding box size.
exposedField	MFNode	children	[ ]	Nodes included in group.
eventIn	MFNode	addChildren		Add nodes to group.
eventIn	MFNode	removeChildren		Remove nodes from group.

VRML 1 SYNTAX

```
Group {
}
```

This node has no fields in VRML v1.0.

NODE GEOMETRY

■ The **bboxCenter** field defines the center of a bounding box that encloses all children nodes of the group.

■ The **bboxSize** field defines the size of the bounding box.

■ The **children** field contains all nodes held by this group.

■ To add nodes to the group, use the **addChildren** eventIn.

■ To remove nodes from the group, use the **removeChildren** eventIn.

TIPS

■ Node is identical to the **Transformation** node, except for transformation fields.

■ The bounding box defined by **bboxCenter** and **bboxSize** should be large enough to enclose children nodes, plus fog, light, and sound nodes of the group.

RELATED NODES

Anchor	Loads another world or viewpoint.
Billboard	Rotates a group about an axis to always faces the camera.
Inline	Groups nodes together from around the World Wide Web.
LOD	Level of detail.
Switch	Switches between zero or more children.
Transform	Transforms the coordinate system of a group of nodes.

VRML F-G

ImageTexture { }

Defines an image map and its parameters (*formerly Texture2; an Appearance node*).

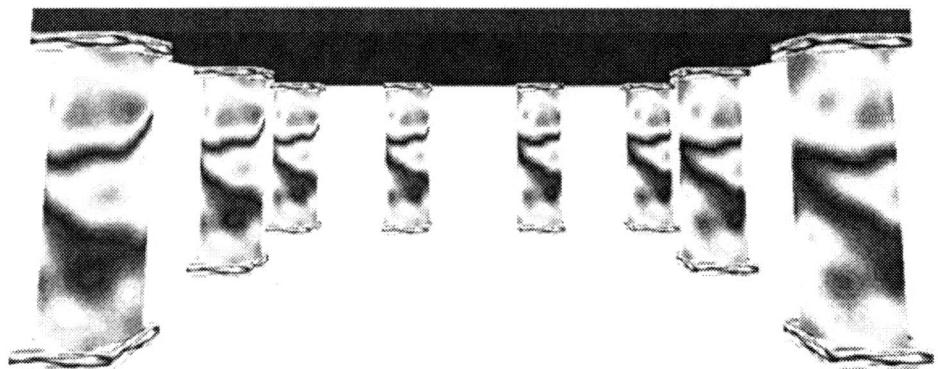

*An image map, Chrome.Gif, was applied to the columns using the **Texture2** node.
Temple.Wrl from Jeff Sonstein's Web site.*

VRML 2 SYNTAX

```
ImageTexture  {
  url          [ ]
  repeatS      TRUE
  repeatT      TRUE
}
```

Field	Type	Name	Default	Meaning
exposedField	MFString	url	[ ]	Texture map source file.
field	SFBool	repeatS	TRUE	Repeat map in S-direction.
field	SFBool	repeatT	TRUE	Repeat map in T-direction.

VRML 1 SYNTAX

```
Texture2  {
  url          [ ]
  wrapS        REPEAT
  wrapT        REPEAT
  image        0 0 0
}
```

- Where **wrapS** and **wrapT** are:

  REPEAT   Repeat the texture over and over.

  CLAMP   Prevent text from repeating.

- And where **image** is for creating pixel patterns (the **PixelTexture** node in VRML v2.0)

NODE GEOMETRY

- The **url** field specifies the source of the texture map's filename in URL format.

- The **repeatS** and **repeatT fields** specify whether the texture map repeats itself:

repeat	Meaning
FALSE	Texture map is applied only once.
TRUE	Texture map repeats to fill the shape; the default.

TIPS

- Set the **url** field to [ ] (no value) to turn off texture mapping.

- The browser should support GIF, JPEG, and PNG file formats.

- The browser may not be able to handle applying a texture map and a material.

RELATED NODES

Material   Specifies the material look for a surface texture.

MovieTexture   Applies a movie file as a texture map.

PixelTexture   Applies a pixel pattern as a texture map.

TextureTransform

                  Transforms the texture map.

IndexedFaceSet { }

Creates a 3D shape from polygons (*a Geometry node*).

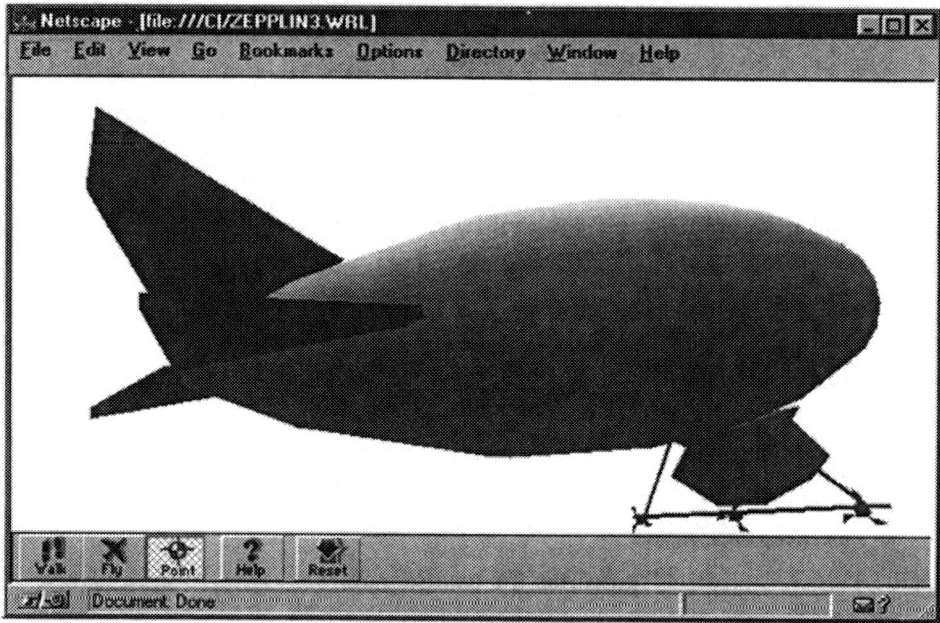

Zepplin3.Wrl modeled by Dave K. from http://www.newcollege.edu/vrmLab/Warehouse.

VRML 2 SYNTAX

```
IndexedFaceSet {
  set_colorIndex
  set_coordIndex
  set_normalIndex
  set_texCoordIndex
  coord              NULL
  coordIndex         [ ]
  texCoord           NULL
  texCoordIndex      [ ]
  color              NULL
  colorIndex         [ ]
  colorPerVertex     TRUE
  normal             NULL
  normalIndex        [ ]
  normalPerVertex    TRUE
  ccw                TRUE
  solid              TRUE
  convex             TRUE
  creaseAngle        0
}
```

Field	Type	Name	Default	Meaning
eventIn	MFInt32	set_colorIndex		Assign a color.
eventIn	MFInt32	set_coordIndex		Assign face indices.
eventIn	MFInt32	set_normalIndex		Assign normal indices.
eventIn	MFInt32	set_texCoordIndex		Assign texture coordinate.
exposedField	SFNode	coord	NULL	Vertices of polygon faces.
field	MFInt32	coordIndex	[ ]	Indices of the faces.
exposedField	SFNode	texCoord	NULL	Generate texture coords.
field	MFInt32	texCoordIndex	[ ]	Use coordIndex array.
exposedField	SFNode	color	NULL	Color node.
field	MFInt32	colorIndex	[ ]	Choose color.
field	SFBool	colorPerVertex	TRUE	Colors of vertices.
exposedField	SFNode	normal	NULL	Generate normals.
field	MFInt32	normalIndex	[ ]	Index of normals.
field	SFBool	normalPerVertex	TRUE	Normal per index.
field	SFBool	ccw	TRUE	Direction of normals.
field	SFBool	solid	TRUE	Defines a solid object.
field	SFBool	convex	TRUE	Convex surface.
field	SFFloat	creaseAngle	0	Smooth shading angle.

VRML 1 SYNTAX

```
IndexedFaceSet {
  coordIndex           0
  materialIndex       -1
  normalIndex         -1
  textureCoordIndex   -1
}
```

NODE GEOMETRY

■ The **coordIndex** field specifies the polygonal faces.

■ An index of -1 flags the start of the next face.

■ When the largest value in **coordIndex** is n, then the **Coordinate** node must contain $n+1$ coordinates, indexed starting from 0.

■ The **ccw** field indicates vertex ordering when the shape is viewed from the outside:

ccw	Meaning
TRUE	Counterclockwise direction; the default.
FALSE	Clockwise or unknown direction.

■ The **solid** field indicates the type of shape:

solid	Meaning
TRUE	The shape encloses a volume; the default.
FALSE	Nothing is known about the shape.

■ The **convex** field indicates:

convex	Meaning
TRUE	All faces in the shape are convex; the default.
FALSE	Nothing is known about the faces.

■ The **creaseAngle** field determines which edges should be smoothly shaded and which have a sharp crease.

RELATED EQUATIONS

Area of a triangle

$$= \frac{1}{2} * base * height$$

Area of a parallelogram (opposing sides are parallel)

$$= base * height$$

Area of a trapezoid (two sides are not parallel)

$$= \frac{1}{2} * (lowerbase + upperbase) * height$$

TIPS

■ Use this node to create arbitrary shapes, such as a face, a mountain, or a pressure wave.

■ Every index is matched to a coordinate triplet; the **IndexedFaceSet** node then uses the index numbers to create the shape. For example, the four corners of a unit square have the following coordinates and index numbers:

x,y,z-Coordinates	Index #
0, 0, 0	1
1, 0, 0	2
1, 1, 0	3
0, 1, 0	4

To draw a unit triangle instead, specify any three of the four index numbers, such as:

x,y,z-Coordinates	Index #
0, 0, 0	1
1, 1, 0	3
0, 1, 0	4

RELATED NODES

ElevationGrid	Creates a 3D terrain-like surface.
Extrusion	Extrudes a 2D shape along a 3D spine.
IndexedLineSet	Creates a complex object from 3D lines.
PointSet	Creates a 3D point cloud.
Color	Specifies the RGB colors of points, lines, and faces.
Coordinate	Specifies the 3D x,y,z-coordinates of points, lines, and faces.
Normal	Specifies the normals for faces and grids.
TextureCoordinate	
	Specifies the 2D texture coordinates for faces and grids.

IndexedLineSet { }

Creates a 3D polyline from a list of vertices (*a Geometry node*).

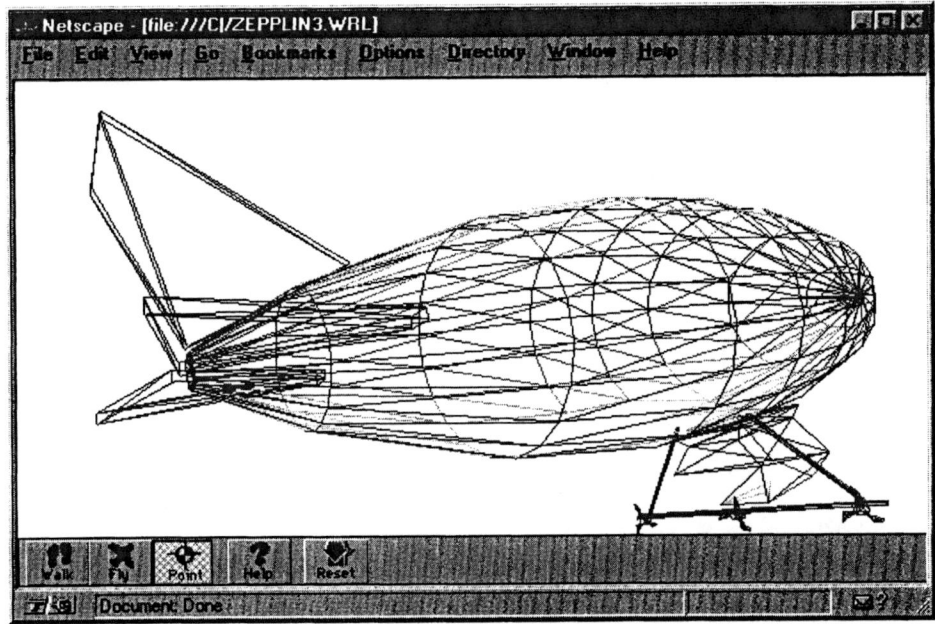

Zepplin3.Wrl modeled by Dave K. from http://www.newcollege.edu/vrmLab/Warehouse.

VRML 2 SYNTAX

```
IndexedLineSet {
  set_colorIndex
  set_coordIndex
  coord              NULL
  coordIndex         [ ]
  color              NULL
  colorIndex         [ ]
  colorPerVertex     TRUE
}
```

Field	Type	Name	Default	Meaning
eventIn	MFInt32	set_colorIndex		Assign color index.
eventIn	MFInt32	set_coordIndex		Assign coordinate index.
exposedField	SFNode	coord	NULL	Vertices of line segments.
field	MFInt32	coordIndex	[ ]	Indices of the segments.
exposedField	SFNode	color	NULL	Color node.
field	MFInt32	colorIndex	[ ]	Choose color.
field	SFBool	colorPerVertex	TRUE	Colors applied to vertices; when **FALSE**, color applied to segment.

VRML 1 SYNTAX

```
IndexedLineSet {
  coordIndex           0
  materialIndex        -1
  normalIndex          -1
  textureCoordIndex    -1
}
```

NODE GEOMETRY

■ This node forms a 3D shape by combining polylines from the vertices that are listed in the **coord** field.

■ An **index** value of -1 indicates the beginning of the next polyline.

RELATED EQUATION

■ Length of a line (where the coordinates of one endpoint are x_1,y_1,z_1 and the coordinates of the other endpoint is x_2,y_2,z_2)

$$= sqrt ((x_2 - x_1)^2 + (y_2 - y_1)^2 + (z_2 - z_1)^2)$$

TIPS

■ This node can be used to create complex lines, wireframe objects, and string-type art.

■ For example, here the **Coordinate** node is used with the **IndexedFaceSet** node:

```
Coordinate {
  point [ -1.223653 2.402087 -2.128398,
          -1.028676 2.400000 -2.728398,
          -1.642742 2.152785 -2.483273,
          . . .
          0.333486 1.686486 -0.231100,
          1.457810 0.562162 -0.231100 ]
}
IndexedFaceSet {
  coordIndex [ 0, 1, 2, -1, 3, ... 119, -1 ]
}
```

RELATED NODES

Extrusion	Extrudes a 2D shape along a 3D spine.
Color	Specifies the RGB colors of points, lines, and faces.
Coordinate	Specifies the 3D x,y,z-coordinates of points, lines, and faces.
ElevationGrid	Creates an topographical grid.
IndexedLineSet	Creates a complex object from 3D lines.
PointSet	Creates a 3D point cloud.

Inline { }

Creates a group from nodes exterior to the scene (*formerly the WWWInline node; a Group node*).

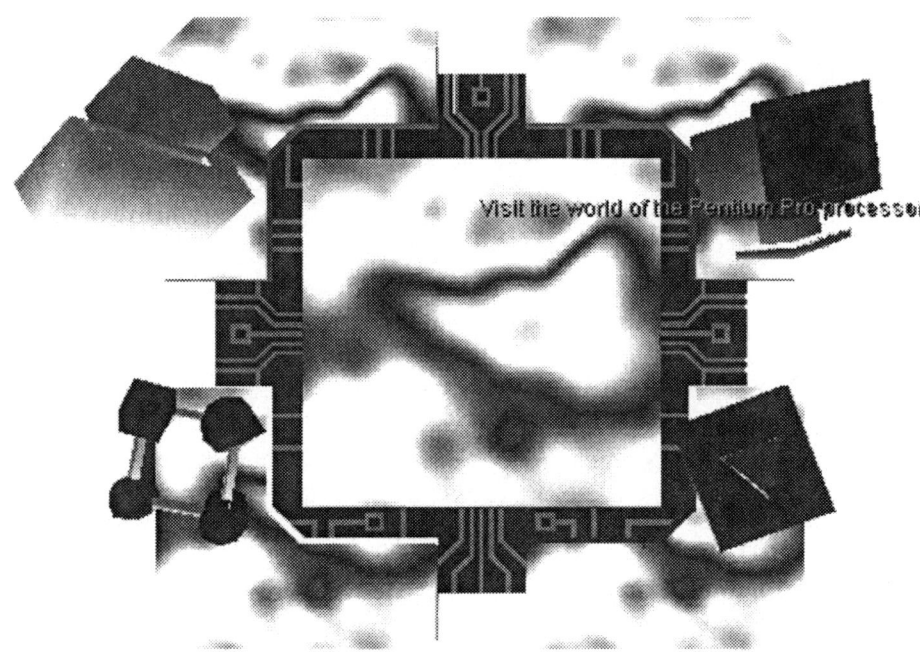

This is a 3D interface with five links to other VRML nodes on the Internet. VRML image from the www.intel.com Web site.

VRML 2 SYNTAX

```
Inline {
  url          [ ]
  bboxSize     -1 -1 -1
  bboxCenter   0 0 0
}
```

Field	Type	Name	Default	Meaning
exposedF•field	MFString	url	[ ]	Uniform resource locator.
field	SFVec3f	bboxSize	-1 -1 -1	Bounding box size.
field	SFVec3f	bboxCenter	0 0 0	Bounding box center.

VRML 1 SYNTAX

```
WWWInline {
  name         [ url ]
  bboxSize     -1 -1 -1
  bboxCenter   0 0 0
}
```

NODE GEOMETRY

■ The **url** field must refer to a valid VRML-format file that contains some grouping or a leaf node.

■ The **bboxSize** and **bboxCenter** fields provide a hint of the anticipated size of the inline'd objects.

TIPS

■ Where as the **Group** node collects objects from within the current scene, the **Inline** node is collects objects from anywhere on the World Wide Web.

■ This node is undefined when the **url** field refers to files other than in VRML format; it is also undefined when the url'ed file lacks a grouping or leaf node.

■ When the **url** field lists more than one URL, they are listed in descending order of preference; the browser will load the first file it is able to.

RELATED NODES

Anchor	Loads another world or viewpoint (previously the **WWWAnchor** node).
Billboard	Rotates a group about an axis to always faces the camera.
Group	Groups nodes together without performing a transformation.
Switch	Switches between zero or more children.
Transform	Transforms the coordinate system of a group of nodes.

LOD { }

Changes the representation of a group of nodes (*short for Level Of Detail; a Grouping node*).

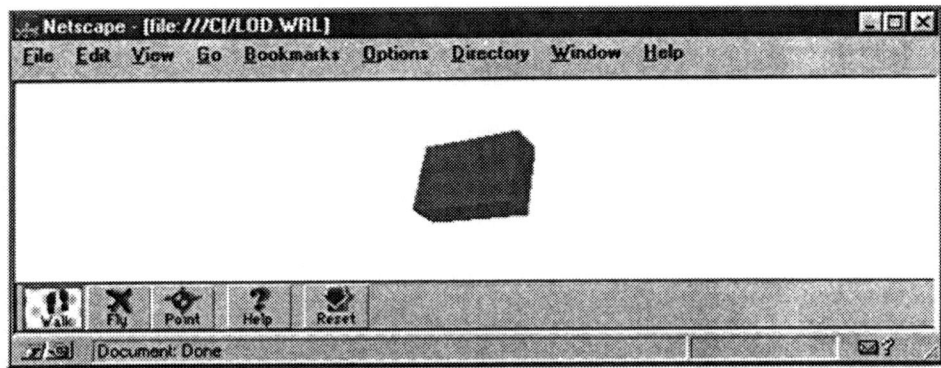

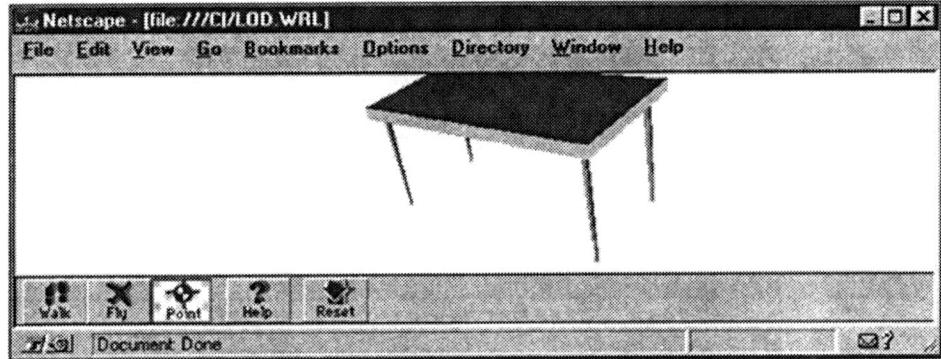

A table (above) represented by the LOD node looks like a box when further away (top).

VRML 2 SYNTAX

```
LOD {
  range    [ ]
  center   0 0 0
  level    [ ]
}
```

Field	Type	Name	Default	Meaning
field	MFFloat	range	[ ]	
field	SFVec3f	center	0 0 0	Center point of the group.
exposedField	MFNode	level	[ ]	Level of detail.

VRML 1 SYNTAX

```
LOD {
  range    [ ]
  center   0 0 0
}
```

NODE GEOMETRY

■ The **range** field specifies the distance at which to display a group in the **level** field, such as **range [10, 30]** represents 10 and 30 meters, respectively.

■ The **center** field specifies the center x,y,z-coordinates of the group; **LOD** uses this coordinate to calculate the range.

■ The **level** field specifies the group to display, based on the range value.

TIPS

■ This node is meant to represent the same group of objects with details varying from highest detail to lowest; however, this need not be the case.

■ For example, the following code displays three levels of detail:

```
LOD {
  range [10, 30]
  level [
    Group {
      ... more detailed nodes ...
    }
    Group {
      ... less detailed nodes ...
    }
    Shape { }
  ]
}
```

1. Range is 10m or less: display the more detailed group of nodes.

2. Range is between 10m and 30m: display the less detailed group of nodes.

3. Range is greater than 30m: display nothing via the **Shape { }** node.

■ *Special case:* When the **range** field is empty, the browser should choose a level of detail to maintain a constant display rate, such as **range [ ]** .

■ **LOD** is useful for speeding up the VRML browser's display speed by reducing the amount of data to display.

■ While you might be tempted to use **LOD** to make a door appear to open, use **ProximitySensor** instead.

■ For *n* values in the **range** field, there should be *n*+1 nodes in the **level** field, since one level applies when the range is greater than the largest value specified by the **range** field.

■ Each value in the **range** field must be greater than the previous value; if a value is less, the result is undefined.

■ When the distance from camera to the center coordinate is less than the first value in the **range** field, then the first level of the LOD is displayed; when the distance matches the second range value, the second level of detail is displayed.

■ When too few levels are specified, the last level is displayed repeatedly; when too many levels are specified, the extra levels are ignored.

RELATED NODES

Anchor	Loads another world or viewpoint.
Billboard	Rotates a group about an axis to always faces the camera.
Fog	Decreases visibility in the distance.
Group	Groups nodes together without performing a transformation.
Inline	Groups nodes together from around the World Wide Web.
Switch	Switches between zero or more children.
Transform	Transforms the coordinate system of a group of nodes.

Material { }

Defines surface properties of associated objects (*an Appearance node*).

A pair of spheres with a Material {specularColor} (left) and Material {diffuseColor}, right.

VRML 2 SYNTAX

```
Material {
    diffuseColor        0.8 0.8 0.8
    ambientIntensity    0.2
    specularColor       0 0 0
    emissiveColor       0 0 0
    shininess           0.2
    transparency        0
}
```

Field	Type	Name	Default	Meaning
exposedField	SFColor	diffuseColor	.8 .8 .8	Reflective light.
exposedField	SFFloat	ambientIntensity	0.2	Ambient light.
exposedField	SFColor	specularColor	0 0 0	Specular highlight.
exposedField	SFColor	emissiveColor	0 0 0	Radiosity.
exposedField	SFFloat	shininess	0.2	Sharper highlights.
exposedField	SFFloat	transparency	0	See through.

VRML 1 SYNTAX

```
Material {
    diffuseColor        0.8 0.8 0.8
    ambientColor        0.2 0.2 0.2
    specularColor       0 0 0
    emissiveColor       0 0 0
    shininess           0.2
    transparency        0
}
```

NODE GEOMETRY

■ The **diffuseColor** field specifies the RGB color for all reflective lights; the default of **0.8 0.8 0.8** is light gray.

■ The **ambientIntensity** field specifies the amount ambient light to reflect:

ambientIntensity	Meaning
0	No ambient light reflected.
0.2	Some abient light reflected; default.
1	All ambient light reflected.

■ The **specularColor** field specifies the shinny spots on metallic and plastic objects.

■ The **emissiveColor** field specifies the radiosity of objects (objects glow with their own light and color).

■ The **shininess** field also affect the shinny spots: a low shininess value (such as 0.2) produces a softer glows; a higher value produces a more defined, smaller highlight.

■ The **transparency** field specifies how see-though an object is:

transparency	Meaning
0	Opaque; the default.
1	Transparent.

RELATED NODES

ImageTexture   Applies a GIF, JPEG, or PNG file as a texture map.

MovieTexture   Applies a movie file as a texture map.

PixelTexture   Applies a pixel pattern as a texture map.

TextureTransform Transforms the texture map.

VRML M

MovieTexture { }

Defines an animated movie texture map (*an Appearance node*).

VRML 2 SYNTAX

```
MovieTexture {
    url                  [ ]
    speed                1
    loop                 FALSE
    startTime            0
    stopTime             0
    repeatS              TRUE
    repeatT              TRUE
    duration_changed
    isActive
}
```

Field	Type	Name	Default	Meaning
exposedField	MFString	url	[ ]	Movie file source.
exposedField	SFFloat	speed	1	Speed of playback.
exposedField	SFBool	loop	FALSE	Repeat movie.
exposedField	SFTime	startTime	0	Time to start movie.
exposedField	SFTime	stopTime	0	Time to stop movie.
field	SFBool	repeatS	TRUE	Repeat in S-direction.
field	SFBool	repeatT	TRUE	Repeat in T-direction.
eventOut	SFFloat	duration_changed		Length of movie.
eventOut	SFBool	isActive		Movie is playing.

VRML 1 SYNTAX
Node is new to VRML v2.0.

NODE GEOMETRY
- The **url** field is the source filename for the movie file in URL format; see Appendix A.
- The **speed** field specifies the speed to playback the movie, in frames per second:

speed	Meaning
1	Playback movie at normal frame rate; default.
2	Playback movie at double frame rate.
positive	Start with first frame.
negative	Start with last frame.

- The **loop** field repeats the movie over and over:

loop	Meaning
FALSE	Movie file is played once; the default.
TRUE	Movie file is played over and over.

- The **startTime** field is the time to begin playing the movie file.

- The **stopTime** field is the time to stop the movie file.

- The **duration_changed** field reports the length of the time to play the movie file, in seconds; the duration_changed eventOut is sent as soon as the movie begins playing.

TIPS

- The **url** field can specify more than one URL so that the browser can choose the movie file that best suits its own capabilities.

- At the minimum, the browser should support the MPEG1-System for audio and video or MPEG1-Video (video-only) movie file formats.

- *Special case*: When **speed** is set to **0** the movie is played at the fastest speed possible.

- *Special case*: When **duration_changed** is set to **-1** the movie has not yet been loaded or is unavailable.

RELATED NODES

All Animation nodes, plus:

ImageTexture   Applies a GIF, JPEG, or PNG file as a texture map.

Material   Specifies the material look for a surface texture.

PixelTexture   Applies a pixel pattern as a texture map.

TextureTransform Transforms the texture map.

VRML M

NavigationInfo { }

Describes to the viewer how the user will interact with the scene (*a Bindable Leaf node*).

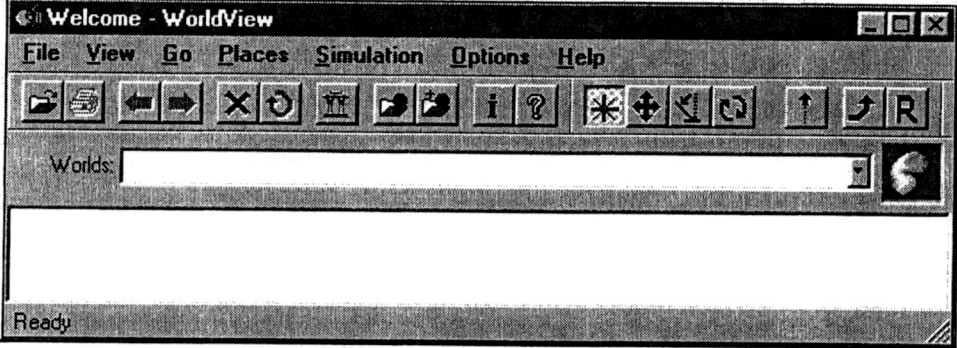

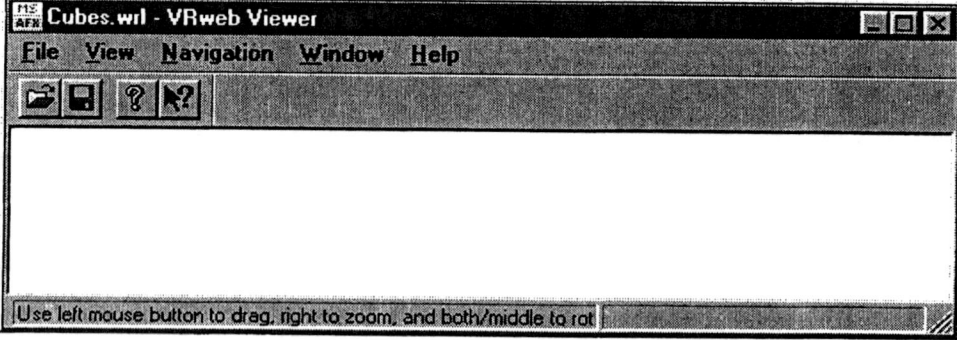

The user interfaces of three VRML browsers. From top to bottom:
Netscape Live3D
InterVista WorldView
IICM VRweb

VRML 2 SYNTAX

```
NavigationInfo {
  avatarSize           [ 0.25, 1.6, 0.75 ]
  headlight            TRUE
  speed                1.0
  type                 "WALK"
  visibilityLimit      0.0
  set_bind
  isBound
}
```

Field	Type	Name	Default	Meaning
exposedField	MFFloat	avatarSize	[0.25, 1.6, 0.75]	
				Collision parameters.
exposedField	SFBool	headlight	TRUE	Turn on headlight.
exposedField	SFFloat	speed	1.0	Travel speed, m/sec.
exposedField	MFString	type	"WALK"	Type of transportation.
exposedField	MFFloat	visibilityLimit	0.0	Maximum viewing distance.
eventIn	SFBool	set_bind		Activates node.
eventOut	SFBool	isBound		Signals change in binding.

VRML 1 SYNTAX

Node is new to VRML v2.0.

NODE GEOMETRY

■ The **avatarSize** field holds one or more parameters for collision detection:

avatarSize	Meaning
n1	Distance before a collision is detected (default = 0.25 meter).
n2	Camera height above the terrain (default = 1.6 meter).
n3	Tallest height camera can step over (default = 0.75 meter).

■ The **headlight** field determines whether a directional light will always display in the direction of the viewer:

headlight	Meaning
TRUE	Headlight is turned on (default).
FALSE	Headlight is turned off.

■ The **speed** field specifies the default speed of movement, in units per second.

- The **type** field is one of the following modes of transportation:

type	Meaning
"WALK"	Is limited by some amount of gravity (default).
"EXAMINE"	Look at and spin individual objects.
"FLY"	Has no gravitational limits.
"NONE"	Remove all viewer controls.

- The **visibilityLimit** field specifies the furthest distance, in meters, that the user can see.
- The **set_bind** field is a Boolean:

set_bind	Meaning
TRUE	The **NavigationInfo** node is activated.
FALSE	The node is deactivated.

- The **isBound** field indicates when the binding has changed.

isBound	Meaning
TRUE	The **NavigationInfo** node is activated.
FALSE	The node is deactivated.

TIPS

- This node occurs only within the **appearance** field of the **Shape** node.

- The **type** field allows viewing methods specific to a browser.

- The **type** field can hold more than one value so that the browser can use a specific or standard viewing method as a fall-back.

- *Special case*: a value of **0.0** for the **visibilityLimit** means no limit to viewing distance.

- The **headlight** should have the following specifications: **intensity 1** (full brightness), color **1 1 1** (white), and **direction 0 0 -1** (facing into the screen).

- NavigationInfo nodes after the first one are ignored.

RELATED NODES

Anchor	Hyperlink to another world.
Collision	Defines collision parameters.
Inline	Display an inline object.

Normal { }

Defines a set of 3D surface normal vectors (*a Geometry node*).

When normals are not correctly specified, part of the model disappears, as shown by the back of the lamp shade.
Lamp.Wrl is included with InterVista's WorldView VRML browser software.

VRML 2 SYNTAX

```
Normal {
  vector   [ ]
}
```

Field	Type	Name	Default	Meaning
exposedField	MFVec3f	vector	[ ]	Direction of normals.

VRML 1 SYNTAX

```
Normal {
  vector 0.0  0.0  1.0
}
```

NODE GEOMETRY

■ The **vector** field holds the 3D surface normal vectors.

TIPS

■ The browser should be able to automatically calculate normals, so this node should be unnecessary.

■ This node is used in the **normal** field of the **IndexedFaceSet** and **ElevationGrid** nodes.

■ Normals must be *unit* length (length = 1.0 units).

RELATED NODES

Color   Specifies the RGB colors of points, lines, and faces.

Coordinate   Specifies the 3D x,y,z-coordinates of points, lines, and faces.

TextureCoordinate Specifies the 2D texture coordinates for faces and grids.

ElevationGrid   Creates an topographical grid.

IndexedFaceSet   Creates a complex object from 3D faces.

NormalInterpolator { }

Interpolates between a set of multi-valued **Vec3f** values for transforming normal vectors (*an Interpolator node*).

VRML 2 SYNTAX

```
NormalInterpolator {
  key            [ ]
  keyValue       [ ]
  set_fraction
  value_changed
}
```

Field	Type	Name	Default	Meaning
exposedField	MFFloat	key	[ ]	Parameterized normals.
exposedField	MFVec3f	keyValue	[ ]	Normal values.
eventIn	SFFloat	set_fraction		Triggers interpolation.
eventOut	MFVec3f	value_changed		Returns results.

VRML 1 SYNTAX

Node is new to VRML v2.0.

NODE GEOMETRY

- The **key** field holds parameterized normal values from **0.0** to **1.0**.
- The **keyValue** field holds the normal values in **MFVect3f** format.
- The **set_fraction** field causes the interpolator function to operate.
- The **value_changed** field returns the interpolated color value in **MFVec3f** format.

TIPS

- This node can be used to transform normals.
- The interpolator nodes are meant to be used to create linear, keyframed animation.
- Values in the **key** field must increase and cannot repeat.
- The number of coordinates in the **keyValue** field must have the same number of normals as the keyframe times in the **key** field.

RELATED NODES

ColorInterpolator	Linearly interpolates along a set of **MFColor** values.
CoordinateInterpolator	Linearly interpolates along a set of **MFVec3f** values.
OrientationInterpolator	Interpolates along a set of **SFRotation** values.
PositionInterpolator	Linearly interpolates along a set of **SFVec3f** values.
ScalarInterpolator	Linearly interpolates along a set of **SFFloat** values.

OrientationInterpolator { }

Interpolates among a set of **SFRotation** values (*an Interpolator node*).

VRML 2 SYNTAX

```
OrientationInterpolator {
    key              [ ]
    keyValue         [ ]
    set_fraction
    value_changed
}
```

Field	Type	Name	Default	Meaning
exposedField	MFFloat	**key**	[ ]	Parameterized rotations.
exposedField	MFRotation	**keyValue**	[ ]	Rotation values.
eventIn	SFFloat	**set_fraction**		Trigger interpolation.
eventOut	SFRotation	**value_changed**		Report results.

VRML 1 SYNTAX
Node is new to VRML v2.0.

NODE GEOMETRY
- The **key** field holds parameterized rotation values from **0.0** to **1.0**.
- The **keyValue** field holds the rotation values in **MFRotation** format.
- The **set_fraction** field causes the interpolator function to operate.
- The **value_changed** field returns the interpolated color value in **SFRotation** format.

TIPS
- The interpolator nodes are meant to be used to create linear, keyframed animation.
- Values in the **key** field must increase and cannot repeat.
- The number of coordinates in the **keyValue** field must have the same number of rotations as the keyframe times in the **key** field.

RELATED NODES

ColorInterpolator	Linearly interpolates along a set of **MFColor** values.
CoordinateInterpolator	Linearly interpolates along a set of **MFVec3f** values.
NormalInterpolator	Interpolates along a set of multivalue **Vec3f** values.
PositionInterpolator	Linearly interpolates along a set of **SFVec3f** values.
ScalarInterpolator	Linearly interpolates along a set of **SFFloat** values.

VRML N-O

PixelTexture { }

Defines a 2D image-based texture map (*an Appearance node*).

VRML 2 SYNTAX

```
PixelTexture {
  image        0 0 0
  repeatS      TRUE
  repeatT      TRUE
}
```

Field	Type	Name	Default	Meaning
exposedField	SFImage	image	0 0 0	Pixel pattern.
field	SFBool	repeatS	TRUE	Repeat in s-direction.
field	SFBool	repeatT	TRUE	Repeat in t-direction.

VRML 1 SYNTAX

The **image** field of the **Texture2** node provides pixel texturing in VRML v1.0:

```
Texture2 {
  url       [ ]
  wrapS     REPEAT
  wrapT     REPEAT
  image     0 0 0
}
```

- Where **wrapS** and **wrapT** are:

  REPEAT   Repeat the texture over and over.

  CLAMP   Prevent text from repeating.

- And where **image** is for creating pixel patterns (the **PixelTexture** node in VRML v2.0)

NODE GEOMETRY

- The **image** field specifies a pattern of pixels in grayscale, grayscale plus transparency, full RGB color, or full RGB color and transparency.

- The **repeatS** and **repeatT** fields specify whether the pixel pattern repeats (**TRUE**, the default) or not (**FALSE**).

RELATED NODES

ImageTexture   Applies a GIF, JPEG, or PNG file as a texture map.

Material   Specifies the material look for a surface texture.

MovieTexture   Applies a movie file as a texture map.

TextureTransform Transforms the texture map.

PlaneSensor { }

Maps dragging motion into a translation in the x,y-plane (*a Sensor node*).

VRML 2 SYNTAX

```
PlaneSensor {
  minPosition          0 0
  maxPosition          -1 -1
  enabled              TRUE
  offset               0 0 0
  autoOffset           TRUE
  isActive
  trackPoint_changed
  translation_changed
}
```

Field	Type	Name	Default	Meaning
exposedField	SFVec2f	minPosition	0 0	X,y-coordinates of plane.
exposedField	SFVec2f	maxPosition	-1 -1	X,y-coordinates of plane.
exposedField	SFBool	enabled	TRUE	Toggles sensor on and off.
exposedField	SFRotation	offset	0 0 0	Offset added to output.
exposedField	SFBool	autoOffset	TRUE	Send to last output value.
eventOut	SFBool	isActive		Cursor is on the plane.
eventOut	SFVec3f	trackPoint_changed		Position of cursor.
eventOut	SFVec3f	translation_changed		Position of cursor.

VRML 1 SYNTAX
Node is new to VRML v2.0.

NODE GEOMETRY
■ The **minPosition** and **maxPosition** fields are x,y-coordinates that limit the size of the plane.

■ The **enabled** field toggles the **PlaneSensor** node on and off:

enabled	Meaning
FALSE	PlaneSensor is off.
TRUE	PlaneSensor is on (default).

■ The **trackPoint_changed** field reports the cursor's current position on the surface of the plane.

■ The **isActive** field reports whether the cursor is on the plane:

onActive	Meaning
FALSE	Cursor has been dragged off plane.
TRUE	Cursor has been dragged on plane.

■ The **translation_changed** field reports the cursor's position on the surface of the plane, limited by the **minPosition** and **maxPosition** coordinates.

TIPS

■ You create a line (one-dimensional) sensor by setting the x (or y) coordinate the same in the **minPosition** and **maxPosition** fields.

■ When **minPosition**'s coordinates are greater than **maxPosition**'s coordinates, then the data reported by **translation_changed** field is *unclamped* and is equivalent to the **trackPosition_changed** field.

RELATED NODES

CylinderSensor Maps dragging motion about the y-axis.

SphereSensor Maps dragging motion into free rotation about its center.

ProximitySensor Generates events when camera enters, moves inside, and exits 3D space.

TimeSensor Generate events as time passes.

TouchSensor Generates events as the cursor passes over child geometry nodes.

VisibilitySensor Generates events when a bounding box enters and leaves the viewing frustum.

PointLight { }

A light source with omnidirectional light beams (*a Leaf node*).

Three spheres illuminated by a single PointLight node.

VRML 2 SYNTAX

```
PointLight {
   on                    TRUE
   intensity             1
   ambientIntensity      0
   color                 1 1 1
   location              0 0 0
   radius                1
   attenuation           1 0 0
}
```

Field	Type	Name	Default	Meaning
exposedField	SFBool	on	TRUE	Toggles light on and off.
exposedField	SFFloat	intensity	1	Intensity of the light.
exposedField	SFFloat	ambientIntensity	0	Ambient intensity.
exposedField	SFColor	color	1 1 1	Color of the light.
exposedField	SFVec3f	location	0 0 0	Location of the light.
exposedField	SFFloat	radius	1	Radius of light beams.
exposedField	SFVec3f	attenuation	1 0 0	Attenuation of light.

VRML 1 SYNTAX

```
PointLight {
   on                    TRUE
   intensity             1
   color                 1 1 1
   location              0 0 0
}
```

Fields have the same meaning as in VRML v2.0.

NODE GEOMETRY

- The **on** field turns the light on (when set to **TRUE**) and off (set to **FALSE**).
- The intensity field controls the brightness of the light:

intensity	Meaning
0.0	Light is off; no light.
1.0	Full intensity; default value.
> 1.0	Can create an overbright light.
< 0.0	Can add darkness; an anti-light.

- The **ambientIntensity** field determines the amount of ambient light, light that is reflected off surfaces and creates an overall illumination.
- The color field determines the color of the light using RGB notation:

color	Meaning
1 1 1	White light; the default.
0 0 0	No light.
1 0 0	Red light.
0 1 0	Green light.
0 0 1	Blue light.

- The **location** field specifies the location of the light; the default of **0 0 0** locates the light at the origin.
- The **radius** field specifies how far the light beams travel from the location.
- The **attenuation** field determines the fall-off of light intensity from the origin.

RELATED EQUATION

The illumination of an object **r** distance from the light

$$= (^1/_{attenuation}) + (attenuation * r) + (attenuation * r^2)$$

TIPS

- Since a point light has omnidirectional light beams, the light needs no direction, only a location.
- Shapes do no cast shadows in VRML since that is too computational intensive; you can simulate shadows with flat objects colored gray or black.
- It can be tricky to set up lights appropriately; for this reason, you may want to install many lights, then turn off (set **on** to **FALSE**) the ones you don't need.

RELATED NODES

DirectionalLight A light source with parallel beams.

Fog   An axis-aligned, ellipsoid of colored atmosphere.

Shape   Holds **appearance** and **geometry** fields (formerly the **ShapeHints** node).

Sound   Position and spatial presentation of a sound.

SpotLight   A cone-shaped, directional light source.

PointSet { }

Displays points in 3D space (*a Geometry node*).

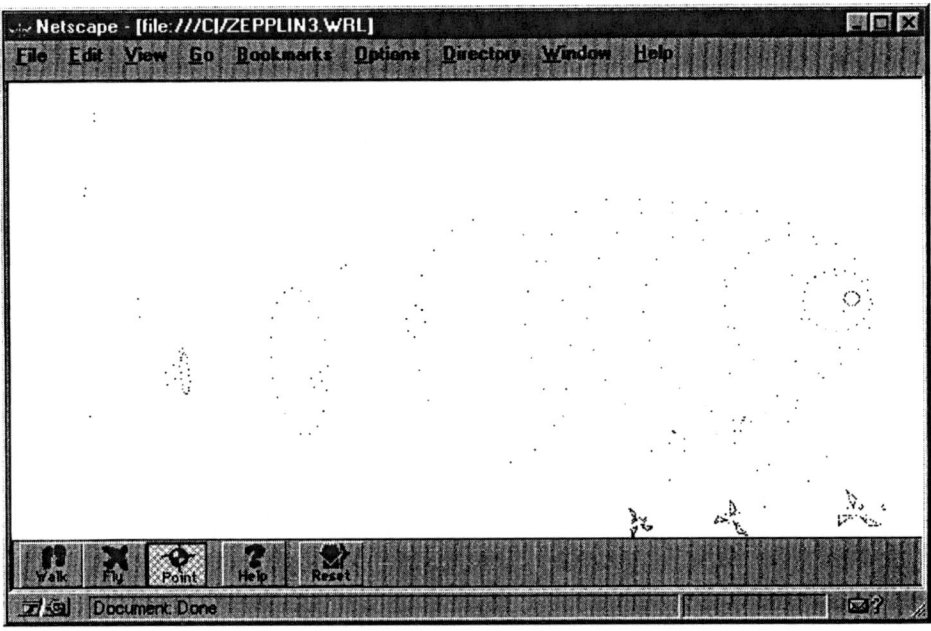

Zepplin3.Wrl modeled by Dave K. from http://www.newcollege.edu/vrmLab/Warehouse.

VRML 2 SYNTAX

```
PointSet {
  coord      NULL
  color      NULL
}
```

Field	Type	Name	Default	Meaning
exposedField	SFNode	**coord**	NULL	Coordinates of points.
exposedField	SFNode	**color**	NULL	Color of the points.

VRML 1 SYNTAX

```
PointSet {
  startIndex   0
  numPoints   -1
}
```

Points are previously specified by the **Coordinate3** node.

VRML P

NODE GEOMETRY

■ This node displays all the points listed in the **coord** field.

■ Points are listed in order they occur; there is no indexing feature.

■ There are no default values for the **PointSet** node.

TEXTURE MAPPING

■ Points are not rendered, cannot be texture mapped, and cannot avoid collisions; however, points may be individually colored.

TIPS

■ To create a starry expanse, create a random set of point coordinates.

■ Some browsers have an option to display all geometry as points

RELATED NODES

Coordinate   Contains a list of 3D points; formerly the **Coordinate3** node.

ElevationGrid   Creates a 3D terrain-like surface.

Extrusion   Extrudes a 2D shape along a 3D spine.

IndexedFaceSet   Creates a 3D surface from multiple polyfaces.

IndexedLincSct   Creates a 3D shape from multiple polylines.

PositionInterpolator { }

Interpolates linearly a set of SFVec3f values (*an Interpolator node*).

VRML 2 SYNTAX

```
PositionInterpolator {
  key            [ ]
  keyValue       [ ]
  set_fraction
  value_changed
}
```

Field	Type	Name	Default	Meaning
exposedField	MFFloat	key	[ ]	Parameterized positions.
exposedField	MFVec3f	keyValue	[ ]	Position values.
eventIn	SFFloat	set_fraction		Trigger interpolation.
eventOut	SFVec3f	value_changed		Return results.

VRML 1 SYNTAX
Node is new to VRML v2.0.

NODE GEOMETRY
■ The **key** field holds parameterized position values from **0.0** to **1.0**.

■ The **keyValue** field holds the position values in **MFVect3f** format.

■ The **set_fraction** field causes the interpolator function to operate.

■ The **value_changed** field returns the interpolated color value in **SFVec3f** format.

TIPS
■ This node can be used to create a transition.

■ These interpolator nodes are meant to be used to create linear, keyframed animation.

■ Values in the **key** field must increase and cannot repeat.

■ The number of coordinates in the **keyValue** field must have the same number of position as the keyframe times in the **key** field.

RELATED NODES
ColorInterpolator	Linearly interpolates along a set of **MFColor** values.
CoordinateInterpolator	Linearly interpolates along a set of **MFVec3f** values.
NormalInterpolator	Interpolates along a set of multivalue **Vec3f** values.
OrientationInterpolator	Interpolates along a set of **SFRotation** values.
ScalarInterpolator	Linearly interpolates along a set of **SFFloat** values.

VRML P

PROTO

Defines a prototype node within the file.

VRML 2 SYNTAX

```
PROTO name
  [
    field     fieldType name   defaultValue
    eventIn   fieldType name
    eventOut  fieldType name
  ]
  { implementation }
```

Field	Type	Name	Default	Meaning
field	...	*fieldtype*	...	Parameters.
eventIn	...	*eventtype*	...	Input.
eventOut	...	*eventtype*	...	Output.

VRML 1 SYNTAX

Keyword is new to VRML v2.0.

TIPS

- The **PROTO** allows you to define a new node in terms of other, pre-defined nodes.

- You can use **PROTO** to protect an object.

- PROTOs are a convenient way to package geometry and behavior.

- To save bandwith, use the **PROTO** to define a structure (such as a column) once, then reuse.

RELATED KEYWORDS

DEF/USE   Defines an instance.

EXTERNPROTO Allows the creation of user-definable nodes external to the file.

ROUTE   Takes the eventOut value from one node and inputs it to the eventIn of another node.

ProximitySensor { }

Generate an event each time the cursor enters, moves around, and exits a 3D space (*a Sensor node*).

VRML 2 SYNTAX

```
ProximitySensor {
  center                  0 0 0
  size                    0 0 0
  enabled                 TRUE
  isActive
  position_changed
  orientation_changed
  enterTime
  exitTime
}
```

Field	Type	Name	Default	Meaning
exposedField	SFVec3f	center	0 0 0	Center of the sensor.
exposedField	SFVec3f	size	0 0 0	Size of the sensor.
exposedField	SFBool	enabled	TRUE	Toggle to turn on and off.
eventOut	SFBool	isActive		Reports sensor is on.
eventOut	SFVec3f	position_changed		Reports position.
eventOut	SFRotation	orientation_changed		Reports orientation.
eventOut	SFTime	enterTime		Reports entry time.
eventOut	SFTime	exitTime		Reports exit time.

VRML 1 SYNTAX
Node is new to VRML v2.0.

NODE GEOMETRY

- The **center** and **size** fields determines the location and size of the sensor.

- The **enabled** field toggles the **ProximitySensor** on and off:

enabled	Meaning
FALSE	ProximitySensor is off.
TRUE	ProximitySensor is on (default).

- The **isActive** field reports to other nodes that the **ProximitySensor** is active.

- The **position_changed** field reports the cursor's current position in the sensor.

- The **orientation_changed** field reports the angle of rotation in the sensor.

- The **enterTime** and **exitTime** fields reports the time when the **isActive** event becomes TRUE and FALSE, respectively.

VRML P

RELATED NODES

TimeSensor	Generate events as time passes.
TouchSensor	Generates events as the cursor passes over child geometry nodes.
VisibilitySensor	Generates events when a bounding box enters and leaves the viewing frustum.
CylinderSensor	Maps dragging motion about the y-axis.
PlaneSensor	Maps dragging motion into the x,y-plane.
SphereSensor	Maps dragging motion into free rotation about its center.

ROUTE

Connects a node's eventOut with another node's eventIn field.

VRML 2 SYNTAX

```
ROUTE NodeName.eventOutName_changed TO
NodeName.set_eventInName
```

Name	Meaning
NodeName	Name of node.
.	Connects field with node name.
eventOutName_changed	**eventOut** name.
exposedFieldname	**exposedField** name.
TO	Direction clarifier.
set_eventIn	**eventIn** name.

VRML 1 SYNTAX

Keyword is new to VRML v2.0.

TIPS

■ Events are sent from node to node with the **ROUTE** keyword.

■ A VRML file can contain any number of **ROUTE** keywords.

■ The **ROUTE** statement is flexible: it can appear at the top-level of a VRML file, or within a prototype implementation, or inside a node wherever fields appear.

■ A route can only be established only from eventOuts to eventIns:

Modifier	Meaning
prefix **set_**	Explicitly defines an eventIn.
suffix **_changed**	Explicitly defines an eventOut.
no prefix or suffix	Explictly defines an exposedField.

■ Several exceptions are made to improve readability:

   ■ The **SFBool** and **MFBool** eventIns and eventOuts are prefixed **is**, such as **isActive**.

   ■ The **SFTime** and **MFTime** eventIns and eventOuts are suffixed **Time**, such as **enterTime**.

   ■ The eventIns for adding and removing children are **addChildren** and **removeChildren**.

■ The type of eventIn and eventOut must match exactly; for example, an SFFloat must be routed to another SFFloat; it cannot route to an MFFloat.

■ The second and following repetitive routings are ignored.

RELATED KEYWORDS

DEF/USE   Defines an instance.

EXTERNPROTO Allows the creation of user-definable nodes external to the file.

PROTO   Creates user-definable nodes.

ScalarInterpolator { }

Interpolates linearly between a set of **SFFloat** values (*an Interpolator node*).

VRML 2 SYNTAX

```
ScalarInterpolator {
  key              [ ]
  keyVvalue        [ ]
  set_fraction
  value_changed
}
```

Field	Type	Name	Default	Meaning
exposedField	MFFloat	key	[ ]	Parameterized scalars.
exposedField	MFFloat	keyValue	[ ]	Scalar values.
eventIn	SFFloat	set_fraction		Trigger interpolation.
eventOut	SFFloat	value_changed		Report results.

VRML 1 SYNTAX

Node is new to VRML v2.0.

NODE GEOMETRY

- The **key** field holds parameterized scalar values from **0.0** to **1.0**.

- The **keyValue** field holds the scalar values in **MFFloat** format.

- The **set_fraction** field causes the interpolator function to operate.

- The **value_changed** field returns the interpolated color value in **SFFloat** format.

TIPS

- This node can be used to interpolate single values, such as radius, height, brightness, and pitch.

- These interpolator nodes are meant to be used to create linear, keyframed animation.

- Values in the **key** field must increase and cannot repeat.

- The number of coordinates in the **keyValue** field must have the same number of scalars the keyframe times in the **key** field.

RELATED NODES

ColorInterpolator	Linearly interpolates along a set of **MFColor** values.
CoordinateInterpolator	Linearly interpolates along a set of **MFVec3f** values.
NormalInterpolator	Interpolates along a set of multivalue **Vec3f** values.
OrientationInterpolator	Interpolates along a set of **SFRotation** values.
PositionInterpolator	Linearly interpolates along a set of **SFVec3f** values.

Script { }

Programs behavior into the scene (*a Global node*).

VRML 2 SYNTAX

```
Script {
  url              [ ]
  mustEvaluate     FALSE
  directOutput     FALSE

  # One or more of the following:
  eventName
  fieldName        initialValue
  eventName
}
```

Field	Type	Name	Default	Meaning
field	MFString	url	[ ]	Source of script.
field	SFBool	mustEvaluate	FALSE	When to evaluate.
field	SFBool	directOutput	FALSE	How to evaluate.

Optional events:

eventIn	eventTypeName	eventName		
field	fieldTypeName	fieldName	initialValue	
eventOut	eventTypeName	eventName		

VRML 1 SYNTAX
Node is new to VRML v2.0.

NODE GEOMETRY
■ The **url** field accesses the script via a URL.

■ The **mustEvaluate** field should be kept **FALSE** (the default) so that the browser delays sending input events to the script until output is needed by the browser.

■ The **directOutputs** field is **FALSE** by default, which means the script only affect the scene by events sent through the **eventOuts** field.

■ The **eventTypeName** and **fieldName** fields contains the data sent to (eventIn) and received from (eventOut) the script.

■ The scripting language is permitted to define the **eventsProcessed** routine; it is called after a set of events are received.

TIPS
■ A script is typically a VRMLscript or JavaScript program that reacts to input and creates some sort of output.

■ When **mustEvaluate** is TRUE, the browser sends input events to the script immediately, even when outputs is not needed; this consumes CPU cycles and should not be used.

■ When **directOutputs** is TRUE, the script is permitted send events to any node to which it has access.

- Any **exposedField** can be read and written by a **Script** node.

- Any **exposedField** and **eventOut** name can be prefixed with *get_* to read the current value, whether with a **Script** node or via an external API.

- For example, **enabled** is an **exposedField** of the **SphereSensor** node:

```
SphereSensor {
  enabled TRUE
  isActive
  trackPoint_changed
  rotation_changed
}
```

To read the value of **enabled**, use the **get_enabled** function within the **Script** node.

RELATED NODES

Anchor   Loads another world or viewpoint.

Switch   Switches between zero or more children.

WorldInfo   Holds information about the world.

VRMLscript NOTES

The syntax of VRMLscript is based on JavaScript; both scripting languages were under development at the time of writing. For the most up-to-date specification for VRMLscript, check the Web site **http://vrml.sgi.com/moving-worlds/spec/scriptref.html**. Contact rikk@best.com , cmarrin@sgi.com, or gavin@acm.org with questions or comments.

Some differences between VRMLscript and JavaScript are:

- Semicolon required at end of expressions (optional in JavaScript).

- Optional keyword **var** not allowed.

- Neither the [ ] notation nor the . notation are allowed since VRML uses them.

- Break and **continue** syntax not supported.

- VRMLscript supports the following JavaScript objects: Math and date object.

Place the { and } characters around multiple statements in a body, separating the statements with the semicolon (;). Variables defined within the block go out of scope at the end of the block.

VRMLscript EXPRESSIONS

■ Some of JavaScript's built-in objects are supported in VRMLscript, plus the unique **Browser** object that gives access to the VRML browser:

getName() Get name of VRML browser (a string).

getVersion() Get browser version number (a string).

getCurrentSpeed() Get user's travel rate (in floating point).

getCurrentFrameRate()

Get instantaneous frame rate of scene rendering (in frames per second, floating point).

getWorldURL() Get URL of the currently loaded world (a string).

loadWorld(*url***)** Load the *url* as a new world.

replaceWorld(*nodes***)**

Replace current world with the passed list of *nodes*.

createVRMLFromURL(*url, node, event***)**

Parse the *url* to a VRML scene; when complete, send the passed *event* to the passed *node* (*event* is a string with the name of an **MFNode** eventIn in the passed *node*).

createVRMLFromString(*vrmlSyntax***)**

Parse the passed *vrmlSyntax* into a VRML scene; return a list of root nodes from the resulting scene.

addRoute(*fromNode, fromEventOut, toNode, toEventIn***)**

Add a route from the passed *eventOut* to the passed *eventIn*.

deleteRoute(*fromNode, fromEventOut, toNode, toEventIn***)**

Remove the route between the passed *eventOut* and passed *eventIn*, if one exists.

■ Logical expressions evaluate to 0 (false) or 1 (true):

&& Logical AND.

|| Logical OR.

! Logical NOT.

< Less than.

<= Less than or equal to.

== Equal to.

!= Not equal to.

>= Greater than or equal to.

> Greater than.

```
r < 8
h > 9 && s > 7
```

- Arithmetic expressions:

&	And.
|	Or.
^	Exclusive or .
~	Not.
-	Negation.

- Operators:

+	Addition.
-	Subtraction.
*	Multiplication.
/	Division.
%	Integer division.

- Expressions to control looping:

for　　Contains three expressions to control the looping behavior:

- First expression is evaluated once before loop execution, such as initializing the loop counter.

- Second expression is evaluated before each loop (if expression evaluates to 0, exit the loop).

- Evaluation of the third expression, such as incrementing the counter.

```
for (i = 0; i < 100; ++i)
  <statement>
```

return　　Immediate return from the function.

```
if (r == 0) {
  g = 1956;
  return 5 + g;
}
```

Assigns the result.

```
r = 31;
```

Shape { }

Holds the **appearance** and **geometry** nodes (*a Leaf node*).

VRML 2 SYNTAX

```
Shape {
  appearance  NULL
  geometry    NULL
}
```

Field	Type	Name	Default	Meaning
field	SFNode	appearance	NULL	Holds Material, texture and TextureTransform.
field	SFNode	geometry	NULL	Holds the Geometry node.

VRML 1 SYNTAX

Node is new to VRML v2.0.

NODE GEOMETRY

- The **appearance** field holds:

  - the **Material** node;

  - the **TextureTransform** node; and

  - the **texture** field, which, in turn, holds:

    - the **ImageTexture** node; or

    - the **MovieTexture** node; or

    - the **PixelTexture** node.

- The **geometry** field holds the **Geometry** node.

TIPS

- An empty **Shape { }** node creates an invisible object.

- The three-way decomposition of a **Shape** — shape, appearance, geometry — allows three-way sharing: of the entire shape, of the shape's geometry, or of just the properties. For example, the nodes of a wood chair and marble table create a wooden table, which uses the texture of the wood chair and the geometry of the marble table.

RELATED NODES

Appearance	Holds the **Material, Texture,** and **textureTransform** nodes.
ImageTexture	Defines a texture map and its parameters.
Material	Assigns a material to an object.
MovieTexture	Defines an animated movie map and its parameters.
PixelTexture	Defines a repetitive pixel map and its parameters.
TextureTransform	Applies a 2D transformation to a texture.

Sound { }

Specifies the position and spatial presentation of a sound (*a Leaf node*).

VRML 2 SYNTAX

```
Sound {
    source       NULL
    intensity    1
    priority     0
    location     0 0 0
    direction    0 0 1
    minFront     1
    maxFront     10
    minBack      1
    maxBack      10
    spatialize   TRUE
}
```

Field	Type	Name	Default	Meaning
exposedField	SFNode	source	NULL	Source of the sound.
exposedField	SFFloat	intensity	1	Sound volume.
exposedField	SFFloat	priority	0	Priority of sound clip.
exposedField	SFVec3f	location	0 0 0	Location of sound source.
exposedField	SFVec3f	direction	0 0 1	Direction of the sound.
exposedField	SFFloat	minFront	1	Max volume in front.
exposedField	SFFloat	maxFront	10	Min volume in front.
exposedField	SFFloat	minBack	1	Max volume in back.
exposedField	SFFloat	maxBack	10	Min volume in back.
field	SFBool	spatialize	TRUE	Mono/stereo sound toggle.

VRML 1 SYNTAX

Node is new to VRML v2.0.

NODE GEOMETRY

■ The **source** field must point to an **AudioClip** node or **MovieTexture** node (which must refer to a movie format that supports sound).

■ The **intensity** field sets the volume of the sound source:

intensity	Meaning
0.0	Silence.
1.0	Maximum volume of sound source; the default.

■ The **priority** field sets the priority of the sound since many sounds at the same time are simply confusing:

priority	Meaning
0	Normal setting; the default.
1	Highest priority.

■ The **location** of the sound in 3D space; the default of **0 0 0** is at the origin.

- The **direction** of the sound; the default of **0 0 1** is toward the viewer.
- The **minFront** field determines the region of full intensity in front of the sound.
- The **minBack** field determines the region of full intensity behind of the sound.
- The **maxFront** field determines the limit of the sound.
- The **maxBack** field determines the limit of the sound.
- The **spatialize** field determines how the sound is played back:

spatialize	Meaning
TRUE	Monaural sound from a single point.
FALSE	Ambient, stereo sound.

RELATED EQUATIONS

- The availability of sound (and multiple sound sources) depends on the computer's sound capabilities. When not enough sound channels available, the VRML specification recommends that "the browser sort the active sounds into an ordered list using the following sort keys:

  1. Decreasing **priority.**

  2. Increasing current time and **startTime** (for sounds with priority greater than 0.5).

  3. Decreasing **intensity** at the viewer location

  $$= \text{intensity} / \text{distance}^2 \text{ ."}$$

- To create omnidirectional sound (the **direction** field is ignored):

  $$\text{minFront} = \text{minBack and maxFront} = \text{maxBack}$$

TIPS

- Sound can emit in a spherical (omnidirectional) or ellipsoid (directional) pattern.
- When the distance is set to the maximum value, the sound is heard throughout the entire VRML scene.
- When the **source** field is set to NULL, no sound is emitted.
- A **priority** field set to **1** ise used only for a short-duration cue sound (like a beep).
- The **minFront and minBack** fields are the foci of an *inner* ellipsoid; the **maxFront** and **maxBack** fields are the foci of an *outer* ellipsoid.
- Inside the inner ellipsoid, sound is played at full intensity.
- Between the two ellipsoids, sound intensity drops off proportionally by the inverse square of the distance from the **location** field.
- Outside the outer ellipsoid, sound is not heard.
- An *ellipsoid* is a 3D ellipse.

RELATED NODES

AudioClip   Plays an audio file.

MovieTexture   Plays a movie file, which may contain sound.

Sphere { }

Creates a 3D sphere (*a Geometry node*).

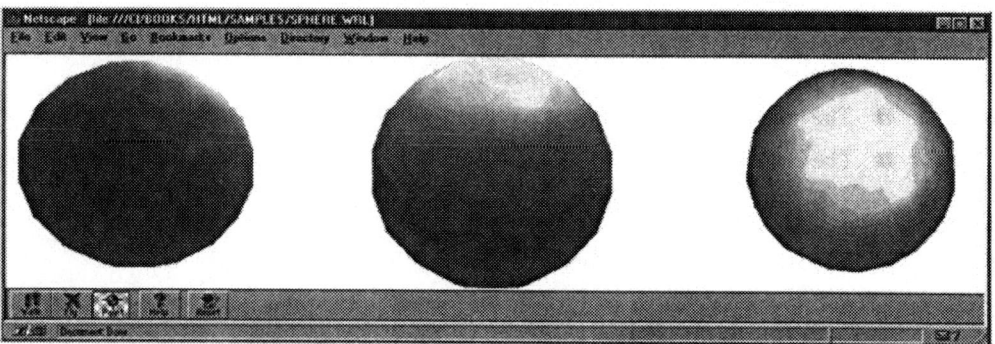

VRML 2 SYNTAX

```
Sphere {
  radius  1
}
```

Field	Type	Name	Default	Meaning
field	SFFloat	radius	1	Radius of the sphere.

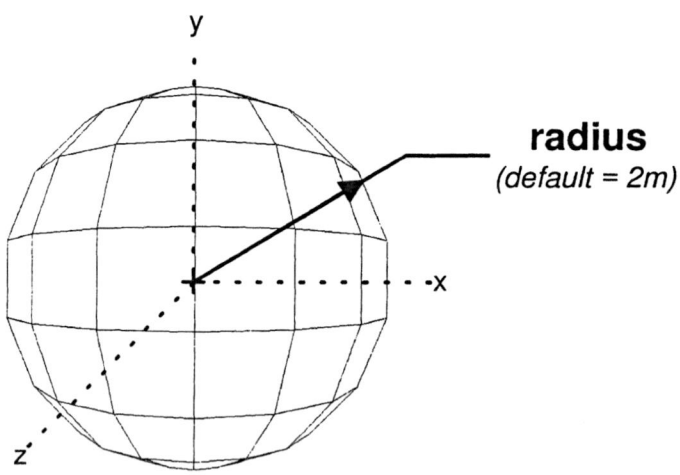

radius
(default = 2m)

VRML 1 SYNTAX

```
Sphere {
  radius  1
}
```

NODE GEOMETRY

■ This node is centered at the origin (0,0,0) and has a default radius of 1.

■ The **Sphere** node generates its own normal.

RELATED EQUATIONS

pi = 3.141

Surface area of a sphere

$$= 4 * pi * \textbf{radius}^2$$

Volume of a sphere

$$= {}^4/_3 * pi * \textbf{radius}^3$$

TEXTURE MAPPING

■ The texture map covers the entire surface.

■ The texture wraps counterclockwise from the back of the sphere, with a seam down the back, along the y,z-plane.

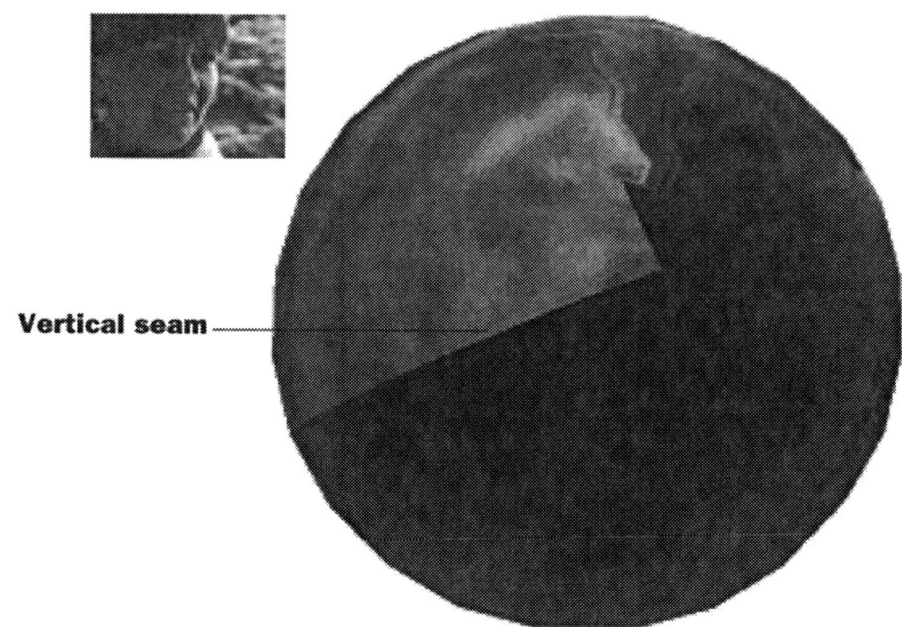

Vertical seam

*The texture map (upper left) applied to the **Sphere** node.*

TIP

■ There isn't too much you can do with a **Sphere** node, other than make it larger or smaller, or combine it with other shapes — but it does make a dandy planet.

RELATED NODES

Box	Creates a 3D box; formerly the **Cube** node.
Cone	Creates a 3D cone.
Cylinder	Creates a 3D cylinder.
ElevationGrid	Creates a 3D terrain-like surface.
Extrusion	Extrudes a 2D shape along a 3D spine.
IndexedFaceSet	Creates a 3D surface from multiple polyfaces.
IndexedLineSet	Creates a 3D shape from multiple polylines.
PointSet	Creates a 3D space from multiple dots.
Text	Creates 3D text; formerly the **AsciiText** node.

SphereSensor { }

Maps dragging motion into a free rotation about its center (*a Sensor node*).

VRML 2 SYNTAX

```
SphereSensor {
  enabled              TRUE
  offset               0 1 0 0
  autoOffset           TRUE
  isActive
  trackPoint_changed
  rotation_changed
}
```

Field	Type	Name	Default	Meaning
exposedField	SFBool	enabled	TRUE	Toggles sensor on or off.
exposedField	SFRotation	offset	0 1 0 0	Offset added to output.
exposedField	SFBool	autoOffset	TRUE	Send to last output value.
eventOut	SFBool	isActive		Reports sensor is active.
eventOut	SFVec3f	trackPoint_changed		Position of cursor.
eventOut	SFRotation	rotation_changed		Rotation, in radians.

VRML 1 SYNTAX

Node is new to VRML v2.0.

NODE GEOMETRY

■ The **enabled** field toggles the **SphereSensor** on and off:

enabled	Meaning
FALSE	SphereSensor is off.
TRUE	SphereSensor is on (default).

■ The **isActive** field sends a Boolean event to other nodes:

isActive	Meaning
TRUE	SphereSensor is active; the mouse cursor is within the sphere.
FALSE	Cursor has left the sphere.

■ The **trackPoint_changed** field reports the cursor's current position on the surface of the sphere.

■ The **rotation_changed** field reports the angle of rotation, in radians.

TIPS

- When **isActive** is TRUE, other pointing device sensors cannot generate events.

- While **isActive** is TRUE, this node generates **trackPoint_changed** and **rotation_changed** events.

- If **CylinderSensor, PlaneSensor, SphereSensor,** and **TouchSensor** are nested, the lowest sensor in the graph is activated and sends outputs; parent sensors are ignored.

- Sibling sensors act independently, outputting simultaneously.

RELATED NODES

CylinderSensor Maps dragging motion about the y-axis.

PlaneSensor Maps dragging motion into the x,y-plane.

ProximitySensor Generates events when camera enters, moves inside, and exits 3D space.

TimeSensor Generate events as time passes.

TouchSensor Generates events as the cursor passes over child geometry nodes.

VisibilitySensor Generates events when a bounding box enters and leaves the viewing frustum.

SpotLight { }

A cone-shaped light source (*a Leaf node*).

VRML 2 SYNTAX

```
SpotLight {
    on                  TRUE
    intensity           1
    ambientIntensity    0
    color               1 1 1
    location            0 0 0
    direction           0 0 -1
    beamWidth           1.570796
    cutOffAngle         0.785398
    radius              100
    attenuation         1 0 0
}
```

Field	Type	Name	Default	Meaning
exposedField	SFBool	on	TRUE	Toggles light on and off.
exposedField	SFFloat	intensity	1	Intensity of the light.
exposedField	SFFloat	ambientIntensity	0	Ambient intensity.
exposedField	SFColor	color	1 1 1	Color of the light.
exposedField	SFVec3f	location	0 0 0	Location of the light.
exposedField	SFVec3f	direction	0 0 -1	Direction of the light.
exposedField	SFFloat	beamWidth	1.570796	Angle of beam width.
exposedField	SFFloat	cutOffAngle	0.785398	Angle of beam cutoff.
exposedField	SFFloat	radius	100	Radius of light.
exposedField	SFVec3f	attenuation	1 0 0	Attenuation of light.

VRML 1 SYNTAX

```
SpotLight {
    on              TRUE
    intensity       1
    color           1 1 1
    location        0 0 0
    direction       0 0 -1
    dropOffRate     0
    cutOffAngle     0.785398
}
```

■ Where **dropOffRate** determines the rate at which the light diminishes at the edges of the cone; the default value of 0 means almost instant lack of illumination beyond the cone.

NODE GEOMETRY

- The **on** field turns the light on (when set to **TRUE**) and off (set to **FALSE**).
- The **intensity** field controls the brightness of the light:

intensity	Meaning
0.0	Light is off; no intensity.
1.0	Full intensity; default value.
> 1.0	Can create an overbright light.
< 0.0	Can add darkness; an anti-light.

- The **ambientIntensity** field determines the amount of ambient light, light that is reflected off surfaces and creates an overall illumination.
- The **color** field determines the color of the light using RGB notation:

color	Meaning
1 1 1	White light; the default.
0 0 0	No light.
1 0 0	Red light.
0 1 0	Green light.
0 0 1	Blue light.

- The **location** field specifies the location of the light; the default of **0 0 0** locates the light at the origin.
- The **direction** field specifies the direction of the light; the default of **0 0 -1** points the light straight ahead.
- The **beamWidth** field is the width of a cone of light, measured in radians; the default of 1.570796 radians represents 90 degrees.
- The **cutOffAngle** field determines where the cone of light is cut off, measured in radians; the default of 0.785398 radians represents 45 degrees.
- The **radius** field specifies how far the light beams travel from the location, 100 meters by default.
- The **attenuation** field determines the fall-off of light intensity from the origin.

RELATED EQUATIONS

360 degrees = 2 * *pi* = 6.23813 radians

- The illumination of an object **r** distance from the light

$$= (^1/_{attenuation}) + (attenuation * r) + (attenuation * r^2)$$

- According to the Moving Worlds specification, "renderers that attenuate using a cosine raised to a power, should use an exponent of exponent

$$= 0.5 * \log (0.5) / \log (\cos (beamWidth))$$

"When **beamWidth** >= $^{pi}/_2$ the illumination is uniform up to the cutoff angle, which is the default."

TIPS

■ Since a spot light has a cone-shaped light beam, this light node has the largest number of parameters.

■ The **cutOffAngle** field controls the angular distribution of light; beyond which illumination is zero.

■ The **beamWidth** field controls the angle at which the beam starts to fall off.

■ The light is brightest within the **beamWidth** angle, gets dimmer between the **beamWidth** and **cutOffAngle** angles; and is nonexistent beyond the **cutOffAngle** angle:

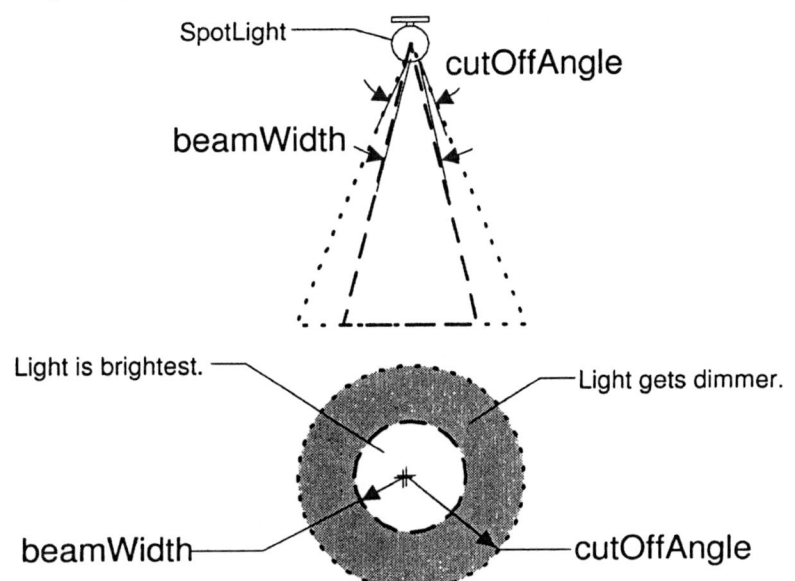

■ Shapes do not cast shadows in VRML, since that is too computational intensive; you simulate shadows with flat objects colored gray or black.

■ It can be tricky to set up lights appropriately; for this reason, you may want to install many lights, then turn off (set **on** to **FALSE**) the ones you don't need.

RELATED NODES

DirectionalLight A light source with parallel beams.

Fog   An axis-aligned, ellipsoid of colored atmosphere.

PointLight   An omnidirectional light source.

Shape   Holds **appearance** and **geometry** fields (formerly the **ShapeHints** node).

Sound   Position and spatial presentation of a sound.

Switch { }

Switches between zero or more children (*a Group node*).

VRML 2 SYNTAX
```
Switch {
  whichChild   -1
  choice       [ ]
}
```

Field	Type	Name	Default	Meaning
exposedField	SFInt32	whichChild	-1	Child to choose.
exposedField	MFNode	choice	[ ]	Children to choose from.

VRML 1 SYNTAX
```
Switch {
  whichChild   -1
}
```

Where the **Separator** node is used to group children.

NODE GEOMETRY
- The value of **whichChild** determines which child to choose:

whichChild	Meaning
0	First child.
-1	Skip over all children; the default.
-3	Read all children.

- The **choice** field holds children nodes.

TIPS
- This node is like the light switch in a car: by changing the position of the switch, you turn on a different set of lights: no lights, interior lights, parking lights, or headlights. Similarly, the value of **whichChild** determines which child node the browser switches to.

- The number of the first child is 0, not one.

- *Special case*: When **whichChild** is set to -1 (the default), the browser skips over all children in this node and continues with the next node following.

- *Special case*: When **whichChild** is set to -3 or is greater than the number of children, the browser reads all children in this node, performing all actions specified by children in this node.

RELATED NODES

Anchor	Loads another world or viewpoint.
Billboard	Rotates a group about an axis to always faces the camera.
Collision	Prevents navigation through an object.
Group	Groups nodes together without performing a transformation.
Inline	Groups nodes together from around the World Wide Web.
LOD	Level of detail.
Transform	Transforms the coordinate system of a group of nodes.

Text { }

Creates 3D text (*formerly AsciiText; a Geometry node*).

VRML 2 SYNTAX

```
Text {
  string        [ ]
  fontStyle     NULL
  maxExtent     0.0
  length        [ ]
}
```

Field	Type	Name	Default	Meaning
exposedField	MFString	string	[ ]	Text to be displayed.
field	SFNode	fontStyle	NULL	Contains **FontStyle** node.
field	SFFloat	maxExtent	0.0	Measured length of string.
field	MFFloat	length	[ ]	Length of string, in chars.

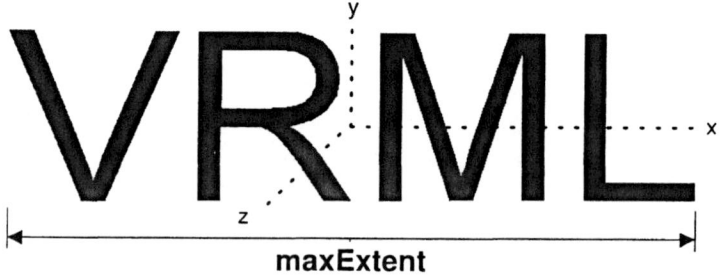

maxExtent

VRML 1 SYNTAX

```
AsciiText {
    string          [ ]
    justification   LEFT
    width           0.0
    spacing         [ ]
}
```

- ■ Where **justification** is LEFT, RIGHT, or CENTER.

NODE GEOMETRY

- ■ The **string** field holds one or more strings of the text to be displayed; strings are stored in visual order.

- ■ The **fontStyle** field contains the **FontStyle** node.

- ■ The **maxExtent** field limits and scales the length of the string; if the string is shorter than this value, the text is unaffected.

- ■ The **length** field indicates the number of characters in the string.

TEXTURE MAPPING

- ■ The origin of the texture map is at the origin of the first string (affected by the justification.

- ■ The texture map is equally scaled the s- and t-directions:

Map	Meaning
s	Increases to the right.
t	Increases up.

- ■ One unit = the font's height.

*The texture map (lower left) applied to the **Text** node.*

TIPS

■ This node is starts at the origin (0,0,0) depending on the justification.

■ To display two or more lines of text, enclose them in square brackets ([and]) and separate strings with a comma (,), as follows:

```
Text {
   string      ["Virtual Reality", "Modeling Language"]
}
```

■ The **Text** node follows the UTF-8 encoding specified by ISO 10646-1:1993 standard plus pDAM 1-5.

■ The purpose of the **maxExtent** field is to limit and scale the text string if the normal length longer than the value in **maxExtent**; the string is not changed when it is shorter than **maxExtent**.

■ The purpose of the **length** field is to scale the string to fit a sentence; when too short, the string is stretched; when too long, the string is compressed. Stretching and compressing is done by either by scaling the text or by adding/subtracting space between characters.

■ When **maxExtent** and/or **length** are 0 or missing, the string is allowed to be its full length.

RELATED NODE

FontStyle   Specifies the font size, family, style, direction, and language.

TextureCoordinate { }

Defines a set of 2D coordinates to map textures to the vertices of geometry nodes (*formerly **TextureCoordinate2**; a Geometric Property node*).

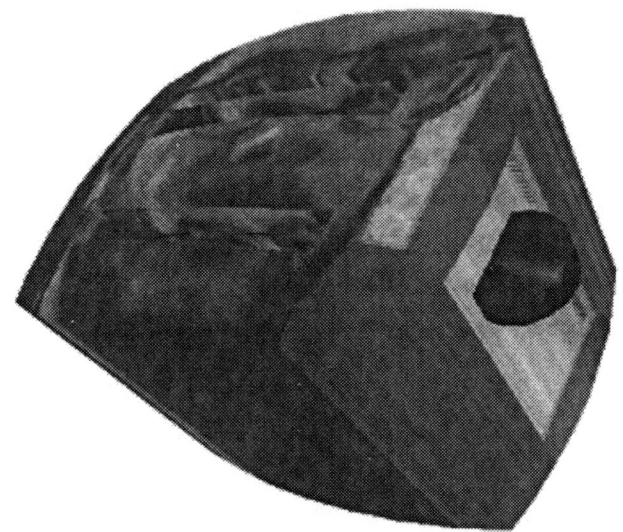

A photograph of the author texture mapped to the surface of a toaster.
Toaster.Wrl obtained from the CadKey, Inc. Web site: http://www.cadkey.com.

VRML 2 SYNTAX

```
TextureCoordinate {
  point   []
}
```

Field	Type	Name	Default	Meaning
exposedField	MFVec2f	**point**	[ ]	2D texture coordinates.

VRML 1 SYNTAX

```
TextureCoordinate2 {
  point   0 0
}
```

NODE GEOMETRY

■ The **point** field specifies the 2D texture coordinates in a range of 0 to 1, with the S-coordinate followed by the T-coordinate.

TIPS

■ This node is only used in the **texCoord** field of the **IndexedFaceSet** and **ElevationGrid** nodes.

■ The S-coordinate specifies the horizontal (x) direction.

■ The T-coordinate specifies the vertical (y) direction.

RELATED NODES

Color   Specifies the RGB colors of points, lines, and faces.

Coordinate   Specifies the 3D x,y,z-coordinates of points, lines, and faces.

Normal   Specifies the normals for faces and grids.

ElevationGrid   Creates an topographical grid.

IndexedFaceSet Creates a complex object from 3D faces.

TextureTransform { }

Defines a 2D transformation applied to texture coordinates (*formerly Texture2Transform; an Appearance node*).

VRML 2 SYNTAX

```
TextureTransform {
  translation        0 0
  rotation           0
  scale              1 1
  center             0 0
}
```

Field	Type	Name	Default	Meaning
exposedField	SFVec2f	translation	0 0	X and y offset.
exposedField	SFFloat	rotation	0	Rotation angle.
exposedField	SFVec2f	scale	1 1	Scale factors.
exposedField	SFVec2f	center	0 0	Center of scale & rotation.

VRML 1 SYNTAX

```
Texture2Transform {
  translation        0 0
  rotation           0
  scaleFactor        1 1
  center             0 0
}
```

NODE GEOMETRY

- The **translation** field an offset in the x- and y-directions, in units.
- The **rotation** field specifies an angle of rotation, in radians.
- The **scale** field specifies scaling factors in the x- and y-directions.
- The **center** field specifies the x,y-coordinates for the **rotation** and **scale** fields.

TIPS

- This node is used only in the **textureTransform** field of the **Appearance** node
- This node affects how a texture is applied to the surface of associated geometry.

RELATED NODES

Appearance	Specifies the appearance of associated geometry.
ImageTexture	Applies a GIF, JPEG, or PNG file as a texture map.
Material	Specifies the material look for a surface texture.
MovieTexture	Applies a movie file as a texture map.
PixelTexture	Applies a pixel pattern as a texture map.

VRML T

TimeSensor { }

Generate events as time passes (*a Sensor node*).

VRML 2 SYNTAX
```
TimeSensor {
    cycleInterval        1
    enabled              TRUE
    loop                 FALSE
    stopTime             0
    startTime            0
    isActive
    fraction_changed
    time
    cycleTime
}
```

Field	Type	Name	Default	Meaning
exposedField	SFTime	cycleInterval	1	Duration.
exposedField	SFBool	enabled	TRUE	Sensor is enabled.
exposedField	SFBool	loop	FALSE	Generate time events.
exposedField	SFTime	stopTime	0	Time to stop sensing.
exposedField	SFTime	startTime	0	Time to start sensing.
eventOut	SFBool	isActive		Sensor is active.
eventOut	SFFloat	fraction_changed		Reports relative time.
eventOut	SFTime	time		Reports absolute time.
eventOut	SFTime	cycleTime		Reports start of cycle.

VRML 1 SYNTAX
Node is new to VRML v2.0.

NODE GEOMETRY
- The **cycleInterval** field specifies the duration of the time sensor.
- The **enabled** field toggles the **TimeSensor** on and off:

enabled	Meaning
FALSE	TimeSensor is off.
TRUE	TimeSensor is on (default).

- The **isActive** field reports to other nodes that the **TimeSensor** is active.

- The **loop** field determines how long **TimeSensor** runs:

loop	Meaning
FALSE	`TimeSensor` stops generating events when time = `startTime + cycleInterval`
TRUE	`TimeSensor` loops continuously.

- The **stopTime** field is the time the sensor should stop.

- The **startTime** field is the time the sensor begins.

- The **faction_changed** field outputs a floating-point value in the range from 0.0 to 1.0:

fraction	Meaning
0.0	Corresponds to `startTime` field.
1.0	Corresponds to `startTime+cycleInterval` fields.

- The **time** field reports the absolute time.

- The **cycleTime** field sends a TRUE event when a cycle is about to begin.

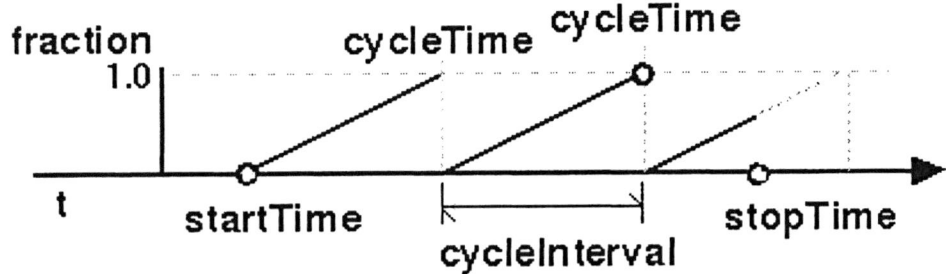

A diagram of the TimeSensor node from http://vag.vrml.org

TIPS

- The **time** field contains the number of seconds since 12 midnight GMT January 1, 1970.

- You can use **TimeSensor** as a stop watch that start and stop time-based nodes, such as interpolators.

- This node is inactive until it reaches **startTime**.

- This node generates time and fraction-of-time events that can drive simulated behaviors.

- The **stopTime** node is ignored when it is less than or equal to the value of **startTime** node.

- This node sets **isActive** to FALSE when **stopTime** or **startTime** + **cycleInterval** (when **loop** is FALSE) is reached.

- The **cycleTime** field is useful for synchronizing with other time-based objects in the scene.

- Whenever **fraction_changed** equals 0.0, **cycleTime** outputs the current time. This is the beginning of an interval; it can be used for synchronization of several events.

$$\text{fraction\_changed} = \text{fmod} (\text{now} - \textbf{startTime}, \textbf{cycleInterval})$$

RELATED NODES

ProximitySensor Generates events when camera enters, moves inside, and exits 3D space.

TouchSensor Generates events as the cursor passes over child geometry nodes.

VisibilitySensor Generates events when a bounding box enters and leaves the viewing frustum.

CylinderSensor Maps dragging motion about the y-axis.

PlaneSensor Maps dragging motion into the x,y-plane.

SphereSensor Maps dragging motion into free rotation about its center.

TouchSensor { }

Generates events as the cursor passes over geometry (*a Sensor node*).

VRML 2 SYNTAX

```
TouchSensor {
    enabled                TRUE
    isOver
    isActive
    hitPoint_changed
    hitNormal_changed
    hitTexCoord_changed
    touchTime
}
```

Field	Type	Name	Default	Meaning
exposedField	SFBool	enabled	TRUE	Toggles node on and off.
eventOut	SFBool	isOver		Cursor is over geometry.
eventOut	SFBool	isActive		Mouse button is pressed.
eventOut	SFVec3f	hitPoint_changed		x,y,z-coordinates.
eventOut	SFVec3f	hitNormal_changed		Normal vector.
eventOut	SFVec2f	hitTexCoord_changed		Texture coordinates.
eventOut	SFTime	touchTime		Time touch occurred.

VRML 1 SYNTAX

Node is new to VRML v2.0.

NODE GEOMETRY

- The **enabled** field

- The **isOver** field generates an event:

isOver	Meaning
FALSE	Cursor is *not* near associated geometry.
TRUE	Cursor is over the associated geometry.

- The **isActive** field reports the state of the primary (left) mouse button:

isActive	Meaning
FALSE	Mouse button is released.
TRUE	Mouse button is pressed.

- The **hitPoint_changed** field reports the 3D x,y,z-coordinates of the underlying geometry at the current cursor location.

- The **hitNormal_changed** field reports the surface normal of the underlying geometry at the current cursor location.

VRML T

- The **hitTexCoord_changed** field reports the texture coordinates of the underlying surface at the current cursor location.

- The **touchTime** field reports the time when the geometry was touched.

TIPS

- The TRUE and FALSE events are generated by the **isOver** field when the pointing device is moving.; the events are *not* generated when the geometry moves under the cursor.

- When the **isOver** field is set to TRUE, every mouse movement generates a **hitPoint**, **hitNormal**, and **hitTexCoord** event.

- The **touchTime** field generates an event only all three occur: (1) the cursor is over geometry; (2) **isOver** is TRUE; and (3) **isActive** is FALSE.

RELATED NODES

ProximitySensor Generates events when camera enters, moves inside, and exits 3D space.

TimeSensor Generate events as time passes.

VisibilitySensor Generates events when a bounding box enters and leaves the viewing frustum.

CylinderSensor Maps dragging motion about the y-axis.

PlaneSensor Maps dragging motion into the x,y-plane.

SphereSensor Maps dragging motion into free rotation about its center.

Transform { }

Transforms the coordinates of a group of nodes (*replaces the **Rotation**, **Scale**, and **Translation** nodes of VRML v1; a **Group** node*).

*This pencil was created by using the **Transform** node to position the **Cone** and **Cylinder** nodes.*
Pen.Wrl by permission of Jeff Sonstein from http://www.newcollege.edu/vrmLab/Warehouse/BooksAndPens.

VRML 2 SYNTAX

```
Transform {
  bboxCenter            0 0 0
  bboxSize              -1 -1 -1
  translation           0 0 0
  rotation              0 0 1 0
  scale                 1 1 1
  scaleOrientation      0 0 1 0
  center                0 0 0
  children              [ ]
  addChildren
  removeChildren
}
```

Field	Type	Name	Default	Meaning
field	SFVec3f	bboxCenter	0 0 0	Bounding box center.
field	SFVec3f	bboxSize	-1 -1 -1	Bounding box size.
exposedField	SFVec3f	translation	0 0 0	Move in the x,y,z-axes.
exposedField	SFRotation	rotation	0 0 1 0	Rotate.
exposedField	SFVec3f	scale	1 1 1	Scale in the x,y,z-axes.
exposedField	SFRotation	scaleOrientation	0 0 1 0	Scale and rotate.
exposedField	SFVec3f	center	0 0 0	Center of the translation.
exposedField	MFNode	children	[ ]	Nodes included in group.
eventIn	MFNode	addChildren		Add nodes to group.
eventIn	MFNode	removeChildren		Remove nodes from group.

VRML 1 SYNTAX

```
Transform {
  translation           0 0 0
  rotation              0 0 1 0
  scaleFactor           1 1 1
  scaleOrientation      0 0 1 0
  center                0 0 0
}
```

VRML v2.0 eliminates the separate **Rotation**, **Scale**, and **Translation** nodes found in the VRML v1.0 specification.

VRML T

NODE GEOMETRY
- The **bboxCenter** and **bboxSize** fields define a bounding box that encloses all children nodes of the group.

- The **translation** field moves the object in the x, y, and/or z-direction (by default, the object doesn't move at all); the values **0 0 0** represent the x, y, and z-axes respectively.

- The **rotation** field rotates the object about the three axes (by default, the object doesn't rotate at all); the values **0 0 1 0** represent the x, y, z, and degrees to rotate, respectively.

- The **scale** field scales the object in the x, y, and/or z-direction (by default, the object doesn't scale at all); the values **1 1 1** represent the x, y, and z-axes respectively.

- The **scaleOrientation** field allows you to scale and rotate independently of the **rotation** field (by default, it doesn't do anything); the values 0 0 1 0 represent the x, y, z-axes and the scale factor, respectively.

- The **center** field is crucial, since it determines the point from which rotation, scaling, and translation takes place.

- The **children** field contains all nodes held by this group.

- To add nodes to the group, use the **addChildren** eventIn; to remove nodes from the group, use the **removeChildren** eventIn.

TIPS
- Use this node to reposition shape nodes (box, cone, cylinder, etc.) from their default positions.

- This node is identical to the **Group** node with the exception of the transformation fields.

- The bounding box defined by **bboxCenter** and **bboxSize** should be large enough to enclose children nodes, plus fog, light, and sound nodes of the group.

- A too-small bounding box is undefined.

- Scaling can be nonuniform; this allows you to create an elliptical cylinder, for example.

RELATED NODES
Anchor	Loads another world or viewpoint.
Billboard	Rotates a group about an axis to always faces the camera.
Collision	Prevents navigation through an object.
Group	Groups nodes together without performing a transformation.
Inline	Groups nodes together from around the World Wide Web.
LOD	Level of detail.
Switch	Switches between zero or more children.

Viewpoint { }

Defines a specific viewpoint (*a Bindable Leaf node*).

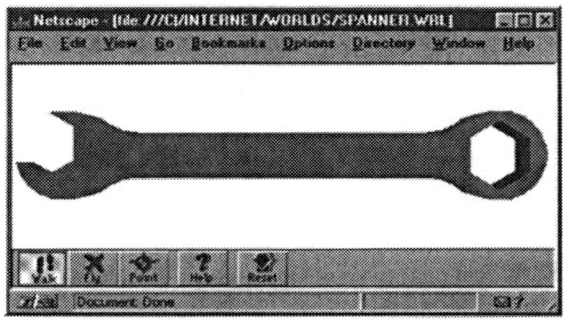

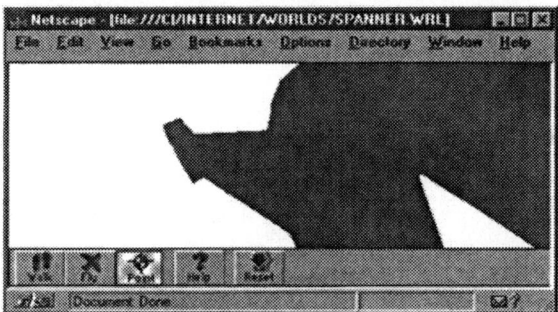

Three different viewpoints of a wrench.
Spanner.Wrl by permission of Jeff Sonstein from http://www.newcollege.edu/vrmLab/Warehouse.

VRML 2 SYNTAX

```
Viewpoint {
    position              0 0 0
    orientation           0 0 1 0
    fieldOfView           0.785398
    description           " "
    jump                  TRUE
    set_bind
    bindTime_changed
    isBound
}
```

Field	Type	Name	Default	Meaning
exposedField	SFVec3f	position	0 0 0	Origin of viewpoint.
exposedField	SFRotation	orientation	0 0 1 0	Rotation of viewpoint.
exposedField	SFFloat	fieldOfView	0.785398	Angle of view, radians.
field	SFString	description	""	Description of viewpoint.
exposedField	SFBool	jump	TRUE	Jump to viewpoint.
eventIn	SFBool	set_bind		Make current viewpoint.
eventOut	SFTime	bindTime_changed		Time of binding.
eventOut	SFBool	isBound		Camera is at viewpoint.

VRML 1 SYNTAX

Node is new to VRML v2.0.

NODE GEOMETRY

■ The **position** field specifies the position of the viewpoint relative to the origin of the coordinate system, 0 0 0.

■ The **orientation** field specifies a rotation relative to the default orientation

■ The **fieldOfView** field specifies the angle of view, in radians:

fieldOfView	Meaning
0	Minimum field of view.
0.785398	Default; 45 degrees.
pi	Maximum field of view; 180 degrees.

■ The **description** field is a text field to describe the viewpoint, possibly via a menu selection.

■ The jump field specifies whether the browser's user view is jumped:

jump	Meaning
	When set_bind is TRUE:
TRUE	Browser must parent the user's view under the **Viewpoint** and move the user view such that it matches the **Viewpoint**'s **position, orientation,** and **fieldOfView** fields.
FALSE	Browser parents the user view under the **Viewpoint** without changing the user view.
	When set_bind is FALSE:
TRUE	**Viewpoint** is popped from the stack and sends **isBound** FALSE and **bindTime_changed** events; next entry in stack becomes current and user view is moved to this location.

■ When the **set_bind** field is set to **TRUE**, this **Viewpoint** node become the current viewpoint (is pushed to the top of the browser's viewpoint stack).

■ The **bindTime_changed** reports the time at which the Viewpoint node was bound.

■ The **isBound** field is set to **TRUE** when the browser has arrived at the viewpoint.

TIPS

■ The VRML browser should recognize that the URL syntax **vrml.wrl#*viewname*** specifies the initial view when first displaying the Vrml.Wrl file.

■ The default **orientation** is looking down the -z-xis, with the +x-axis to the right, and +y-axis up.

■ The **bindTime_changed** field is useful for starting an animation or script when a given **Viewpoint** node becomes active.

RELATED NODES

Collision   Defines collision parameters.

NavigationInfo   Default values for transportation around the VRML scene.

VRML V-W

VisibilitySensor { }

Generates an event when any portion of a bounding box enters the viewing frustum (*a Sensor node*).

VRML 2 SYNTAX

```
VisibilitySensor {
   center      0 0 0
   size        0 0 0
   enabled     TRUE
   isActive
   enterTime
   exitTime
}
```

Field	Type	Name	Default	Meaning
exposedField	SFVec3f	center	0 0 0	Center of bounding box.
exposedField	SFVec3f	size	0 0 0	Size of bounding box.
exposedField	SFBool	enabled	TRUE	Toggles sensor on and off.
eventOut	SFBool	isActive		Box is within frustum.
eventOut	SFTime	enterTime		Enter box time.
eventOut	SFTime	exitTime		Exit box time.

VRML 1 SYNTAX

Node is new to VRML v2.0.

NODE GEOMETRY

- The **center** field specifies the center of the bounding box.

- The **bboxSize** fields specifies the size of the bounding box.

- The **enabled** field turns the **VisibilitySensor** on and off:

enabled	Meaning
FALSE	VisibilitySensor is turned off.
TRUE	VisibilitySensor is turned on; the default.

- The **isActive** field reports the status of the bounding box:

isVisible	Meaning
FALSE	Box is fully out of viewing frustum.
TRUE	Any part of the box in within the frustum.

- The **enterTime** field generates the time that **isActive** becomes TRUE.

- The **exitTime** field generates the time that **isActive** becomes FALSE.

TIPS

- This node detects when an object becomes visible to you, and when you become visible to the object.

- Every **VisibilitySensor** node is independent of other **VisibilitySensor** nodes.

RELATED NODES

ProximitySensor   Generates events when camera enters, moves inside, and exits 3D space.

TimeSensor   Generate events as time passes.

TouchSensor   Generates events as the cursor passes over child geometry nodes.

CylinderSensor   Maps dragging motion about the y-axis.

PlaneSensor   Maps dragging motion into the x,y-plane.

SphereSensor   Maps dragging motion into free rotation about its center.

VRML V-W

WorldInfo { }

Holds information about the VRML file (*formerly the **Info** node; a Global node*).

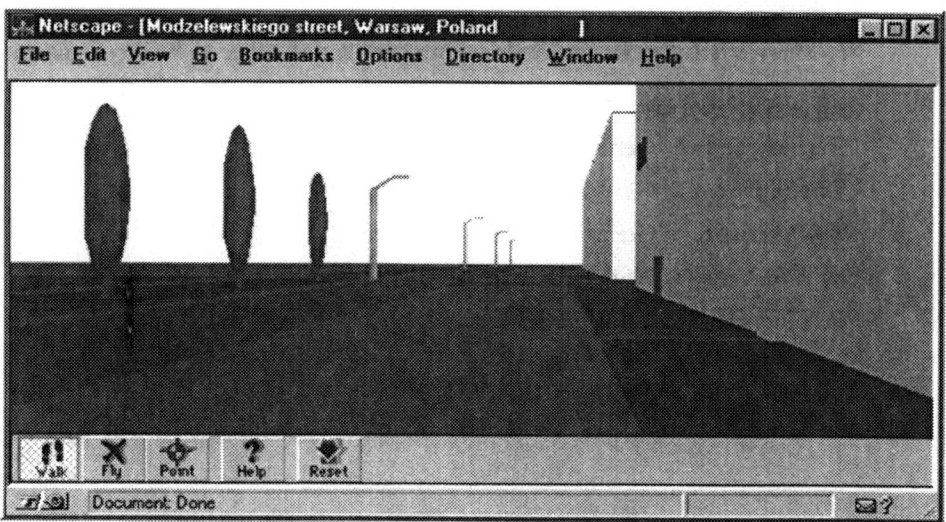

*This scene uses the **Info** node to display a title on the VRML browser's title bar.*
Modzel.Wrl designed by Jacek Szamrej in 1995, Institute for Social Studies, Warsaw University.

VRML 2 SYNTAX

```
WorldInfo {
   title      ""
   info       [ ]
}
```

Field	Type	Name	Default	Meaning
field	SFString	title	""	Title of the scene.
field	MFString	info	[ ]	Comment field.

VRML 1 SYNTAX

```
Info {
   string     ""
}
```

■ Where **string** is any text.

NODE GEOMETRY

■ The **title** field displays the title of the scene on the title bar of the VRML browser.

■ The **info** field is a general purpose comment field.

TIPS

■ VRML v1.0 uses the Info node to set the background color:

```
DEF BackgroundColor Info {string "1 1 1"}
```

■ Use the info node to describe copyright and other information, such as:

```
WorldInfo {
  title     "My Favorite Places"
  info      ["Copyright 1996 by Ralph Grabowski",
            "Created 22 April, 1997"]
}
```

■ An alternative to the **WorldInfo** node is the # (hash mark) comment, such as:

```
# Copyright 1996 by Ralph Grabowski
# Created 22 April, 1997
```

RELATED NODES

Anchor   Hyperlinks to other scenes.

NavigationInfo   Provides information on viewing the scene.

URL Syntax

HTML and VRML use a standardized method of accessing files called URL, short for Uniform Resource Locator. Using URL, files can be accessed from anywhere on the Internet, an intranet, and your own computer.

The generic syntax of a resource locator consists of up to six components:

scheme://net_loc/path;params?query#fragment

Component	Meaning
scheme:	Scheme name.
//net_loc	Network location and login information.
/path	One or more URL paths.
;params	Object parameters.
?query	Query information.
#fragment	Fragment identifier.

URL SCHEMES

The following schemes access specific resources on the Internet:

Scheme	Meaning
mailto	Electronic mail.
news	USENET news.
telnet	TELNET protocol for interactive sessions.
gopher	Gopher and Gopher+ protocols.
prospero	Prospero directory service.
wais	Wide Area Information Servers protocol.
file	Host-specific files.
ftp	File Transfer Protocol.
http	HyperText Transfer Protocol.
nntp	USENET news using NNTP access.

APPENDICES

HTML Character Codes

Since HTML uses the < and > characters to markup the document, you need a replacement for those two characters. This is done via the *numeric code reference*, which uses ASCII codes, plus a prefix and suffix:

Code	Meaning
&#	Prefix; alerts HTML to the numeric code.
nnn	ASCII code number, representing 256 characters.
;	(Semicolon) Suffix, terminates numeric code.

SAMPLE MARKUP

■ To display an HTML tag in an HTML document:

```
The &#60;H1&#62; tag is for creating headline text.
```

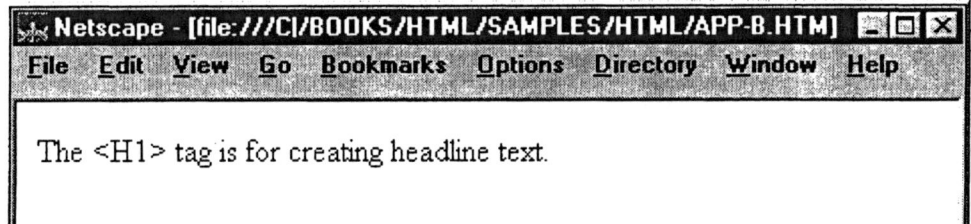

TIPS

■ Use < to display < (left angle bracket) and > to display > (right angle bracket) in an HTML document.

■ Good HTML coding convention recommends using & in place of & (ampersand).

■ A common error is to leave out the ; (semicolon) suffix.

■ Alternatives to the numeric codes:

Alternative	Meaning
&amp;	Ampersand (&)
&cent;	Cent symbol (¢).
&copy;	Copyright symbol (©)
&gt;	Greater-than symbol (>)
&lt;	Less-than symbol (<)
&quote;	Quotation (")

APPENDICES

Code	Character	Meaning
		&#00; through &#08 are not used.
			Horizontal tab.

		Line feed.

		&#11; through &#31; are not used.
 		Space.
!	!	Exclamation mark.
"	"	Quotation mark.
#	#	Number sign.
$	$	Dollar sign.
%	%	Percent sign.
&	&	Ampersand.
'	'	Apostrophe.
(	(	Left parenthesis.
)	)	Right parenthesis.
*	*	Asterisk.
+	+	Plus sign.
,	,	Comma.
-	-	Hyphen.
.	.	Period.
/	/	Forward slash (solidus).
0	0	Digit 0.
1	1	Digit 1.
2	2	Digit 2.
3	3	Digit 3.
4	4	Digit 4.
5	5	Digit 5.
6	6	Digit 6.
7	7	Digit 7.
8	8	Digit 8.
9	9	Digit 9.
:	:	Colon.
;	;	Semicolon.
<	<	Less than.
=	=	Equals sign.
>	>	Greater than.
?	?	Question mark.
@	@	At.
A	A	Uppercase A.
B	B	Uppercase B.
C	C	Uppercase C.
D	D	Uppercase D.
E	E	Uppercase E.

Code	Character	Meaning
F	F	Uppercase F.
G	G	Uppercase G.
H	H	Uppercase H.
I	I	Uppercase I.
J	J	Uppercase J.
K	K	Uppercase K.
L	L	Uppercase L.
M	M	Uppercase M.
N	N	Uppercase N.
O	O	Uppercase O.
P	P	Uppercase P.
Q	Q	Uppercase Q.
R	R	Uppercase R.
S	S	Uppercase S.
T	T	Uppercase T.
U	U	Uppercase U.
V	V	Uppercase V.
W	W	Uppercase W.
X	X	Uppercase X.
Y	Y	Uppercase Y.
Z	Z	Uppercase Z.
[	[	Left square bracket.
\	\	Backslash (reverse solidus).
]	]	Right square bracket.
^	^	Caret.
_	_	Underscore.
`	'	Acute accent.
a	a	Lowercase a.
b	b	Lowercase b.
c	c	Lowercase c.
d	d	Lowercase d.
e	e	Lowercase e.
f	f	Lowercase f.
g	g	Lowercase g.
h	h	Lowercase h.
i	i	Lowercase i.
j	j	Lowercase j.
k	k	Lowercase k.
l	l	Lowercase l.
m	m	Lowercase m.
n	n	Lowercase n.
o	o	Lowercase o.
p	p	Lowercase p.
q	q	Lowercase q.

Code	Character	Meaning
r	r	Lowercase r.
s	s	Lowercase s.
t	t	Lowercase t.
u	u	Lowercase u.
v	v	Lowercase v.
w	w	Lowercase w.
x	x	Lowercase x.
y	y	Lowercase y.
z	z	Lowercase z.
{	{	Left curly brace.
|	|	Vertical bar.
}	}	Right curly brace.
~	~	Tilde.
		&#127; through are not used.
¡	¡	Inverted exclamation.
¢	¢	Cent sign.
£	£	Pound sterling.
¤	¤	General currency sign.
¥	¥	Yen sign.
¦	¦	Broken vertical bar.
§	§	Section sign.
¨	¨	Umlaut (dieresis).
©	©	Copyright symbol.
ª	ª	Feminine ordinal.
«	«	Left angle quote (guillemot left).
¬	¬	Not sign.
­	-	Soft hyphen.
®	®	Registered trademark symbol.
¯	¯	Macron accent.
°	°	Degree sign.
±	±	Plus or minus.
²	²	Superscript two.
³	³	Superscript three.
´	´	Acute accent.
µ	µ	Micro or micron.
¶	¶	Paragraph marker.
·	·	Middle dot.
¸	¸	Cedilla.
¹	¹	Superscript one.
º	º	Masculine ordinal.
»	»	Right angle quote (guillemot right).
¼	¼	One-quarter.
½	½	One-half.
¾	¾	Three-quarters.
¿	¿	Inverted question mark.

Code	Character	Meaning
À	À	Uppercase A, acute accent.
Á	Á	Uppercase A, grave accent.
Â	Â	Uppercase A, circumflex accent.
Ã	Ã	Uppercase A, tilde.
Ä	Ä	Uppercase A dieresis (umlaut).
Å	Å	Uppercase A ring.
Æ	Æ	Uppercase AE (dipthong ligature).
Ç	Ç	Uppercase C cedilla.
È	È	Uppercase E acute accent.
É	É	Uppercase E grave accent.
Ê	Ê	Uppercase E circumflex accent.
Ë	Ë	Uppercase E dieresis (umlaut).
Ì	Ì	Uppercase I acute accent.
Í	Í	Uppercase I grave accent.
Î	Î	Uppercase I circumflex accent.
Ï	Ï	Uppercase I dieresis (umlaut).
Ð	Ð	Uppercase Eth Icelandic.
Ñ	Ñ	Uppercase N tilde.
Ò	Ò	Uppercase O acute accent.
Ó	Ó	Uppercase O grave accent.
Ô	Ô	Uppercase O circumflex accent.
Õ	Õ	Uppercase O tilde.
Ö	Ö	Uppercase O dieresis (umlaut).

Code	Character	Meaning
×	×	Multiplication symbol.

Code	Character	Meaning
Ø	Ø	Uppercase O slash.
Ù	Ù	Uppercase U acute accent.
Ú	Ú	Uppercase U grave accent.
Û	Û	Uppercase U circumflex accent.
Ü	Ü	Uppercase U dieresis (umlaut).
Ý	Ý	Uppercase Y acute accent.
Þ	Þ	Uppercase Thorn Icelandic.

Code	Character	Meaning
ß	ß	Lowercase sharp s (German sz ligature).
à	à	Lowercase a acute accent.
á	á	Lowercase a grave accent.
â	â	Lowercase a circumflex accent.
ã	ã	Lowercase a tilde.
ä	ä	Lowercase a dieresis (umlaut).
å	å	Lowercase a ring.
æ	æ	Lowercase ae dipthong (ligature).
ç	ç	Lowercase c cedilla.
è	è	Lowercase e acute accent.
é	é	Lowercase e grave accent.

Code	Character	Meaning
&#234;	ê	Lowercase e circumflex accent.
&#235;	ë	Lowercase e dieresis (umlaut).
&#236;	ì	Lowercase i acute accent.
&#237;	í	Lowercase i grave accent.
&#238;	î	Lowercase i circumflex accent.
&#239;	ï	Lowercase i dieresis (umlaut).
&#240;	ð	Lowercase eth Icelandic.
&#241;	ñ	Lowercase n tilde.
&#242;	ò	Lowercase o acute accent.
&#243;	ó	Lowercase o grave accent.
&#244;	ô	Lowercase o circumflex accent.
&#245;	õ	Lowercase o tilde.
&#246;	ö	Lowercase o dieresis (umlaut).
&#247;	÷	Division symbol.
&#248;	ø	Lowercase o slash.
&#249;	ù	Lowercase u acute accent.
&#250;	ú	Lowercase u grave accent.
&#251;	û	Lowercase u circumflex accent.
&#252;	ü	Lowercase u dieresis (umlaut).
&#253;	ý	Lowercase y acute accent.
&#254;	þ	Lowercase thorn Icelandic.
&#255;	ÿ	Lowercase y dieresis (umlaut).

Language and Country Codes

HTML v3 uses the <LANG> tag and **LANG** attribute to define the language to be displayed by the browser via a two-letter language and country code defined by ISO 639 and ISO 3166, respectively. The format is *la-st*, where *la* is the language code, followed by *st*, which is one or more subtags, which can be the country code, a dialect, or script variation.

SAMPLE MARKUPS

■ To specify the language for an HTML v3 document:

```
<LANG> In American slang, </LANG>
```

■ To display a portion of a document in a specific language:

```
<B LANG="en-US"> In American slang,</B>
```

TIPS

■ Private language codes use **x**. For example, the Romulan language is:

```
x-romulan
```

■ The country codes are the same ones used for Internet domain names. For example, http://bcferries.bc.**ca** is the Web site for BC Ferries in Canada (country code = **ca**).

■ The registration authority for ISO 3166 country codes is:

> Deutches Institut für Normung
> Burggrafenstraße 6
> Postfach 1107
> D-10787 Berlin
> Germany.

■ The registration authority for ISO 639 language codes is:

> Infoterm
> Osterreiches Normungsinstitut (ON)
> Postfach 130
> A-1021 Vienna
> Austria.

APPENDICES

COUNTRY CODES

Country	Code
Afghanistan	af
Albania	al
Algeria	dz
American Samoa	as
Andorra	ad
Angola	ao
Anguilla	ai
Antarctica	aq
Antigua and Barbuda	ag
Argentina	ar
Armenia	am
Aruba	aw
Australia	au
Austria	at
Azerbaijan	az
Bahamas	bs
Bahrain	bh
Bangladesh	bd
Barbados	bb
Belarus	by
Belgium	be
Belize	bz
Benin	bj
Bermuda	bm
Bhutan	bt
Bolivia	bo
Bosnia and Herzegowina	ba
Botswana	bw
Bouvetisland	bv
Brazil	br
British Indian Ocean Territory	io
Brunei Darussalam	bn
Bulgaria	bg
Burkinafaso	bf
Burundi	bi
Cambodia	kh
Cameroon	cm
Canada	ca
Cape Verde	cv
Cayman Islands	ky
Central African Republic	cf
Chad	td

Country	Code
Chile	cl
China	cn
Christmas island	cx
Cocos (Keeling) Islands	cc
Colombia	co
Comoros	km
Congo	cg
Cook Islands	ck
Costa Rica	cr
Cote d'Ivoire	ci
Croatia (Hrvatska)	hr
Cuba	cu
Cyprus	cy
Czech Republic	cz
Denmark	dk
Djibouti	dj
Dominica	dm
Dominican Republic	do
East Timor	tp
Ecuador	ec
Egypt	eg
El Salvador	sv
Equatorial Guinea	gq
Eritrea	er
Estonia	ee
Ethiopia	et
Falkland Islands (Malvinas)	fk
Faroe Islands	fo
Fiji	fj
Finland	fi
France	fr
Metropolitan France	fx
French Guiana	gf
French Polynesia	pf
French Southern Territories	tf
Gabon	ga
Gambia	gm
Georgia	ge
Germany	de
Ghana	gh

Country	Code
Gibraltar	gi
Greece	gr
Greenland	gl
Grenada	gd
Guadeloupe	gp
Guam	gu
Guatemala	gt
Guinea	gn
Guinea-Bissau	gw
Guyana	gy
Haiti	ht
Heard and McDonald Islands	mm
Honduras	hn
Hong Kong	hk
Hungary	hu
Iceland	is
India	in
Indonesia	id
Iran	ir
Iraq	iq
Ireland	ie
Israel	il
Italy	it
Jamaica	jm
Japan	jp
Jordan	jo
Kazakhstan	kz
Kenya	ke
Kiribati	ki
Korea, North	kp
Korea, South	kr
Kuwait	kw
Kyrgyzstan	kg
Lao	la
Latvia	lv
Lebanon	lb
Lesotho	ls
Liberia	lr
Libyan Arab Jamahiriya	ly
Liechtenstein	li
Lithuania	lt
Luxembourg	lu

Country	Code
Macau	mo
Macedonia	mk
Madagascar	mg
Malawi	mw
Malaysia	my
Maldives	mv
Mali	ml
Malta	mt
Marshall Islands	mh
Martinique	mq
Mauritania	mr
Mauritius	mu
Mayotte	yt
Mexico	mx
Micronesia	fm
Moldova	md
Monaco	mc
Mongolia	mn
Montserrat	ms
Morocco	ma
Mozambique	mz
Myanmar	mm
Namibia	na
Nauru	nr
Nepal	np
Netherlands	nl
Netherland Santilles	an
New Caledonia	nc
New Zealand	nz
Nicaragua	ni
Niger	ne
Nigeria	ng
Niue	nu
Norfolk Island	nf
Northern Mariana Islands	mp
Norway	no
Oman	om
Pakistan	pk
Palau	pw
Panama	pa
Papua New Guinea	pg
Paraguay	py
Peru	pe

Country	Code		Country	Code
Philippines	ph		Tanzania	tz
Pitcairn	pn		Thailand	th
Poland	pl		Togo	tg
Portugal	pt		Tokelau	tk
Puerto Rico	pr		Tonga	to
			Trinidad and Tobago	tt
Qatar	qa		Tunisia	tn
			Turkey	tr
Reunion	re		Turkmenistan	tm
Romania	ro		Turks and Caicos Islands	tc
Russian Federation	ru		Tuvalu	tv
Rwanda	rw			
			Uganda	ug
Saint Kitts and Nevis	kn		Ukraine	ua
Saint Lucia	lc		United Arab Emirates	ae
Saint Vincent and the			United Kingdom	gb
Grenadines	vc		United States	us
Samoa	ws		US Minor Outlying	
Sanmarino	sm		Islands	um
Sao Tome and Principe	st		Uruguay	uy
Saudi Arabia	sa		Uzbekistan	uz
Senegal	sn			
Seychelles	sc		Vanuatu	vu
Sierra Leone	sl		Vatican	va
Singapore	sg		Venezuela	ve
Slovakia	sk		Viet Nam	vn
Slovenia	si		British Virgin Islands	vg
Solomon Islands	sb		US Virgin Islands	vi
Somalia	so			
South Africa	za		Wallis and Futuna	
South Georgia and the			Islands	wf
South Sandwich Island	sg		Western Sahara	eh
Spain	es			
Sri Lanka	lk		Yemen	ye
St. Helena	sh		Yugoslavia	yu
St. Pierre and Miquelon	pm			
Sudan	sd		Zaire	zr
Suriname	sr		Zambia	zm
Svalbard and Jan Mayen			Zimbabwe	zw
Islands	sj			
Swaziland	sz			
Sweden	se			
Switzerland	ch			
Syrian Arab Republic	sy			
Taiwan	tw			
Tajikistan	tj			

LANGUAGE CODES

Language	Code	Language	Code
Afan, Oromo	om	Guarani	gn
Abkhazian	ab	Gujarati	gu
Afar	aa		
Afrikaans	af	Hausa	ha
Albanian	sq	Hebrew	iw
Amharic	am	Hindi	hi
Arabic	ar	Hungarian	hu
Armenian	hy		
Assamese	as	Icelandic	is
Aymara	ay	Indonesian	in
Azerbaijani	az	Interlingua	ia
		Interlingue	ie
Bashkir	ba	Inupiak	ik
Basque	eu	Irish	ga
Bengali, Bangla	bn	Italian	it
Bhutani	dz		
Bihari	bh	Japanese	ja
Bislama	bi	Javanese	jw
Breton	br		
Bulgarian	bg	Kannada	kn
Burmese	my	Kashmiri	ks
Byelorussian	be	Kazakh	kk
		Kinyarwanda	rw
Cambodian	km	Kirghiz	ky
Catalan	ca	Kirundi	rn
Chinese	zh	Korean	ko
Corsican	co	Kurdish	ku
Croatian	hr		
Czech	cs	Laothian	lo
		Latin	la
Danish	da	Latvian, Lettish	lv
Dutch	nl	Lingala	ln
		Lithuanian	lt
English	en		
Esperanto	eo	Macedonian	mk
Estonian	et	Malagasy	mg
		Malay	ms
Faeroese	fo	Malayalam	ml
Fiji	fj	Maltese	mt
Finnish	fi	Maori	mi
French	fr	Marathi	mr
Frisian	fy	Moldavian	mo
		Mongolian	mn
Galician	gl		
Georgian	ka	Nauru	na
German	de	Nepali	ne
Greek	el	Norwegian	no
Greenlandic	kl		

APPENDICES

Language	Code
Occitan	oc
Oriya	or
Pashto, Pushto	ps
Persian	fa
Polish	pl
Portuguese	pt
Punjabi	pa
Quechua	qu
Rhaeto-Romance	rm
Romanian	ro
Russian	ru
Samoan	sm
Sangro	sg
Sanskrit	sa
Scots, Gaelic	gd
Serbian	sr
Serbo-Croatian	sh
Sesotho	st
Setswana	tn
Shona	sn
Sindhi	sd
Singhalese	si
Siswati	ss
Slovak	sk
Slovenian	sl
Somali	so
Spanish	es
Sundanese	su
Swahili	sw
Swedish	sv

Language	Code
Tagalog	tl
Tajik	tg
Tamil	ta
Tatar	tt
Tegulu	te
Thai	th
Tibetan	bo
Tigrinya	ti
Tonga	to
Tsonga	ts
Turkish	tr
Turkmen	tk
Twi	tw
Ukrainian	uk
Urdu	ur
Uzbek	uz
Vietnamese	vi
Volapuk	vo
Welsh	cy
Wolof	wo
Xhosa	xh
Yiddish	ji
Yoruba	yo
Zulu	zu

HTML Color Codes

HTML uses a hexadecimal notation to represent a total of 16.7 million colors. The notation, such as #FF0000 for red, uses the # (hash mark) to altert the browser that hexadecimal number pairs follow, representing red, green, and blue. Each hexadecimal pair ranges from 00 to FF (0 to 255, in decimal), representing 256 possible shades for each basic color. By combining the 256 levels of red, green, and blue, a total of 16,777,216 colors are possible, including black (#000000), white (#FFFFFF) and 254 shades of gray (from #010101 to #FEFEFE).

SAMPLE MARKUPS
■ To display the background of a document in yellow (red plus green):

```
<BODY BGCOLOR="#FFFF00">
```

■ To display the background of a document in white (red plus green plus blue):

```
<BODY BGCOLOR="#FFFFFF">
```

TIPS
■ The hexadecimal characters range from 0 to 15, using the first six letters of the alphabet to represent numbers 10 through 15: 0 1 2 3 4 5 6 7 8 9 A B C D E F.

■ Hexadecimal number notation is case-insenstive: the browser understands #ffffff as well as #FFFFFF.

■ A common error is to leave out the # (hash mark) prefix.

■ Use the tables on the following pages for: (1) mapping Microsoft color names to hexadeciamal equivalents; and (2) creating a corporate standard for the use and naming of colors in HTML documents.

■ On the following pages are the names for 500 hexadecimal color codes.

APPENDICES

Color Name	Hex Code	Color Name	Hex Code
alice blue	#F0F8FF	chocolate	#D2691E
antique white	#FAEBD7	chocolate 1	#FF7F24
antique white 1	#FFEFDB	chocolate 2	#EE7621
antique white 2	#EEDFCC	chocolate 3	#CD661D
antique white 3	#CDC0B0	chocolate 4	#8B4513
antique white 4	#8B8378	coral	#FF7F50
aquamarine	#7FFFD4	coral 1	#FF7256
aquamarine 2	#76EEC6	coral 2	#EE6A50
aquamarine 3	#66CDAA	coral 3	#CD5B45
aquamarine 4	#458B74	coral 4	#8B3E2F
azure	#F0FFFF	cornflower blue	#6495ED
azure 2	#E0EEEE	cornsilk	#FFF8DC
azure 3	#C1CDCD	cornsilk 2	#EEE8CD
azure 4	#838B8B	cornsilk 3	#CDC8B1
		cornsilk 4	#8B8878
beige	#F5F5DC	cyan	#00FFFF
bisque	#FFE4C4	cyan 2	#00EEEE
bisque 2	#EED5B7	cyan 3	#00CDCD
bisque 3	#CDB79E	cyan 4	#008B8B
bisque 4	#8B7D6B		
black	#000000	dark goldenrod	#B8860B
blanched almond	#FFEBCD	dark goldenrod 1	#FFB90F
blue	#0000FF	dark goldenrod 2	#EEAD0E
blue 2	#0000EE	dark goldenrod 3	#CD950C
blue 4	#00008B	dark goldenrod 4	#8B6508
blue violet	#8A2BE2	dark green	#006400
brown	#A52A2A	dark khaki	#BDB76B
brown 1	#FF4040	dark olive green	#556B2F
brown 2	#EE3B3B	dark olive green 1	#CAFF70
brown 3	#CD3333	dark olive green 2	#BCEE68
brown 4	#8B2323	dark olive green 3	#A2CD5A
burlywood	#DEB887	dark olive green 4	#6E8B3D
burlywood 1	#FFD39B	dark orange	#FF8C00
burlywood 2	#EEC591	dark orange 1	#FF7F00
burlywood 3	#CDAA7D	dark orange 2	#EE7600
burlywood 4	#8B7355	dark orange 3	#CD6600
		dark orange 4	#8B4500
cadet blue	#5F9EA0	dark orchid	#9932CC
cadet blue 1	#98F5FF	dark orchid 1	#BF3EFF
cadet blue 2	#8EE5EE	dark orchid 2	#B23AEE
cadet blue 3	#7AC5CD	dark orchid 3	#9A32CD
cadet blue 4	#53868B	dark orchid 4	#68228B
chartreuse	#7FFF00	dark salmon	#E9967A
chartreuse 2	#76EE00	dark sea green	#8FBC8F
chartreuse 3	#66CD00	dark sea green	#8FBC8F
chartreuse 4	#458B00		

Color Name	Hex Code		Color Name	Hex Code
dark sea green 2	#B4EEB4		goldenrod 4	#8B6914
dark sea green 3	#9BCD9B		gray	#BEBEBE
dark sea green 4	#698B69		gray 01	#030303
dark slate blue	#483D8B		gray 02	#050505
dark slate gray	#2F4F4F		gray 03	#080808
dark slate gray 1	#97FFFF		gray 04	#0A0A0A
dark slate gray 2	#8DEEEE		gray 05	#0D0D0D
dark slate gray 3	#79CDCD		gray 06	#0F0F0F
dark slate gray 4	#528B8B		gray 07	#121212
dark turquoise	#00CED1		gray 08	#141414
dark violet	#9400D3		gray 09	#171717
darksea green 1	#C1FFC1		gray 10	#1A1A1A
deep pink	#FF1493		gray 11	#1C1C1C
deep pink	#FF1493		gray 12	#1F1F1F
deep pink 2	#EE1289		gray 13	#212121
deep pink 3	#CD1076		gray 14	#242424
deep pink 4	#8B0A50		gray 15	#262626
deep skyblue	#00BFFF		gray 16	#292929
deep skyblue 2	#00B2EE		gray 17	#2B2B2B
deep skyblue 3	#009ACD		gray 18	#2E2E2E
deep skyblue 4	#00688B		gray 19	#303030
dim gray	#696969		gray 20	#333333
dodger blue	#1E90FF		gray 21	#363636
dodger blue 2	#1C86EE		gray 22	#383838
dodger blue 3	#1874CD		gray 23	#3B3B3B
dodger blue 4	#104E8B		gray 24	#3D3D3D
			gray 25	#404040
firebrick	#B22222		gray 26	#424242
firebrick 1	#FF3030		gray 27	#454545
firebrick 2	#EE2C2C		gray 28	#474747
firebrick 3	#CD2626		gray 29	#4A4A4A
firebrick 4	#8B1A1A		gray 30	#4D4D4D
floral white	#FFFAF0		gray 31	#4F4F4F
forest green	#228B22		gray 32	#525252
			gray 33	#545454
gainsboro	#DCDCDC		gray 34	#575757
ghost white	#F8F8FF		gray 35	#595959
gold	#FFD700		gray 36	#5C5C5C
gold 2	#EEC900		gray 37	#5E5E5E
gold 3	#CDAD00		gray 38	#616161
gold 4	#8B7500		gray 39	#636363
goldenrod	#DAA520		gray 40	#666666
goldenrod 1	#FFC125		gray 41	#696969
goldenrod 2	#EEB422		gray 42	#6B6B6B
goldenrod 3	#CD9B1D		gray 43	#6E6E6E

Color Name	Hex Code	Color Name	Hex Code
gray 44	#707070	gray 89	#E3E3E3
gray 45	#737373	gray 90	#E5E5E5
gray 46	#757575	gray 91	#E8E8E8
gray 47	#787878	gray 92	#EBEBEB
gray 48	#7A7A7A	gray 93	#EDEDED
gray 49	#7D7D7D	gray 94	#F0F0F0
gray 50	#7F7F7F	gray 95	#F2F2F2
gray 51	#828282	gray 96	#F5F5F5
gray 52	#858585	gray 97	#F7F7F7
gray 53	#878787	gray 98	#FAFAFA
gray 54	#8A8A8A	gray 99	#FCFCFC
gray 55	#8C8C8C	green	#00FF00
gray 56	#8F8F8F	green 2	#00EE00
gray 57	#919191	green 3	#00CD00
gray 58	#949494	green 4	#008B00
gray 59	#969696	green yellow	#ADFF2F
gray 60	#999999		
gray 61	#9C9C9C	honeydew	#F0FFF0
gray 62	#9E9E9E	honeydew 2	#E0EEE0
gray 63	#A1A1A1	honeydew 3	#C1DCC1
gray 64	#A3A3A3	honeydew 4	#838B83
gray 65	#A6A6A6	hot pink	#FF69B4
gray 66	#A8A8A8	hot pink 1	#FF6EB4
gray 67	#ABABAB	hot pink 2	#EE6AA7
gray 68	#ADADAD	hot pink 3	#CD6090
gray 69	#B0B0B0	hot pink 4	#8B3A62
gray 70	#B3B3B3		
gray 71	#B5B5B5	indian red	#CD5C5C
gray 72	#B8B8B8	indian red 1	#FF6A6A
gray 73	#BABABA	indian red 2	#EE6363
gray 74	#BDBDBD	indian red 3	#CD5555
gray 75	#BFBFBF	indian red 4	#8B3A3A
gray 76	#C2C2C2	ivory	#FFFFF0
gray 77	#C4C4C4	ivory 2	#EEEEE0
gray 78	#C7C7C7	ivory 3	#CDCDC1
gray 79	#C9C9C9	ivory 4	#8B8B83
gray 80	#CCCCCC		
gray 81	#CFCFCF	khaki	#F0E68C
gray 82	#D1D1D1	khaki 1	#FFF68F
gray 83	#D4D4D4	khaki 2	#EEE685
gray 84	#D6D6D6	khaki 3	#CDC673
gray 85	#D9D9D9	khaki 4	#8B864E
gray 86	#DBDBDB		
gray 87	#DEDEDE	lavender	#E6E6FA
gray 88	#E0E0E0	lavender blush	#FFF0F5
		lavender blush 2	#EEE0E5

Color Name	Hex Code
lavender blush 3	#CDC1C5
lavender blush 4	#8B8386
lawn green	#7CFC00
lemon chiffon	#FFFACD
lemon chiffon 2	#EEE9BF
lemon chiffon 3	#CDC9A5
lemon chiffon 4	#8B8970
light blue	#ADD8E6
light blue 1	#BFEFFF
light blue 2	#B2DFEE
light blue 3	#9AC0CD
light blue 4	#68838B
light coral	#F08080
light coral	#F08080
light cyan	#E0FFFF
light cyan 2	#D1EEEE
light cyan 3	#B4CDCD
light cyan 4	#7A8B8B
light goldenrod	#EEDD82
light goldenrod 1	#FFEC8B
light goldenrod 2	#EEDC82
light goldenrod 3	#CDBE70
light goldenrod 4	#8B814C
light goldenrod 5	#FAFAD2
light gray	#D3D3D3
light pink	#FFB6C1
light pink 1	#FFAEB9
light pink 2	#EEA2AD
light pink 3	#CD8C95
light pink 4	#8B5F65
light salmon	#FFA07A
light salmon 2	#EE9572
light salmon 3	#CD8162
light salmon 4	#8B5742
light sea green	#20B2AA
light sky blue	#87CEFA
light sky blue 1	#B0E2FF
light sky blue 2	#A4D3EE
light sky blue 3	#8DB6CD
light sky blue 4	#607B8B
light slate blue	#8470FF
light slate gray	#778899
light steel blue	#B0C4DE
light steel blue 1	#CAE1FF
light steel blue 2	#BCD2EE

Color Name	Hex Code
light steel blue 3	#A2B5CD
light steel blue 4	#6E7B8B
light yellow	#FFFFE0
light yellow 2	#EEEED1
light yellow 3	#CDCDB4
light yellow 4	#8B8B7A
lime green	#32CD32
linen	#FAF0E6
magenta	#FF00FF
magenta 2	#EE00EE
magenta 3	#CD00CD
magenta 4	#8B008B
maroon	#B03060
maroon 1	#FF34B3
maroon 2	#EE30A7
maroon 3	#CD2990
maroon 4	#8B1C62
medium aquamarine	#66CDAA
medium blue	#0000CD
medium orchid	#BA55D3
medium orchid 1	#E066FF
medium orchid 2	#D15FEE
medium orchid 3	#B452CD
medium orchid 4	#7A378B
medium purple	#9370DB
medium purple 1	#AB82FF
medium purple 2	#9F79EE
medium purple 3	#8968CD
medium purple 4	#5D478B
medium sea green	#3CB371
medium slate blue	#7B68EE
medium spring green	#00FA9A
medium turquoise	#48D1CC
medium violet red	#C71585
midnight blue	#191970
mint cream	#F5FFFA
misty rose	#FFE4E1
misty rose 2	#EED5D2
misty rose 3	#CDB7B5
misty rose 4	#8B7D7B
moccasin	#FFE4B5
navajo white	#FFDEAD
navajo white 2	#EECFA1
navajo white 3	#CDB38B

Color Name	Hex Code	Color Name	Hex Code
navajo white 4	#8B795E	pink 2	#EEA9B8
navy	#000080	pink 3	#CD919E
		pink 4	#8B636C
old lace	#FDF5E6	plum	#DDA0DD
olive drab	#6B8E23	plum 1	#FFBBFF
olive drab 1	#C0FF3E	plum 2	#EEAEEE
olive drab 2	#B3EE3A	plum 3	#CD96CD
olive drab 3	#9ACD32	plum 4	#8B668B
olive drab 4	#698B22	powder blue	#B0E0E6
orange	#FFA500	purple	#A020F0
orange 2	#EE9A00	purple 1	#9B30FF
orange 3	#CD8500	purple 2	#912CEE
orange 4	#8B5A00	purple 3	#7D26CD
orange red	#FF4500	purple 4	#551A8B
orange red 2	#EE4000		
orange red 3	#CD3700	red	#FF0000
orange red 4	#8B2500	red 2	#EE0000
orchid	#DA70D6	red 3	#CD0000
orchid 1	#FF83FA	red 4	#8B0000
orchid 2	#EE7AE9	rosy brown	#BC8F8F
orchid 3	#CD69C9	rosy brown 1	#FFC1C1
orchid 4	#8B4789	rosy brown 2	#EEB4B4
pale goldenrod	#EEE8AA	rosy brown 3	#CD9B9B
pale green	#98FB98	rosy brown 4	#8B6969
pale green 1	#9AFF9A	royal blue	#4169E1
pale green 2	#90EE90	royal blue 1	#4876FF
pale green 3	#7CCD7C	royal blue 2	#436EEE
pale green 4	#548B54	royal blue 3	#3A5FCD
pale turquoise	#AFEEEE	royal blue 4	#27408B
pale turquoise 1	#BBFFFF		
pale turquoise 3	#96CDCD	saddle brown	#8B4513
pale turquoise 4	#668B8B	salmon	#FA8072
pale violet red	#DB7093	salmon 1	#FF8C69
pale violet red 1	#FF82AB	salmon 2	#EE8262
pale violet red 2	#EE799F	salmon 3	#CD7054
pale violet red 3	#CD6889	salmon 4	#8B4C39
pale violet red 4	#8B475D	sandy brown	#F4A460
papaya whip	#FFEFD5	sea green	#2E8B57
peach puff	#FFDAB9	sea green 1	#54FF9F
peach puff 2	#EECBAD	sea green 2	#4EEE94
peach puff 3	#CDAF95	sea green 3	#43CD80
peach puff 4	#8B7765	seashell	#FFF5EE
peru	#CD853F	seashell 2	#EEE5DE
pink	#FFC0CB	seashell 3	#CDC5BF
pink 1	#FFB5C5	seashell 4	#8B8682
		sienna	#A0522D

Color Name	Hex Code
sienna 1	#FF8247
sienna 2	#EE7942
sienna 3	#CD6839
sienna 4	#8B4726
sky blue	#87CEEB
sky blue 1	#87CEFF
sky blue 2	#7EC0EE
sky blue 3	#6CA6CD
sky blue 4	#4A708B
slate blue	#6A5ACD
slate blue	#6A5ACD
slate blue 1	#836FFF
slate blue 2	#7A67EE
slate blue 3	#6959CD
slate blue 4	#473C8B
slate gray	#708090
slate gray 1	#C6E2FF
slate gray 2	#B9D3EE
slate gray 3	#9FB6CD
slate gray 4	#6C7B8B
snow	#FFFAFA
snow 2	#EEE9E9
snow 3	#CDC9C9
snow 4	#8B8989
spring green	#00FF7F
spring green 2	#00EE76
spring green 3	#00CD66
spring green 4	#008B45
steel blue	#4682B4
steel blue 1	#63B8FF
steel blue 2	#5CACEE
steel blue 3	#4F94CD
steel blue 4	#36648B
tan	#D2B48C
tan 1	#FFA54F
tan 2	#EE9A49

Color Name	Hex Code
tan 3	#CD853F
tan 4	#8B5A2B
thistle	#D8BFD8
thistle 1	#FFE1FF
thistle 2	#EED2EE
thistle 3	#CDB5CD
thistle 4	#8B7B8B
tomato	#FF6347
tomato 2	#EE5C42
tomato 3	#CD4F39
tomato 4	#8B3626
turquoise	#40E0D0
turquoise 1	#00F5FF
turquoise 2	#00E5EE
turquoise 3	#00C5CD
turquoise 4	#00868B
violet	#EE82EE
violet red	#D02090
violet red 1	#FF3E96
violet red 2	#EE3A8C
violet red 3	#CD3278
violet red 4	#8B2252
wheat	#F5DEB3
wheat 1	#FFE7BA
wheat 2	#EED8AE
wheat 3	#CDBA96
wheat 4	#8B7E66
white	#FFFFFF
white smoke	#F5F5F5
yellow	#FFFF00
yellow 2	#EEEE00
yellow 3	#CDCD00
yellow 4	#8B8B00
yellow green	#9ACD32

VRML Field Types

VRML v2.0 uses 20 different kinds of *fields* to hold the data in a node. Each field type defines the format for the values it writes. There are two classes of fields:

■ **Single-value** fields start with SF.

■ **Multiple-value** fields start with MF. Multiple-value fields are enclosed by square brackets, with each value separated by a comma: [1, 2.3, 3.4]. An empty field has square brackets: [ ]

Fields are accessible to other nodes in four ways:

■ A **field** is not accessible to other nodes.

■ An **exposedField** is accessible to other nodes.

■ An **eventIn** reads in data sent by other nodes.

■ An **eventOut** sends out data for use by other nodes.

SFBool
SFBool contains a single boolean value: **TRUE** or **FALSE**.

SFColor and MFColor
SFColor contains one RGB color: **0.5 0.5 0.5**

MFColor contains zero or more RGB colors: **[0.5 0.5 0.5, 0 1 0, 0.0 1 1]**

SFFloat and MFFloat
SFFloat contains a single-precision, floating point number: **3.141**

MFFloat contains zero or more single-precision, floating point numbers: **[3.1415926, 12.5e-3, .0001]**

SFImage
SFImage contains an uncompressed, two-dimensional, color or grayscale image written to file in this order:

■ Three integers: width, height, and number of components in the image.

■ Hexadecimal value: width * height, representing the total number of pixels in the image.

■ One-component image: one-byte hexadecimal value representing the intensity of the image. For example, 0xFF is full intensity, 0x00 is no intensity.

■ Two-component image: intensity in first, high-order byte; transparency in second, low-order byte.

■ Three-component image: red in first, high-order byte; green in second byte; blue in third byte.

■ Four-component image: red-green-blue bytes followed by transparency byte.

■ Pixels: specified from left to right, bottom to top.

The Web Publisher's Illustrated Quick Reference   ■   **257**

APPENDICES

SFInt32 and MFInt32

SFInt32 contains a single 32-bit integer written to file as an integer in decimal or hexadecimal: **0xF**

MFInt32 contains zero or more 32-bit integers: **[17, -0xE20, -518820]**

SFNode and MFNode

SFNode contains one node or NULL (contains nothing): **Transform {translation 1 0 0}**

MFNode contains zero or more nodes: **[Transform {translation 1 0 0}, Cube { }]**

SFRotation and MFRotation

SFRotation contains one arbitrary rotation: **0 1 0 3.141]** (x,y,z-axis of rotation and right-hand rotation).

MFRotation contains zero or more rotations: **[0 1 0 0.7, 2 4 6 1.4]**

SFString and MFString

SFString contains one text string in UTF-8 format: **"VRML"**

MFString contains zero or more text strings in UTF-8 string: **["VRML", "HTML"]**

SFTime and MFTime

SFTime contains a single time value; an absolute **SFTime** is the number of seconds since the midnight of January 1, 1970 GMT.

MFTime contains zero or more time values.

SFVec2f and MFVec2f

SFVect contains a single two-dimensional vector: **2.3 1.0**

MFVect contains zero or more two-dimensional vectors **[2.3 1.0 , 4.5 6.7]**

SFVec3f and MFVec3f

SFVec3f contains a single three-dimensional vector: **1.0 2.3 4.5**

MFVec3f contains zero or more three-dimensional vectors: **[1.0 2.3 4.5 , 5.6 7.8 9]**

Printed in the United States
108215LV00004B/7-10/A